Only One Way?

*Three Christian Responses
to the Uniqueness of Christ
in a Pluralistic World*

Gavin D'Costa, Paul Knitter &
Daniel Strange

scm press

© Gavin D'Costa, Paul Knitter & Daniel Strange 2011

Published in 2011 by SCM Press
Editorial office
13–17 Long Lane,
London, EC1A 9PN, UK

SCM Press is an imprint of Hymns Ancient and Modern Ltd
(a registered charity)
13A Hellesdon Park Road
Norwich NR6 5DR, UK

www.scm-canterburypress.co.uk

British Library Cataloguing in Publication data

A catalogue record for this book is available
from the British Library

978-0-334-04400-0

Originated by the Manila Typesetting Company
Printed and bound by
CPI Antony Rowe, Chippenham, Wiltshire

Contents

Part 3: The Dialogue Continues

Preface

In Part 1 readers will be presented with three very different approaches by three influential authors in the field: Gavin D'Costa, Paul Knitter and Daniel Strange. The authors give a brief autobiographical background and then outline the theological and practical approaches to other religions in three essays with matching subheadings so that students can see how the topics of philosophical presuppositions, theological presuppositions, creation, fall, God, Christ, Trinity, salvation, eschaton, dialogue, social justice, and mission are handled when related to other religions within these three differing theological approaches. Using these subheadings also creates a unified treatment despite the serious differences between the authors. Part 1 alone will act as a major introduction to this field of study as the authors between them comment on a wide range of approaches other than their own.

In Part 2 each author has written a critique of the other two positions so that the reader will see both questions of method and content being debated in a sophisticated and rigorous manner. This will allow the reader to make their own judgements on questions being discussed as well as facilitate a deeper engagement with contemporary theological debate on these issues. This will also allow for a unique interactive element that will hopefully act as a valuable teaching aid allowing for class or church group discussion, further debate, and even role play by students. Parts 1 and 2 are self-standing and can be used on shorter courses or as basic primary readings and secondary critical readings. Furthermore, Parts 1 and 2 have been designed so that a single theologian's work can be read, and then two critical views of that work can be pursued.

In Part 3 there are three final 'defences against the critics' presented by each author in the light of the critiques presented by their fellow writers. Each theologian sets out to defend and develop their thesis in the light of these criticisms. This level of interaction and in-depth argumentation makes the book especially helpful to thinking through these difficult and important questions.

At the conclusion, each author presents a very brief bibliography for students to engage with further readings related to their approach. We collectively hope that this book will help people reflect upon this pressing and urgent task. As authors we have learnt that in conversation and discussion, we might move closer to the truth. We are grateful to each other for the opportunity to share that process with the reader.

Our thanks to Sven Ensminger for helping with the technical preparation of the manuscript.

Gavin D'Costa

A Brief Note on the Authors

Gavin D'Costa is Professor of Catholic Theology, University of Bristol, UK. Among his recent publications are *The Meeting of Religions and the Trinity* (2000); *Disputed Questions in the Theology of Religions* (2009); co-ed. Becker and Morali, *Catholic Engagement with World Religions* (2010). D'Costa is a Roman Catholic and advises the English and Welsh Catholic bishops as well as the Pontifical Council for Interreligious Dialogue, Vatican City, and has published widely in this field. His work has been translated into seven languages.

Paul Knitter was Paul Tillich Professor of Theology, World Religions and Culture at Union Theological Seminary, New York and Professor Emeritus of Theology at Xavier University, Cincinnati, Ohio, where he taught for 28 years. Knitter serves on the Board of the International, Interreligious Peace Council, formed after the 1993 World Parliament of Religions to promote interreligious peace-making projects. His main publications are *No Other Name?* (1985); *Introducing Theologies of Religions* (2002); and ed. *The Myth of Religious Superiority* (2005).

Daniel Strange is Tutor in Culture, Religion and Public Theology at Oak Hill Theological College in London. His main publications are *The Possibility of Salvation Among the Unevangelised: An Analysis of Inclusivism in Recent Evangelical Theology* (2002); co-ed. David Gibson, *Engaging with Barth: Contemporary Evangelical Critiques* (2008). Strange is a Reformed evangelical concerned with defending and developing an evangelical 'theology of religions'.

PART ONE

Position Papers

I

Christianity and the World Religions: A Theological Appraisal

Gavin D'Costa

Method

I write as a Roman Catholic theologian, which has a variety of entailments – in fact three for the purposes of this chapter. First, this means that my theological job, shaped by the Church's teachings about the role of the theologian, is to convey the teachings of the Catholic Church on the matter at hand.[1] I hope this will not put off readers, as it is my conviction that everyone doing theology comes from 'somewhere' with specific allegiances and commitments, authority sources and special texts and so on. Even the theologian who says they are not aligned to a church and are simply open to truth, not to doctrines of the inerrancy of scripture, are making strategic decisions about their starting point and the assumptions contained within that starting point. This is one of the great insights from postmodern philosophy, or rather it is an insight that helped

---

1 See Congregation for the Doctrine of the Faith, *Instruction on the Ecclesial Vocation of the Theologian*, 1990. (This and all Vatican documents cited, unless otherwise stated, can be found on www.vatican.va website. All websites cited in this chapter were checked in July 2009.) I have developed this view of the theologian in *Theology in the Public Square* (Oxford: Blackwell, 2005), pp. 77–111; and see also Joseph Ratzinger, *The Nature and Mission of Theology: Approaches to Understanding Its Role in the Light of Present Controversy* (San Francisco: Ignatius Press, 1995), which acts as a commentary to the *Instruction*.

call into question one of the 'idols' of modernity: that it is possible to do objective research without any presuppositions or biases.[2] So please do not stop reading if you are not a Catholic theologian. Why? Because as Christians we are called into special conversation and sharing as we have a call from Christ to discover our unity and this can only be done by being truthful with each other and being open to each other's criticisms and corrections – which is precisely one of the objectives of this present book. If you are a Lutheran or Quaker or Baptist or a 'don't know', but a spiritually sensitive person interested in the question at hand, I think I will learn from your criticisms and I hope you will learn from listening to the view of the Catholic Church on these matters, or at least one of its (unofficial) theologians explicating it. What is explicated below is my view as well. To 'think with the Church' allows ample room for critical exploration and development of arguments and engagement with a wide range of issues and is not a simple act of repetition, although the latter is also part of the theologian's job.[3]

If you respond to all this by saying: 'I want to hear what this person Gavin D'Costa thinks, not what some institution thinks', I would argue that the attention to what the individual thinks is a preoccupation of the modern period and it is an important intellectual task to find out what an authoritative body such as the Catholic Church thinks and then engage with a person who identifies themselves within this body and who is willing to engage in serious theological argument.

Second, while it is my primary job to outline what the Church teaches, this is not an easy positivist task: here are the texts, the job is done! With every text we have contestations of interpretation so one of my fellow writers in this volume, and friend, Paul Knitter, has offered very different interpretations of some of the texts we both take seriously (teachings by the magisterium – by which I mean the universal councils of the Church, the bishops speaking

---

2 See Alasdair MacIntyre, *Three Rival Versions of Moral Enquiry* (London: Duckworth, 1990).

3 See Paul Griffiths' challenging thesis on this matter in *Religious Reading: The Place of Reading in the Practice of Religion* (New York: Oxford University Press, 1999).

together, authoritative statements from pontifical offices within the Vatican and also certain teachings by the Pope).[4] For the bewildered Protestant reading this I should add that it is presupposed that all the teachings from these bodies just cited have their authority from scripture, or their teachings are implications deriving from authoritative scriptural teachings as they get unfolded over time. Hence, it can never be a matter of *sola scriptura*, as this scripture actually demands another source of authority to make the judgement. This other source is not a new source of authority but one derived from scripture which after all is a collection of texts that were decided by the Church to be 'canon'. Hence, there is no scripture without church and no church without scripture.[5] There is an intimate reciprocity between these different sources of authority, although all derive their authority finally from Christ; neither scripture nor church nor tradition alone counts.

Third, and finally, you may ask: but what of your experience Gavin? Does it not sometimes call into question the teachings of your Church on these matters? I have to be honest and say that there is a productive tension in ingesting *some* of my Church's teachings, but in terms of dogma, nothing in my experience has called into question the teachings of the Church on other religions. Rather the contrary. I have found the teachings of the Church deeply illuminative of what I have experienced in some fifty years of inter-religious dialogue. It should be said that first and foremost the question about 'other religions' is about dear friends and companions, people I have known. Sometimes, in looking at the formal teachings we can lose sight of human friendship, but that is not the intention

---

4   See Avery Dulles, *Magisterium: Teacher and Guardian of the Faith* (Florida: Sapientia Press, 2007) for a very good discussion of the magisterium and the complex question of establishing the different levels of authority within the magisterium. For Paul Knitter's readings differing from my own see his *No Other Name? A Critical Study of Christian Attitudes to Other Religions* (London: SCM Press, 1985) and *Jesus and the Other Names* (Maryknoll: Orbis, 1996).

5   I have argued this case in 'Revelation, Scripture and Tradition: Some Comments on John Webster's Conception of "Holy Scripture"', *International Journal of Systematic Theology* 6:4 (2004), pp. 337–50.

of Catholic teachings, for Christ's central gift is that of the command to love one another, to form friendships. Hence, the question about other religions might be simply one of how do we learn to love, honour and serve our neighbour who may be a Muslim, Hindu or Buddhist? Given the personal nature of dialogue, I should say a few words about myself.

I was born Roman Catholic into a religious pluralist society in the Asian community of Kenya, East Africa, and had Sikh, Hindu and Muslim neighbours. My family shared in their festivals, and as a child, I specially delighted in sharing in their sweets and celebration. But I also became aware of the goodness, kindness and deep compassion present in these 'non-Christians', a word that I would never have thought of to describe Inderjit, Ravi, Sunder and Mrs Patel, to name a few. In 1968 I came to England with my mum, dad and sister. I have been more 'formally' involved in interfaith theology and practice since I did my first degree at the University of Birmingham under the guidance of John Hick, who theologically stimulated me by criticizing my Catholicism vis-à-vis other religions in always respectful but incisive ways. In Birmingham I worked on schemes to teach people English, and this involved close contact with Chinese and Indian families. I continued interfaith activity through my doctoral days at Cambridge, where I worked on the interfaith approach of John Hick and the Hindu philosopher Sarvapelli Radhakrishnan. I travelled to India for this research and was involved in Cambridge interfaith groups. I was also involved in the Campaign for Nuclear Disarmament, where I worked with many Buddhists and Hindus who belonged to the campaign. After Cambridge I moved to London to teach and was involved in the Catholic Bishops' Conference on interfaith matters and the West London Interfaith Group, which covered an area, Southall, often called 'little India' because of its huge numbers of Hindus and Muslims. Friendships always made me realize that theology of religions was about friends whom I respected and from whose spiritual practices I learnt so much, not least their faithfulness in friendship. Finally, I've spent the last twenty years of my life in Bristol teaching at the university. With a young family I spent less time on interfaith activities, but a lot of time in nourishing friendships with

Hindus and Buddhists within my workplace. One of these friends, Paul Williams, a Buddhist of many years, converted to Catholicism, which was both a surprise and a great joy.[6] One of my best doctoral research students in Bristol, from whom I learnt greatly, is a co-writer in this book, Daniel Strange. It is a great privilege to work with him in this capacity. That is enough on method and certainly enough on me.

The Roman Catholic teaching on other religions

I am going to outline what I take to be the Catholic teaching on other religions and, before that, provide a brief historical background for the reader.[7] To structurally match my fellow authors I'm going to group the 'modern approach' taken by the Catholic Church under the subheadings of creation, fall, God, Christ, Trinity, salvation, church, eschaton, dialogue, social justice and mission, although I shall clump these together to emphasize their interconnections. This will allow some comparison of our positions.

Biblical and early church background

Three interesting attitudes to this religious pluralism are discernible within the first few centuries that continue to shape contemporary Catholicism. First, there was a clear emphasis on the necessity of faith in Christ for salvation, echoing John 14.6: 'I am the way, and the truth, and the life. No one comes to the Father except through me.' This faith had an ecclesial dimension, including the necessity for baptism into Christ's body, so that membership of the Church (in the case of adults, always assuming active faith and love in the

---

6   See Paul Williams, *The Unexpected Way: On Converting from Buddhism to Catholicism* (London: Continuum, 2002).

7   For good overall studies in this area see Louis Capéran, *Le Salut des Infidèles* (Paris: Louis Beauchesne, 1912); and in English the best work is Francis A. Sullivan, *Salvation Outside the Church? Tracing the History of the Catholic Response* (London: Geoffrey Chapman, 1992), and Jacques Dupuis, *Toward a Christian Theology of Religious Pluralism* (Maryknoll: Orbis, 1997).

person's heart) was required for salvation (Acts 2.23, 41; 8.12–13; 16.15, 31–3; Matt. 28.19; 2 Cor. 5.17; Gal. 6.15; 3.27; Rom. 6.3–4). This first emphasis meant that Christianity was a vigorous missionary religion with an explicit desire to convert all peoples. This was formulated in the famous axiom *extra ecclesiam nulla salus* teaching (no salvation outside the Church), which was formally taught at the Council of Florence in the fifteenth century, but originates from as early as the second century and was consolidated by Augustine of Hippo. It is formally still taught in the Roman Catholic Church. This missionary drive excluded no religion or culture, although Jewish rejection of the gospel was always an embarrassment in the early days and eventually led to a strong anti-Jewish polemic. This teaching presupposed that God created the world good and that the fall brought in death and alienation between humans and God (Gen. 3; Rom. 5.2–21; Luke 11.21–2; John 16.11). This breach initiated by Adam and Eve meant that the history of restoration of the broken covenant between God and humans begins in Israel and comes to completion in Christ. It is quite important to note that until the twentieth century there has generally been what might be called a salvation pessimism about the salvation of non-Christians, that is, there is an assumption that because of sin non-Christians will be lost. Our recent history can be characterized by a move to a salvation optimism, which is always in danger of playing down the power of sin and exalting the power of human goodness. Doctrinally, the latter, while being a wonderful reality, is biblically insufficient for salvation: men and women cannot save themselves by their own righteousness.

Second, various early Christian intellectuals had learnt greatly from Greek philosophy and could not help but wonder at the wisdom they had found there: truths that were consonant with revelation, moral exhortation of a high order, and indeed, philosophical frameworks that allowed for the sophisticated explication of Christian revelation and for its defence against philosophical attacks. They developed three crucial theories to explain pagan wisdom: the *prisca theologia* (ancient theology), the *praeparatio evangelica* (the preparation for the gospel), and the *semina verbi* (the seeds of the Word). The first held that all pagan wisdom was actually an explicit or implicit unacknowledged borrowing from the Old Testament – a theory of a form of intellectual plagiarism. The latter two theories, by contrast, argued that God provided knowledge in nature and in cultures that led people to the truth of the gospel, such that it was possible to know God and find truth, goodness, and beauty outside of Christianity although these truths always derived (causally, and sometimes historically) from the Christian revelation. These truths prepared the person for salvation through cultivating the good life but they were not in themselves saving revelation – which came through Christ. These truths found their fulfilment and culmination in Christian revelation.

Third, the early Christians were faced with the question of the righteous of Israel: were they lost because they were born before the time of Christ? This was unthinkable to many of them. The saints of Israel had valid faith in God, for they partook of the very covenant which is the root upon which the Church was grafted (Rom. 11.11–24). Ideas of the justice of God (in tandem with passages like Acts 2.7; Rom. 10.6–7; Eph. 4.8–9; 1 Pet. 3.18–20) led to the notion that these righteous awaited the coming of Christ, who as the creed has it, 'descended into hell', where he preached salvation to those who deserved it so that they might be saved. This scenario led to the idea of the *limbus patrum* (the limbo of the fathers) as a kind of holding tank for the righteous who died before Christ. In the third century Clement of Alexandria and others included righteous pagans in the *limbus patrum*, which suggested the possibility of salvation for all persons, not just Israelites. Augustine likewise insisted on an invisible Church from the time of Abel composed of the righteous. For all these thinkers, the assumption was that after Christ came, no one was in an analogous position to these righteous gentiles and holy pre-Christian Jews.

Together, these three attitudes run throughout Christian history, leading to three widely adopted *theologoumena* in the modern period which are central to Catholic teaching: (1) the necessity of Christ and his Church for salvation; (2) the justice of God towards the righteous before (and obviously after) the coming of Christ, but the application was related to those before Christ; (3) the possibility of goodness, truth, and beauty being present in pagan traditions, but never in a manner equal to Christ and his sacramental presence in his Church in kind or degree. However, the modern period introduces a new hermeneutical context which contextualizes this tradition: that well until the age of discovery in the fifteenth century it was generally assumed by most theologians that after the time of Christ everyone knew the gospel. If a person was not a Christian they had explicitly rejected the truth of God. This meant that Judaism and eventually Islam (from the seventh century on) were both seen as heretical and/or schismatic movements, rather than genuinely 'other' as we tend to view these and other traditions today.

The Middle Ages

The age of discovery also brought on a development in doctrinal theology with the discovery of the 'new world' with millions of women and men who had never heard of the gospel through no fault of their own. It was difficult to rely on Thomas Aquinas' (thirteenth-century) speculation that, were there to be a young boy brought up by wolves (and who thus had never heard the gospel), God's justice would require that an angel would visit him or that he would have interior revelation. The evidence was generally that angels had not visited non-Christian peoples *en masse* and private interior revelation in such circumstances is unrecorded. New thinking was required in a new context. But note the continuity of dogmatic focus on the necessity of Christ and the Church for salvation.

Two sixteenth-century Dominicans of Salamanca, Francisco de Vitoria and Domingo de Soto, laid the seeds for later Catholic theology on this topic in two significant ways. Vitoria was outraged by the behaviour of some of the Spanish missionary *conquistadores* in South America and argued that unless the gospel was presented properly, without violence, threat, and coercion, both before and after its preaching, the hearers were under no obligation to accept it and could not be enslaved. This was a very radical stance, but Vitoria was not the only one to develop this insight. Bartolomé de Las Casas was also savagely critical of the Spanish military and political authorities for their clear exploitative ambitions and disregard for a basically peace-loving civilization reduced to shreds through Spain's violent *encomienda*, whereby entire communities were forcibly reduced to slavery by being entrusted to Spanish conquistadores whom they were required to pay for their tuition in the Spanish language and instruction in the Catholic faith. Much of this socio-political sensitivity would mark modern Catholicism's attention to these matters in mission work. Nevertheless, Catholics should feel shame at the activities of some Catholic missionaries in history, although that should not obscure the many blessings and benefits others brought to millions of people and various cultures. I would not be a Catholic were it not for the sixteenth-century Portuguese missionaries. Second, De Soto argued that implicit faith in Christ would suffice for those 'who had never heard the gospel' but who had followed the natural law evident in creation and through the use of their reason. This meant that the necessity of the Church for salvation was contextualized, while nevertheless still being viewed as binding. This position, with various qualifications, remains the official Catholic position today. Not all Catholics at the time shared these opinions.

The modern period

There are five important factors that mark the modern period that have shaped the Catholic Church's formal teachings on our subject. First, there is the end of 'Christendom'. Europe slowly became secularized, initially through the 'alleged' wars of religions whereby Catholics and Protestants slaughtered each other;[8] and later through the nation-state's overcoming of these differences through a unitary identity found in belonging to the state rather than a particular religion. The second factor that marks the modern is the profound crisis of two world wars fought in the heart of Christian Europe. Christians slaughtered each other savagely. Unsurprisingly many Europeans had no confidence in the cultural

---

8 See William T. Cavanaugh, *Theopolitical Imagination* (Edinburgh: T&T Clark, 2002); and my *Christianity and World Religions: Disputed Questions in the Theology of Religions* (Oxford: Blackwell, 2009), pp. 74–102.

resources of their ancient religion. Many found solace in modern science that was perceived to have more authority than religions in its claims. Science also had vast instrumental power and seemed to offer possibilities of 'redemption' for millions of people in poverty. Others turned to ethics without religion. Some intellectuals turned to the 'East', which had been idealized by German Romanticism. This mythical 'East' seemed to offer something different from war and destruction. A third factor was the Holocaust. The slaughter of nearly six million Jews at the heart of a Christian culture raised deep questions about Christianity's attitude to the religious 'other' as well as its own complicity in European anti-Semitism. A fourth factor was the critique of missions from the viewpoint of secular modernity. Many liberal Europeans saw Christian mission as culturally arrogant, failing to learn from the deep wisdom of the East, bearing responsibility for the destruction of primitive and ancient cultures, and falsely valuing Christianity over other religions. Fifth and finally, many 'prophetic' voices within Catholicism saw the future as requiring a deeper assimilation to modernity. This latter issue is still unresolved in the Catholic Church although Popes John Paul II and Benedict XVI have developed a trenchant critique against many aspects of modernity that should certainly call into question any uncritical assimilation.[9] This background helps in part to understand the importance of our topic for dogmatic, apologetic and pastoral reasons. It is also the background that meant the Second Vatican Council addressed the issue of other religions in three of its documents.

The Second Vatican Council

In the light of these factors the Catholic Church reflected upon its dogmatic heritage and interpreted its teachings in the modern context in the Second Vatican Council (1962–5). I will outline the

---

9 This trajectory is thoughtfully discussed and contextualized in Tracey Rowland, *Culture and the Thomist Tradition: After Vatican II* (London: Routledge, 2003).

major *theologoumena* that relate to my topic.[10] I will argue that we find central dogmatic continuity with the ancient faith but also important innovations and developments in the modern communal thinking-through of these dogmatic issues. Before moving to these texts, I would remind readers that all the teachings advanced below are biblically grounded, but I am unable to attend to that grounding in what follows and take it for granted. For a more robust and extended explication of my position, such a biblical defence would be very necessary.[11]

God, Christ, the Church: the story of the fall and the coming of salvation

The most important dogmatic document (in contrast to a pastoral document or declaration) on this question is The Dogmatic Constitution on the Church 16 (*Lumen Gentium*, 1964 – subsequently *LG*). Before turning to section 16 in detail, it needs contextualizing. *LG* 1–7 reiterates previous teachings. It starts with the basic Catholic plot-line: God created the world, which was good. After the fall humans seek the living God and yearn for that original communion that has been lost. That restoration begins in Israel and the broken relationship is fully and finally restored in the second Adam, Christ,

---

10   For commentaries on the Council see Giuseppe Alberigo (ed.), *History of Vatican II*, 5 vols (Maryknoll: Orbis, 1995, 1997, 2000, 2003, 2006); and Herbert Vorgrimler (ed.), *Commentary on the Documents of Vatican II*, 5 vols (New York: Crossroad, 1967, 1968, 1968, 1969, 1969). For the best single-volume commentary see Matthew L. Lamb and Matthew Levering (eds), *Vatican II: Renewal within Tradition* (Oxford: Oxford University Press, 2008).

11   Dupuis, *Toward*, pp. 29–52 presents a very rich Catholic synopsis of biblical materials employed within the Catholic tradition on this matter, as does Gerald O'Collins, *God's Other Peoples: Salvation for All* (Oxford: Oxford University Press, 2008). While their coverage is excellent, I would disagree with both in their exegesis of various texts and their exclusion of other texts to provide a balanced picture. I have found Ida Glaser's work very helpful: *The Bible and Other Faiths: What Does the Lord Require of Us?* (Leicester: InterVarsity Press, 2005).

who is founder of the Church. As the *Catechism of the Catholic Church* puts it:

> Although to some extent the People of God in the Old Testament had tried to understand the pathos of the human condition in . . . *Genesis*, they could not grasp this story's ultimate meaning, which is revealed only in the light of . . . Christ. We must know Christ as the source of grace in order to know Adam as the source of sin. The Spirit-Paraclete, sent by the risen Christ, came to 'convict the world concerning sin' (Jn. 16:8), by revealing him who is the Redeemer.[12]

The document then expands on the trinitarian foundation of the Church through the Father, and the Son who founded the Church through the power of the Spirit (2–4). It recognizes the way the kingdom is made present in the Church, primarily through its sacramental character but also in the works of charity that follow conversion of the heart, mind and will to God (5). It shows how the Church is prefigured in the Old Testament (6) and then reflects upon New Testament images of the Church (7), leading to the conclusion that the Church is the sacramental mediator of saving grace: 'Christ, the one Mediator, established and continually sustains here on earth His holy Church, the community of faith, hope and charity, as an entity with visible delineation (*)[13] through which He communicated truth and grace to all (8). It is then stated that this unique Church of Christ 'subsists [*subsistit*] in the [Roman] Catholic Church . . .'. This term 'subsists' replaced the term 'is' [*est*] in the original draft, and there has been much discussion about the significance of 'subsists'.[14] The same sentence continues: 'although many elements of sanctification and of truth are found outside of its

---

12   1994, p. 388 (http://www.vatican.va/archive/catechism/ccc_toc.htm).

13   When an * is used within a bracket within a quotation, this signifies a note in the original cited text which I have omitted.

14   See for example Karl Joseph Becker, 'An Examination of *Subsistit in*: A Profound Theological Perspective', *L'Osservatore Romano*, Weekly English Edition, 14 December 2005, p. 11; and Francis Sullivan's response: 'Quaestio disputata: a response to Karl Becker, S.J., on the meaning of *subsistit in*', *Theological Studies* 67 (2006), pp. 395–409.

visible structure. These elements, as gifts belonging to the Church of Christ, are forces impelling toward catholic unity.'

The rest of the document until paragraph 16 delineates the different types of relation and belonging to the Church, first for Catholics and then for other Christians and then finally in section 16 in relation to other religions. Catholics are fully 'incorporated' (*plene incorporantur*) into the Church and catechumens are 'united' (*coniunguntur*) to the Church in virtue of their desire to join the Church (14). The term *voto* (desire) is used solely for catechumens. Then come non-Catholic Christians, who are 'joined' (*coniuncti*) to the Church for various reasons, but are 'incorporated' (*incorporantur*) into Christ. Finally, in paragraph 16 the Council turns to non-Christian religions and non-religions. The stage is now set for our topic and three points are important.

First, *LG* reiterates the ancient teaching: *extra ecclesiam nulla salus* (there is no salvation outside the Church) but with a different phrase: '*Docet autem, sacra scriptura et traditione innixa, Ecclesiam hanc peregrinantem necessariam esse ad salute*' ('Basing itself on scripture and tradition, it teaches that the Church, a pilgrim now on earth, is necessary for salvation').[15] The different Latin phrase outlines an important shift of emphasis: the old dogmatic truth is reiterated – that Christ and his Church are necessary for salvation; but that truth is now expressed not in negative relation to others – no salvation outside Christ and his Church, but as a positive teaching about the Church and its binding force upon Catholics. Hence, this same section ends: 'Whosoever, therefore, knowing that the Catholic Church was made necessary by Christ, would refuse to enter or to remain in it, could not be saved' (14). What was often employed negatively against non-Christians before is now turned into a profound call to Catholic Christians and those who truly hear the gospel message. But it does not negate the objective claim that the Church is necessary for salvation. Rather there is an acknowledgement that

---

15 The Latin texts are taken from Austin Flannery (ed.), *Vatican Council II: The Conciliar and Post Conciliar Documents* (Dublin: Dominican Publications, 1975); and all English translations are taken from the Vatican website – see note 1 above.

hermeneutically, the way this might apply to different groups requires contextualizing and further theological reflection.

Before the Council there had already been clarification on *extra ecclesiam nulla salus* when in 1949 the Holy Office, now called the Congregation for the Doctrine of the Faith, condemned the teachings of Leonard Feeney SJ, who held to a literal interpretation of *extra ecclesiam nulla salus*. Feeney claimed all non-Catholics were damned: including other Christian denominations as well as those in non-Christian religions. The Holy Office issued a letter against Feeney's literal interpretation making it clear that the teaching did not mean damnation for all those who were not Roman Catholics. The letter stressed that all people who had not explicitly rejected the gospel had a possibility of being 'related to the Mystical Body of the Redeemer by a certain unconscious yearning and desire'.[16] This teaching would find different expression in the Council, which dropped the notion of 'unconscious desire' and 'Mystical' Body, as the former was just one model of explaining how this might happen and the Council was not keen to close down discussion in this area, but simply offer a general orientation. It thus still insisted on a connection to the Body of Christ, the Church. The Council also reiterated the clear teaching that those who die not knowing Christ on earth, and even those who do not know God, might still be saved:

> Those also can attain to salvation who through no fault of their own do not know the Gospel of Christ or His Church, yet sincerely seek God and moved by grace strive by their deeds to do His will as it is known to them through the dictates of conscience.(*) Nor does Divine Providence deny the helps necessary for salvation to those who, without blame on their part, have not yet arrived at an explicit knowledge of God and with His grace strive to live a good life. (16)

---

16 Letter: *The True Sense of the Catholic Doctrine that there is no Salvation outside the Church* – which can be accessed in English translation on: http://www.romancatholicism.org/feeney-condemnations.htm#a2 along with other key texts related to this matter.

This is not Pelagianism through the back door, but presumes grace for the possibility of the 'good life'. This is very important to stress, for otherwise the effects of original sin would be gravely eclipsed, undermining dogmatic truth.

Here we have the Christological, trinitarian and ecclesiological *theologoumena* delicately welded together in Catholic theology. Christ, the self-revelation of the triune God, through the power of the Spirit is the source of all salvation. But Christ through the power of the Spirit founds the Church, which is his instrument for salvation to the entire world because the Church is the sacramental body of Christ to the world. Thus all non-Christians who are saved are related to the Church. The relationship of Christ to the Church and precisely how it is to be explained in the context of the salvation of non-Christians is a matter for Catholic theologians to attend to. The Council was simply laying down the legitimate dogmatic parameters for reflection reiterating the tradition. After the Council there have been significant debates about the two central links in this claim: first, whether and how Christ is the sole constitutive cause of all saving grace; and second, whether and how the Church is the means of salvation to those who die outside its visible boundaries but may nevertheless be saved. What is important right now is to state those claims and note that there has been considerable discussion about them.[17]

Second, *LG* 16 addresses the question of non-Christians (those from other religions and none) and distinguishes their relation to the Church not in terms of those 'incorporated', or 'united', or 'joined', but as those 'ordained (*ordinantur* – *) in various ways, to the People of God'. In the footnote to the term *ordinantur*, Aquinas's *Summa Theologica* III, q. 8, a. 3, ad 1 is cited.[18] In that section of the *Summa*, Thomas is discussing the headship of Christ both to the Church and to all humans and is answering the objection that the unbaptized have no relation to the head as they are not part of

---

17 In *The Meeting of Religions and the Trinity* (Maryknoll: Orbis, 2000), pp. 99–142 and in *Christianity and World Religions: Disputed Questions in the Theology of Religions* (Chichester: Wiley-Blackwell, 2009), pp. 161–211, I have explicated these two claims.

18 From the latin *ordo*, to order.

the body (the Church). The answer given by Thomas resists any such decapitation and severance of relation: 'Those who are unbaptized, though not actually in the Church, are in the Church potentially. And this potentiality is rooted in two things – first and principally, in the power of Christ, which is sufficient for the salvation of the whole human race; secondly, in free-will.'[19] It should be recalled that Aquinas's adoption of Aristotelian terms here requires 'potentially' to be understood as referring to something future, which at present exists only as a germ to be evolved. The potentiality has been variously interpreted subsequent to Aquinas as I have noted when looking at the medieval period above. Pius XII used the term *ordinantur* in *Mystici Corporis* (1943) of those who have not been baptized to say they are 'oriented towards [the Church] by a certain unconscious desire and wish' (*inscio quodam desiderio ac voto ad mysticum Redemptoris corpus ordinari*) (103). Here, Thomas's 'potentiality' is given its future orientation towards *actus* (being fulfilled) in terms of 'unconscious desire'.[20] I have spent time on this matter as this issue has been hotly debated since the Council. My own elaboration of the implication of this future actualization of potentiality can be found elsewhere.[21] However, let me make three brief remarks concerning salvation and the eschaton.

If it is clear that salvation is possible for the non-Christian, yet salvation involves the beatific vision (the direct vision of God as Father, Son and Spirit), then I would argue that salvation for the non-Christian is an eschatological event. It cannot be an event that hap-

---

19   I have used the version of the *Summa* to be found at New Advent: http://www.newadvent.org/summa/index.html.

20   This is contrary to Dupuis's exegesis of the term in *Toward*, pp. 348–9, where he concludes that non-Christians can be saved solely in relation to Christ and not in relation to the Church. Dupuis's conclusion was also called into question by the Congregation of the Doctrine of the Faith, *Notification on the book Toward a Christian Theology of Religious Pluralism (Orbis Books: Maryknoll, New York 1997) by Father Jacques Dupuis, S.J.*, 2001: http://www.vatican.va/roman_curia/congregations/cfaith/documents/rc_con_cfaith_doc_20010124_dupuis_en.html. I cite this not to minimize Dupuis's contribution to this debate, but simply to indicate inappropriate avenues for further exploration.

21   See *Christianity and World Religions*, pp. 161–211.

pens in this life for the non-Christian who dies as a non-Christian, not because they are necessarily lost (which is contrary to church teaching), or because they lack nobility, holiness and goodness that might put many a Christian to shame, but simply because to posit the beatific vision for such a person would be epistemologically overriding their freedom, imposing upon them a relation with a reality that they do not know. Ontologically, in God's eyes, this person is known to be saved, but the epistemological reality of this is yet to happen. Does this mean that non-Christians are any the less good and noble? Not at all. Does it mean that as human persons they do not show remarkable courage and deep compassion? Not at all. All that is being claimed here is that salvation as the enjoyment of the beatific vision is something that will be enjoyed only after this life. To further contextualize these remarks, it should also be said that apart from Mary and the saints, the beatific vision will only be enjoyed in the eschaton by most Christians. Most Christians, while being justified by baptism and faith, will die still lacking purity and perfection which is what will be required for their participation in the beatific vision. Hence, this sense of seeing the salvation of non-Christians as a future event does not in any way provide a commentary on the individual person. It is clear that their religion cannot be objectively true although it may contain many elements of goodness, truth and beauty as well as reflect the light that enlightens all men and women.

Second, this individualist manner of speaking about salvation only tells part of the story. Salvation is a deeply corporate and social event, for the body of Christ is not about the salvation of an individual but the salvation of a community. Here Karl Barth's rereading of double predestination is most illuminating. Barth questions Calvin's focus on the individual as the site of predestination but rather sees this double predestination concretized in Jesus Christ. First, as the damned, in so much as Jesus undertakes that which rightly belongs to the damned: death and dereliction. Second, as the redeemed, in so much as Jesus through his resurrection redeems fallen men and women and his being saved by the Father is the first-fruits of God's reconciliation. Barth overstepped the mark, at least the Catholic mark, in then arguing from this to a form of universalism (that all men and women will be saved). Christ's resurrection and transformation of humanity means that all men and women will have the opportunity to be saved, as taught by Vatican II and the tradition, not that all men and women will actually be saved. Universalism compromises the radical nature of human freedom. Its condemnation is only concerned with human freedom, not a meanness of spirit about the numbers who might be saved. As I noted earlier, of course, until the modern period salvation optimism was quite novel.

Third, if we are to uphold Augustine's teaching that conversion cannot happen after death, a teaching that has been upheld my the majority of the tradition since Augustine's days and forms one of the parameters within which we must try and address the question, have we come to a dead end (in a double sense) when dealing with the question of the fate of the non-Christian? Fortunately, there is another route to think through this matter and it is along the route related to the righteous before the coming of Christ. Remembering that this metaphoric language requires careful handling, elements of the tradition teach that Christ descended into hell to save these souls who were destined for paradise but could not yet enter the gates of heaven as they had not yet met Christ. Are there not many millions after Christ who are in an analogous situation? These people have not had the opportunity to hear the gospel but may, through God's Spirit and thus through the promptings of grace, have followed the dictates of their conscience and the good elements within their religions and thereby sought to follow the good at great personal cost. This does not mean that they have received Christ as is sometimes taught by certain theologians, but rather that they would do (as in Thomas's difference between potentiality and actuality) and in this sense, their future salvation may be construed.

This analogical application of an ancient doctrine is not without problems, but has the benefit of keeping intact a non-Christian's freedom, allowing for their decisions in this life (potentiality) to bear full fruit (actuality) in the beatific vision. Clearly, there is thus continuity and discontinuity involved, but we must assume that only God is the just judge who can adjudicate on such questions and how they might be measured. After all, it took the thief on the cross, Dismas, a single moment of recognition to be assured of future salvation. One cannot imagine that after death he had much inner transformation to undergo before final purification was attained. Augustine argued that he was probably someone who had already been baptized and had fallen away from the Church so that his argument about conversion after death was not weakened, but there is little to support such a reading, although there is admittedly little evidence to refute it. Furthermore, to reiterate, it should also be remembered that apart from Mary and the saints, Catholic theology teaches that many who are Christians and are destined for salvation will nevertheless after death enter into an interim stage of further purification and transformation before enjoying the beatific vision. This is called purgatory. Elsewhere I have related these doctrines of purgatory and the *limbus patrum* (the limbo of the fathers, the place where the righteous before Christ awaited his descent into hell and the opening of the gates of heaven) to provide a solution to an unresolved lacuna in Catholic teaching: how a non-Christian who dies as a non-Christian can be said to be saved, when salvation (as beatific vision of the blessed Trinity) entails a state of which they have no consciousness in this life.[22]

The metaphoric complexity of both the limbo of the fathers and purgatory should make us wary of pushing these models too far. When writing about the fires of purgatory, Benedict XVI touches on this deepest of mysteries in his Encyclical *Spes Salvi*:

> Some recent theologians are of the opinion that the fire which both burns and saves is Christ himself, the Judge and Saviour. The encounter with him is the decisive act of judgement. Before his gaze all falsehood melts away. This encounter with him, as it burns us, transforms and frees us, allowing us to become truly ourselves. All that we build during our lives can prove to be mere straw, pure bluster, and it collapses. Yet in the pain of this encounter, when the impurity and sickness of our lives become evident to us, there lies salvation. His gaze, the touch of his heart heals us through an undeniably painful transformation 'as through fire'. But it is a blessed pain, in which the holy power of his love sears

---

22 *Christianity and World Religions*, pp. 161–211.

through us like a flame, enabling us to become totally ourselves and thus totally of God. In this way the inter-relation between justice and grace also becomes clear: the way we live our lives is not immaterial, but our defilement does not stain us for ever if we have at least continued to reach out towards Christ, towards truth and towards love. Indeed, it has already been burned away through Christ's Passion. At the moment of judgement we experience and we absorb the overwhelming power of his love over all the evil in the world and in ourselves. The pain of love becomes our salvation and our joy. It is clear that we cannot calculate the 'duration' of this transforming burning in terms of the chronological measurements of this world. The transforming 'moment' of this encounter eludes earthly time . . . it is the heart's time, it is the time of 'passage' to communion with God in the Body of Christ. (47)

To conclude this section let me summarize: God through Christ is the cause of all salvation and the Church is Christ's body on earth, the means by which all grace is mediated. How this grace might be mediated to those outside the Church is an area that is not defined or resolved, but that this grace is mediated to those outside the Church is a certainty. Catholics can be confident that non-Christians might be saved which is the solemn dogmatic teaching on this matter. There is obviously a lot of work for theologians to do in developing, explicating and defending this teaching, but this is the basic teaching of the Catholic Church on these questions.

The Holy Spirit and the religions

The Council and John Paul II's papal teachings after the Council have developed Catholic teaching in pneumatology in very interesting ways. I do not have space to pay attention to this chronological process, so will here summarize some important pneumatological points, with minor commentary on some of them.

First, the Holy Spirit is acknowledged to be at work from the time of creation and before Christ's incarnation. The Spirit 'blows where he will' (John 3.8). This is most explicitly found in a passage in John Paul's Encyclical, On the Holy Spirit in the Life of the Church and the World (*Dominum et Vivificantem*, 1986), 53:

[W]e cannot limit ourselves to the two thousand years which have passed since the birth of Christ. We need to go further back, to embrace the whole of the action of the Holy Spirit even before Christ – from the beginning, throughout the world, and especially in the economy of the Old Covenant. For this action has been exercised, in every place and at every time, indeed in every individual, according to the eternal plan of salvation, whereby this action was to be closely linked with the mystery of the Incarnation and Redemption, which in its turn exercised its influence on those who believed in the future coming of Christ. This is attested to especially in the Letter to the Ephesians. (See Eph 1:3–14.) Grace, therefore, bears within itself both a Christological aspect and a pneumatological one, which becomes evident above all in those who expressly accept Christ: 'In him [in Christ] you . . . were sealed with the promised Holy Spirit, which is the guarantee of our inheritance, until we acquire possession of it. (Eph 1:13f.) . . .[23]

The Second Vatican Council, centred primarily on the theme of the Church, reminds us of the Holy Spirit's activity also 'outside the visible body of the Church'. The Council speaks precisely of

all people of good will in whose hearts grace works in an unseen way. For, since Christ died for all, and since the ultimate vocation of man is in fact one, and divine, we ought to believe that the Holy Spirit in a manner known only to God offers to every man the possibility of being associated with this Paschal Mystery. (*Gaudium et Spes*, 22; *Lumen Gentium*, n. 16)

We have a twofold direction of activity in the Spirit's operation upon which Christology is dependent: (a) in preparing people for Christ before his coming; and (b) in applying the fruits of Christ to

---

23   *Dominum et Vivificantem*, 1986, 53; drawing on Vatican II: the Decree on the Church's Missionary Activity (*Ad Gentes*, 1965, – subsequently *AG*), 4, 11.

people after his coming, both those who have received him in faith and to others. This leaves open the interesting question: what of those after Christ who do not yet know him – is the Spirit's activity within them as in (a) or of a different quality given that this is now the post-resurrection Spirit? I think the answer is (a) and also of a different quality, given the ontological transformation of all creation in the resurrection, but I am unable to develop this point here.[24]

Second, we find the Holy Spirit can be found in the hearts of non-Christian people and also in their values, cultures and religions.[25] This is an important move, because it allows for both the subjective work of the Holy Spirit in the hearts of women and men as well as the fruits of that activity that is lodged in the cultural institutions, texts, rituals and practices. While these latter are not to be understood sacramentally, in an *ex opere operato* fashion (see below), this does not diminish both the subjective and historical elements of God's grace to be found in the hearts of persons and in visible elements in their religions. Third, the Holy Spirit within these religions can cause Christians deep shame at their disposition to doubt 'truths revealed by God and proclaimed by the Church'.[26] It would follow that if the Spirit is at work in other religions, it can also call into question false practices and beliefs held by Christians who have failed to grasp their own faith properly, when for example the faithfulness in prayer five times a day or fasting at Ramadan in Islam, rightly calls into question the way prayer and fasting are ignored by some Christians. This action of the Spirit will also help a deepening grasp of the truths that have been given to us in revelation. I will

---

24   See my forthcoming 'The Spirit in the World Religions', *Journal of Louvain Studies* 34 (2010).

25   The Redeemer of Man *(Redemptor Hominis,* 1979), 6, 11; drawing on Vatican II: *AG* 11; *LG* 17.

26   *Redemptor Hominis,* 6; drawing on the Pastoral Constitution on the Church in the Modern World *(Gaudium et Spes,* 1965), 92: 'Our thoughts go out to all who acknowledge God and who preserve precious religious and human elements in their traditions; it is our hope that frank dialogue will spur us all on to receive the impulses of the Spirit with fidelity and act upon them with alacrity.'

return to this theme when I deal with mission and inculturation below. Fourth, the Holy Spirit's work serves as a preparation for the gospel (*praeparatio evangelica*) and can only be understood in reference to Christ.[27] This latter emphasis is important in countering those pneumatologies that have been employed to bypass what is sometimes called the Christological 'impasse' in the theology of religions, which end up in danger of being binitarian or unspecific about the nature of the Holy Spirit.[28]

Fifth, the Holy Spirit moves every 'authentic prayer' of those from other religions: 'We can indeed maintain that every authentic prayer is called forth by the Holy Spirit, who is mysteriously present in the heart of every person.'[29] This is a profound acknowledgement that when we speak of the Spirit we speak of the deepest longings and desires within a person, which are to be found in the 'cave of the heart'. Hence, there is no aspect of the non-Christian's life that might be untouched by the Spirit, including of course their scripture. Finally, and related to the discussion above regarding salvation and the eschaton, it is through the Holy Spirit that every person is offered the 'possibility of being associated with this paschal mystery [Christ]' so that all may have the possibility of salvation.[30]

These themes will return in much that will be developed below.

Dialogue and engagement with other religions

What precisely does *LG* say about the different non-Christian religious cultures? Not much, but what it says is very significant. At this point I will also draw from the Declaration on the Relation of the Church to Non-Christian Religions (*Nostra Aetate*, 1965;

---

27 *Redemptoris Missio*, 1991, 29; drawing on AG 11.

28 See Amos Yong, *Beyond the Impasse. Toward a Pneumatological Theology of Religions* (Grand Rapids, MI.: Baker Academic, 2003), although Yong becomes guilty of just the weakness he sees in Spirit approaches that bypass Christ.

29 *Redemptoris Missio*, 29, in which a key address is cited: *Address to Cardinals and the Roman Curia*, 22 December 1986, 11: *AAS* 79 (1987), 1089, where the Pope explained his Assisi meeting.

30 Second Vatican Council: *Gaudium et Spes*, 22; *LG* 16.

subsequently *NA*). A 'declaration' has no dogmatic value but here acts as a commentary with examples on the dogmatic claims in *Lumen Gentium* 16. We must recall that Aquinas had already argued that the minimal condition for salvation, following Hebrews 11.6, was faith in a God who rewards good and punishes evil. Theism and morality are the minimal requirements for saving faith. After all, this had sufficed for Israel before Christ. The Council takes this approach a step forward recognizing the genuine theism (assuming that Jews and Muslims have not knowingly rejected the gospel) in both Judaism and Islam, while recognizing the *sui generis* relationship with the Jewish people. But it moves beyond this in positively affirming Hinduism and Buddhism (developed in *NA*, but only indirectly in *LG* referring to 'shadows' and 'images') in so much as Hindu and Buddhist beliefs and practices are not in contradiction to the gospel. First, let me cite the relevant section in *LG* 16 before interlacing *NA* comment on *LG*:

Finally, those who have not yet received the Gospel are related [*ordinatur*] in various ways to the people of God.(*) In the first place we must recall the people to whom the testament and the promises were given and from whom Christ was born according to the flesh. (See Rom 9:4–5) On account of their fathers this people remains most dear to God, for God does not repent of the gifts He makes nor of the calls He issues (see Rom 11:28–9). But the plan of salvation also includes those who acknowledge the Creator. In the first place amongst these there are the Muslims, who, professing to hold the faith of Abraham, along with us adore the one and merciful God, who on the last day will judge mankind. Nor is God far distant from those who in shadows and images seek the unknown God, for it is He who gives to all men life and breath and all things, (see Acts 17:25–8) and as Saviour wills that all men be saved. (See 1 Tim 2:4)

Let me address each religion in turn interpolating *NA* into the discussion. In *LG* the Catholic Church provides a particular reading of Romans that marks a real advance in formally accepting that God does not revoke God's covenant with Israel. This excludes the notion that Israel's covenant has come to an end with the coming of Christ. However, contrary to various modern commentaries, I would argue that it cannot be assumed that Israel has been faithful to the covenant without further qualification, or that the covenant can be understood without its necessary fulfilment in Christ. [31] But what is significant here is the recognition that the Jewish covenant (for Jews and for Christians) is God-given and thus genuinely related (*ordinatur*) in terms of potentiality to the Church and Christ. *NA* adds three further important points. First, due to the 'common spiritual heritage', referring back to Paul's reading of Romans and the 'Old Testament', the Council enjoins 'mutual understanding and appreciation' (4.e).[32] Given the years of anti-Semitism among Catholic Christians this is a remarkably important and ground-breaking statement. There is a positive call to learn from and appreciate what is present in Judaism, which has flowered in many ways since the Council. Clearly, the Council has no authority over Jews, so this learning can only be seen as an invitation to Jews, but is a duty to Catholics. The foundation of a dicastery in the Vatican related to the Jewish people under the wing of Christian ecumenism compared to the dicastery for non-Christians, which is separate, indicates the serious recognition of Judaism in modern Catholicism. There have been criticisms of Pope Benedict XVI regarding his views on the Jews and his apparent clawing back what the Council affirmed. I do not think these charges can be sustained.[33]

Second, there is a disavowal of the charge of Jewish deicide that has caused so much Christian anti-Semitism: 'neither all Jews indiscriminately at that time, nor Jews today, can be charged with the crimes committed during [Jesus'] passion' (4.d). Third, the Council actively rebukes any form of 'antisemitism levelled at any time or from any source against the Jews'. It took 35 years and John Paul II to produce a formal repentance for the anti-Semitism within

---

31 See *NA* 4.d. See further my 'The Catholic Church and the Jewish People: Recent Reflections from Rome', *Modern Theology* 25:2 (2009), pp. 348–52.

32 Letters after the section numeral denote the paragraph within the section, that is a = first, b = second and so on.

33 See the controversy about the changing of the Good Friday prayers regarding the Jews and the lifting of the excommunication of Bishop Richard Williamson by Benedict XVI.

Catholicism expressed in the Liturgy of the Day of Pardon presided over by the Pope on the First Sunday of Lent in the Millennium.

Of Islam there is an acknowledgement of a genuine theism and a genuine basis for morality, for 'along with us they adore [*adorant*] the one merciful God who will judge humanity on the last day' (*LG* 16). This is an important dogmatic point. *NA* adds three further important points. First, it notes the high esteem in which Jesus is held in Islam and also the honour given to the Virgin Mary, who is 'at times devoutly invoked' (3.b). Of course, there is also the common root of Abraham 'to whose faith Muslims eagerly link their own'. Notice the phrase does not affirm or deny this claim, but states it as a point of possible contact. As with the mention of Jesus, these commonalities operate within the context of a greater and insuperable difference: 'Although not acknowledging [Jesus] as God' is the rightful beginning of the sentence just quoted above.[34] This allows for possible points of contact, or what the document calls 'what men have in common' (1), even amid differences. Second, there is a qualified approval of selective beliefs and practices, rather than some disembodied notion of Islam. Arising out of Muslim belief and worship of the creator God, the Council notes their 'way of prayer, alms-deeds and fasting' (4.b). Third, as with the Jewish people, the Council tries to move forward from periods of very troubled relations between Islam and the Church. The purpose of this move forward is mutual service to the 'common good', as it is the Church's duty to 'foster unity and charity' among individuals, nations, and religions (*NA* 1). It was left to the Liturgy of the Day of Pardon to call for forgiveness for Catholic actions against Islam in the Crusades.

When we turn to the Asian traditions, *LG* 16 is very thin indeed. It uses Paul's speech on the Areopagus regarding the worship of the 'Unknown God' in 'shadows and images' to suggest the wider connection with non-theistic traditions. It also cites 1 Timothy 2.4 regarding God's desire to save all peoples. One should recall *LG* is not concerned to flesh out this skeleton, but only to indicate its

---

34 See Anthony O'Mahony, 'Catholic Theological Perspectives at the Second Vatican Council', *New Blackfriars* 88 (2007), pp. 385–98.

dogmatic existence. The two dogmatic points here are: first, there is an acceptance that non-theistic religions might exemplify a genuine search for God – and in this sense, there is an analogical extension of Aquinas's 'potentiality'. Second, there is a further extension to non-religious cultures that can also be 'orientated' towards the Church. The latter is a remarkable move given the Catholic Church's opposition to communism and secularism right up until the twentieth century, although neither is affirmed *per se*. The Eastern traditions are given a little more flesh in *NA*. In Hinduism, which contains theistic strands that are different from Semitic theism in their cosmological context,[35] it is acknowledged that there is an exploration of the divine mystery in 'myth' and 'philosophy' (beliefs) – and also in practices. This latter is found in the 'ascetical practices' and 'profound meditation' in the non-theistic traditions, and through 'recourse to God in confidence and love' in the *bhakti* devotional traditions. While any scholar of Hinduism might balk at this thin description, one should instead perhaps marvel and rejoice that any positive description is being made at all. It is not at all normal for a Church Council to speak about another religion. Instead, here a door is being opened to serious scholarship and Indology theologically to flesh out and think through these starting points for engagement towards the 'common good'.

Buddhist beliefs and practices are likewise singled out, even though there are no theistic elements within Buddhism. Nevertheless, in Pure Land and other forms of Buddhism there are emphases upon 'divine' aid. Thus *NA* affirms the insight regarding the 'inadequacy of the changing world' and the way Buddhists seek 'perfect liberation' and 'supreme illumination' 'either though their own efforts or by the aid of divine help' (2).

I want to use the example of Buddhism to make a subsidiary point. *NA* is only concerned to encourage positive pastoral orientation. It makes no claims about comprehensive or detailed evaluation of any religious culture. How could it? Hence, it should be

---

35   See for example Julius Lipner, 'The Christian and Vedantic Theories of Originative Causality: A Study in Transcendence and Immanence', *Philosophy East and West* 28:1 (1978), pp. 53–68.

no surprise that two intellectually probing popes after the Council have, in their 'private' writings (that is writings that have no magisterial authority), made negative judgements about Buddhism. For example, Cardinal Ratzinger in an interview with a French newspaper suggested that in Buddhism the self-help involved in meditation and release amounted to salvation by one's own efforts and thus might be compared to 'auto-eroticism'. He is reported as saying: 'If Buddhism is attractive, it is because it appears as a possibility of touching the infinite and obtaining happiness without having any concrete religious obligations. A spiritual auto-eroticism of some sort.'[36] Pope John Paul II, in *Crossing the Threshold of Hope,* raised similar searching questions about Buddhism. For example, he explored the question whether Buddhist meditation and contemplation is at all the same as meditation and contemplation in orthodox Christianity. Buddhist meditation strives to 'wake' one from existential delusions regarding the status of the world. Christian meditation in the Carmelite tradition begins where the Buddha left off. He continues: 'Christian mysticism . . . is not born of a purely negative "enlightenment." It is not born of an awareness of the evil which exists in man's attachment to the world through the senses, the intellect, and the spirit. Instead, Christian mysticism is born of the Revelation of the living God.'[37] Paul Williams, whom I mentioned earlier, an expert in Tibetan Buddhism as well as a Catholic, has further explored these critical probings.[38] Taking the other religion seriously in terms of what it teaches is part of the process of respectful and informed theological engagement. None of these explorations negate the positive outreach towards Buddhism. Other Indologists and theologians have made different judgements about

36 See http://en.wikiquote.org/wiki/Pope_Benedict_XVI – from *L'Express,* 20 March 1997, without the original being cited.

37 *Crossing the Threshold of Hope* (London: Jonathan Cape, 1994), p. 81.

38 'Aquinas Meets the Buddhists: Prolegomenon to an Authentically Thomist Basis for Dialogue', in Jim Fodor and Frederic Christian Bauerschmidt (eds), *Aquinas in Dialogue: Thomas for the Twenty-First Century* (Oxford: Blackwell, 2004), pp. 87–118.

Buddhism[39] and this is an ongoing engagement initiated by Vatican II's attitude to search after points of contact and similarities that might facilitate work together towards the common good.

Vatican II, as I have been trying to illustrate, opened the door to the possibility that scholarship *about* the religions and theological reflection *on* the religions might rightly join hands. There is thus room here for both a theology of religions (which is concerned primarily with the dogmatic questions of Christology, Trinity, Church, grace, salvation and so on) and a theology in engagement with each particular religion (dealing with the different contexts of engagement and thus with often very particular sets of questions). Both feed upon each other, although the former drives the latter.

I should finally note that Vatican II only mentioned some religions. There are so many more in the world such as Sikhism, Confucianism, Taoism, folk and tribal religions and New Religious Movements. While the Council could hardly address all these, it started a process that would orient Catholic scholarship and practice towards a positive and critical engagement with these traditions. 'Positive' in the sense that one is called to seek points of contact that can be harnessed towards working together for the common good, and also positive in terms of learning and listening to the 'Other' knowing that God's Spirit may have already worked within these traditions. Catholics have much to learn from this process about the disciplines and practices that help build up the common good, that help men and women resist evil and despair, and that encourage selflessness and service. But none of these things, however true, good and noble, can displace the necessity of Christ's call to total conversion to the triune God, to rejecting the depths of sin and violence and falling upon his forgiving grace and knowing that only in this grace is there salvation. Nothing allows the Catholic Christian to forgo offering that which is the greatest gift that they themselves know: Jesus Christ, the transforming and redeeming relationship with God and his creation. Thus, engagement with other

---

39   See for example, Paul Knitter, *Without Buddha I Could Not Be A Christian* (Oxford: Oneworld, 2009) and Aloysius Pieris, *Love Meets Wisdom: A Christian Experience of Buddhism* (Maryknoll: Orbis, 1988).

religions is inevitably complex in terms of not only acknowledging and rejoicing in that which is true, good and holy and also the many promptings of the Holy Spirit, but also respectfully questioning and critically engaging with all features of that religion. Elsewhere, I have suggested that this latter process can be modelled well upon Alasdair MacIntyre's understanding of conversations between 'rival communities'.[40]

The meaning of other religions in God's plan of salvation

What is the theological status of these religions in the light of the two sets of discussion above? There is widespread consensus that Vatican II was silent about the theological status of these religions in terms of denying or affirming that they can be viewed as 'salvific means'.[41] The Council itself does use a group of cognate phrases that indicates a reasonably clear answer. In the most important dogmatic document, *LG* 16, we find the important phrases that these positive elements in the religions and non-religions are 'considered by the church as a preparation for the gospel [*praeparatio evangelica*]'.[42] Eusebius and the tradition after him that employed this phrase did not impute any salvific significance to what was to be found in the traditions, but rather that the truth there at least provided a bridge whereby the gospel might be understood and error abandoned. The *prisca theologia* tradition is not invoked, but the *logos spermatikos* or *semina verbi* is. In *NA* 2 it says of the religions that while differing from the Catholic Church's teachings they nevertheless 'often reflect a ray of that truth which enlightens all men [*sic!*]'. This is also found in *AG* 11, which says that Christians

---

40 See *The Meeting of Religions*, pp. 3–15.

41 For a good discussion of this see Dupuis, *Toward*, pp. 165–70; and in contrast Mikka Ruokanen, *The Catholic Doctrine on Non-Christian Religions according to the Second Vatican Council* (Leiden: Brill, 1992).

42 Citing Eusebius of Caesarea, *Preparation for the Gospel* 1.1; see also on this matter the very helpful historical contextualization of Eusebius' approach which properly roots it in a biblical historical worldview: Aaron P. Johnson, *Ethnicity and Argument in Eusebius' Praeparatio Evangelica* (Oxford: Oxford University Press, 2006).

living among non-Christians 'should be familiar with their national and religious traditions and uncover with gladness and respect those seeds of the Word which lie hidden among them'. From Justin Martyr onwards and in the Council, 'seeds' is not used in any way to justify religions *per se* but denotes them as preparatory, like Aquinas's potentiality, for the coming of Christ even while being immersed in error and superstition.[43]

Given the subsequent heated theological debate on this matter after the Council, the magisterium issued a specific declaration on this issue: On the Unicity and Salvific Universality of Jesus Christ and the Church (*Dominus Iesus*, 2000; subsequently *DI*). Paragraphs 20–2 address the intention of the Council teachings and also indicate illegitimate explications from the Council documents. *DI* acknowledges that while the religions may contain truth and goodness moved by the Spirit, nevertheless: 'it is clear that it would be contrary to the faith to consider the Church as *one way* of salvation alongside those constituted by the other religions, seen as complementary to the Church or substantially equivalent to her, even if these are said to be converging with the Church toward the eschatological kingdom of God'. This thereby counters any form of pluralism *de iure* (in principle). It also shows why the other religions cannot be understood as a 'means of salvation' as this term is uniquely applied to the Church precisely because of its Christological foundations. It is for this reason that the document is able to say, despite the many positive teachings that are unhesitatingly repeated, that the other religions *per* se cannot be understood as ways to salvation. Section 21 is important (as are its notes):

Certainly, the various religious traditions contain and offer religious elements which come from God,[85] and which are part of what 'the Spirit brings about in human hearts and in the history

---

43   A good study of Justin's context and intention can be found in Ragnar Holte, 'Logos Spermatikos: Christianity and Ancient Philosophy according to St Justin's Apologies', *Studia Theologica* 12 (1958), pp. 109–68. The patristic tradition is often viewed over-positively in this regard. For a spirited critique of these readings see Paul Hacker, *Theological Foundations of Evangelization* (St Augustin: Steyler Verlag, 1980).

of peoples, in cultures, and religions'.[86] Indeed, some prayers and rituals of the other religions may assume a role of preparation for the Gospel, in that they are occasions or pedagogical helps in which the human heart is prompted to be open to the action of God.[87] One cannot attribute to these, however, a divine origin or an *ex opere operato* salvific efficacy, which is proper to the Christian sacraments.[88] Furthermore, it cannot be overlooked that other rituals, insofar as they depend on superstitions or other errors (cf. *1 Cor* 10:20–21), constitute an obstacle to salvation.[44,89]

The door is thus closed on trying to establish any form of pluralism *de iure*,[45] but it is kept open to explore how these religions might be forms of 'participated mediation' in so much as their positive elements might actually be part of God's plan to lead all people to Christ. These positive elements cannot be viewed as positive in themselves, but only as some form of *praeparatio*. Such a distinction is crucial. *DI* rightly suggests that this is a question that requires serious theological exploration. However, it also needs to be said that the 'positive elements' that might act in this fashion are not necessarily how those religions would interpret themselves. The meaning of religions is not fixed, although one must take the various historical forms seriously that contest what the right interpretation of a religion is. But logically speaking, to turn the situation around, a Muslim has both the epistemological and political right to claim that the true meaning of Christianity is disclosed in the Qur'an and has been misunderstood by mainstream Christianity. The Christian at least would then need to turn to the Qur'an and the Bible to try and refute this claim Quranically, and if they could not, they would

---

44   The sources for the footnotes as given in the document are as following: '(85) These are the seeds of the divine Word (*semina Verbi*), which the Church recognizes with joy and respect (cf. Second Vatican Council, Decree *Ad gentes*, 11; Declaration *Nostra aetate*, 2). (86) JOHN PAUL II, Encyclical Letter *Redemptoris missio*, 29. (87) Cf. *ibid.*; *Catechism of the Catholic Church*, 843. (88) Cf. COUNCIL OF TRENT, *Decretum de sacramentis*, can. 8, *de sacramentis in genere*: *DS* 1608. (89) Cf. JOHN PAUL II, Encyclical Letter *Redemptoris missio*, 55.'

45   See my Christian Orthodoxy and Religious Pluralism: A Response to Terrence W. Tilley, *Modern Theology* 23:3 (2007), pp. 435–46 and the ensuing debate in the same journal on this point.

then have to try and show why Christianity better understands the meaning of Islam. Whether there is any resolution to such arguments is not relevant. That they are required is all-important. For example: many mainstream Jews would resist the affirmation that the Church might give to the positive elements drawn from Judaism. How so? If these affirmations were to end in Christian support for messianic Judaism or Jews for Jesus or Hebrew Christians. Likewise, if a Muslim considered unorthodox because they believed *Isa* (Jesus) to be a fulfilment of the Prophet's teaching. What the Church might deem 'positive elements', as happened with Justin and Eusebius, are not necessarily viewed in the same light by the non-Christian to whose traditions they belong. Of course, in very many cases the positive elements will be mutually affirmed by both Christians and the partner, as in almsgiving and fasting, valued by Muslims and Catholics. And in some cases the positive elements might cause deep shame and also learning and wonder in a Catholic.

To summarize: while other religions might be affirmed in the way outlined above, they can only be seen as part of God's plan in so much as they provide a *praeparatio* to the gospel, but not in themselves as a means of salvation. While saying this latter, there is no implication that non-Christians are damned or that genuine holiness is to be found in adherents, and wisdom in their traditions. We see emerging a nuanced and delicate balance between a group of theological principles that uphold both the ancient orthodox faith of the Catholic Church as well as positively engaging with this new context whereby the religions are seen as other than schismatic and heretical cultural configurations. Of course, that they might contain idolatries of all sorts is also an important continuity in teaching. This point is consistently made in all the documents we have examined. I have been stressing the positive themes, but they cannot be taken seriously and in a balanced manner without taking seriously the reality of sin. *LG* 16 adds this ominous and realistic note after the positive appraisal of the religions:

> But often men, deceived by the Evil One, have become vain in their reasonings and have exchanged the truth of God for a lie, serving the creature rather than the Creator. (See Rom. 1.21, 25) Or some

there are who, living and dying in this world without God, are exposed to final despair. Wherefore to promote the glory of God and procure the salvation of all of these, and mindful of the command of the Lord, 'Preach the Gospel to every creature' (Mark 16.16) the Church fosters the missions with care and attention.

Mission and inculturation

I have touched on these two above, but it is time to be explicit: what does the Council teach about mission? Three things are clear in numerous Council documents. First, it is the nature of the Church to be a light to all nations, to call all men and women to the good news that Christ has come to bring salvation into the world. [46] There is no exception to the extent of evangelization, for to exclude anyone would be to exclude them from God's great gift to all men and women. Second, while there is a call to universal mission, there is also a call to respect the dignity of every human person and thus their freedom of conscience.[47] No one should be coerced to follow Christ, and mission does not call for disrespect or belittling of other beliefs and practices. I have also noted how after the Council, the Church has officially recognized that Catholics have not always followed their own teachings. Third, mission means planting Christian communities in every nation so that all cultures and creation can join in a hymn of praise and thanksgiving to the triune God. Mission involves the gradual transformation of the Church through a critically sifted process of inculturation.

This third point is worth dwelling on further, for it raises the important question: What elements from other religions might transform future Christian practices and beliefs? The answer I think is in principle simple: anything that is good, true, and holy in the cultures of the world can and should be incorporated into the Church. In practice the answer is far more complex. After the discovery of the 'New World', as it was called, Catholic missionaries engaged with

---

46   The document most important here is *Ad Gentes*, but see also *Lumen Gentium* and *Nostra Aetate*.

47   Besides *Ad Gentes,* the key document here is in fact the Declaration on Religious Liberty (*Dignitatis humanae*, 1965), p. 3.

all types of religious cultures, some of which had appalling dark elements and others which elicited high praise and respect. It goes without saying that the same was true for the missionaries' own religious culture. Discerning dark from light is sometimes rather complex and incorporating the good and positive elements likewise. Today, for example, we would not necessarily share the judgement of a Jesuit in India who found in the practice of widow immolation (*sati*) something so noble and dutiful, that it would truly challenge Hindus if Christians could engage in such self-sacrificial martyrdom![48] And Christians might evaluate certain rites very differently. Some Catholic missionaries were perhaps uniquely able to appreciate what some of the Protestant missionaries could only see as Hindu 'idol worship' in the practices of Hindu *puja*. Those Protestant missionaries of course saw idol worship in the practices of Catholicism!

Regarding inculturation (the use of cultures to give shape and form to the proclamation of the gospel) it is a fair generalization to say that within Catholicism the Western Latin tradition dominated for historical and geographical reasons. As Newman has argued, the Latin tradition was a long slow process of critical inculturation of Greek and Roman traditions, practices and conceptualities.[49] Harnack and earlier Reformers judged this to be sometimes the dilution and falsification of Christianity, but since I am accepting the basic dogmatic legitimacy of the Western Latin tradition I am not going to get bogged down in this debate. The inculturation of 'positive elements' from non-Christian traditions forms the historical explication of 'faith', which as 'faith' cannot be reduced to any single culture. Nevertheless the culture through which Christianity was transmitted in the West does takes a privileged but contingent role in that it critically forms that which is called 'tradition', and tradition contains all sorts of normative statements (in Councils, for example) that are determinative for shaping developments and articulations of the faith in different cultural mediums. With the slow

---

48 See Catherine Weinberger-Thomas, *Ashes of Immortality: Widow Burning in India* (Chicago: University of Chicago Press, 1999), p. 18 cites this and other very interesting comparative materials.

49 See John Henry Newman, *An Essay on the Development of Christian Doctrine* (London: Longman, 1890).

crumbling of European economic and political power this issue will become more and more acute in the Western Latin tradition. In 1659, in the early days of the discovery of the New World, the Sacred Congregation for the Propagation of the Faith (now known as the Congregation for the Evangelization of Peoples) issued an instruction to new missionaries to China, regarding the matter of adapting to local customs and respecting the habits of the countries to be evangelized: 'Do not act with zeal, do not put forward any arguments to convince these peoples to change their rites, their customs or their usages, except if they are evidently contrary to the religion and morality. What would be more absurd than to bring France, Spain, Italy or any other European country to the Chinese? Do not bring to them our countries, but instead bring to them the faith, a faith that does not reject or hurt the rites, nor the usages of any people, provided that these are not distasteful, but that instead keeps and protects them.'[50] It might be said that the famous Chinese rites controversy was not entirely about inculturation but rather a battle between the Dominicans and Jesuits. The lifting of the ban of 1705 against using local rites in 1939 by Pius XII was politically motivated regarding the Catholic Church's operations in China.[51]

LG continues in this tradition of respect for cultures but with a sharp critical eye, recognizing that the process of incorporation will often transform the dynamic of that which is incorporated:

> Through her work, whatever good is in the minds and hearts of men, whatever good lies latent in the religious practices and cultures of diverse peoples, is not only saved from destruction but is also cleansed, raised up and perfected unto the glory of God, the confusion of the devil and the happiness of man. (17)

An example from the Asian Church will be helpful here.

---

50   See *Missions étrangères de Paris: 350 ans au service du Christ* (Paris: Editeurs Malesherbes, 2008), p. 5. (English and French cited in the entry on Paris Foreign Missions Society: http://wapedia.mobi/en/Paris_Foreign_Missions_Society?t=5.)

51   See George Minamiki, *The Chinese Rites Controversy: From its Beginning to Modern Times* (Chicago: Loyola University Press, 1985).

Some Catholics employ meditational techniques from the yoga tradition of Hinduism and from Japanese Buddhist practices. Breathing, posture, stillness and concentration, it is sometimes claimed, are immensely helpful ways of stilling the mind to be receptive to God. Examples could be drawn from the French Benedictine Dom Henri Le Saux, later called Swami Abhishiktananda, who learnt meditation under a Hindu guru; or the Trappist monk Thomas Merton, who found great wisdom in Zen meditation resonating with his own contemplative Trappist tradition and engaged deeply with D. T. Suzuki; and my colleague in this book, Paul Knitter, who testifies to how his Catholicism is fed and nourished by Buddhist spirituality.[52] Furthermore, some Asian Catholics are trying to think through dogmatics with the aid of Sankara and Ramanuja in the same way that Aquinas employed Aristotle. Just as Aristotle and Plato were central in shaping the thinking of some early Christian intellectuals, why should Sankara, Ramanuja and Nagarjuna not shape a new generation as they reflect on their 'faith'?[53] As LG put it, all that is good in people's hearts, rites, cultures will be raised and purified in this transformation into a hymn of praise to God when incorporated into a Church which we might find very difficult to recognize.

While there are important and exciting developments, some critical problems should also be registered, for the stream of engagement with other religions and cultures entails complex currents. While legitimately drawing on Sankara, can the Latin heritage simply be

---

52   See Knitter, *Without Buddha*. For Abhishiktananda see: *Hindu–Christian Meeting Point* (Bangalore: CISRS, 1969); *Saccidananda: Christian Approach to Advaitic Experiences* (Dehli: ISPCK, rev. edn, 1998). For Merton see *Asian Journal* (New York: Norton, 1975), and *Zen and the Birds of Appetite* (New York: Norton, 1968).

53   For an excellent guide to early Indian experiments in the nineteenth and twentieth centuries see Joseph Mattam, *The Land of the Trinity: A Study of Modern Christian Approaches to Hinduism* (Bangalore: Theological Publications in India, 1975). The most outstanding Catholic of the early pioneers in terms of theological sophistication was the Jesuit Pierre Johanns, whose Thomist synthesis and analysis are systematically presented in Dean Doyle, *Synthesizing the Vedanta: The Theology of Pierre Johanns S. J.* (Bern: Peter Lang, 2006).

seen as 'European' so that the Indian Church is not tied to this Latin tradition as is argued by some radical Indian theologians?[54] John Paul II argued against such a move in his encyclical *Faith and Reason* (*Fides et Ratio*, 1998), 72: 'the Church cannot abandon what she has gained from her inculturation in the world of Graeco-Latin thought. To reject this heritage would be to deny the providential plan of God who guides his Church down the paths of time and history.' This is not to privilege the Graeco-Latin heritage, but to argue for an organic continuity for the Church in different cultures. He then continues: 'This criterion is valid for the Church in every age, even for the Church of the future, who will judge herself enriched by all that comes from today's engagement with Eastern cultures and will find in this inheritance fresh cues for fruitful dialogue with the cultures which will emerge as humanity moves into the future.' So rather than adopt a Harnackian-like nineteenth-century Liberal Protestant view about the Catholic Church, what is at stake here is valuing cumulative traditions and allowing fresh formulations to be accountable to the Bible and earlier traditions. This does not reify a static monolithic block called 'tradition', which is why I have used 'traditions', but it draws into an organic unity the local and universal Church.

In the West we have seen this issue arise with the employment of Marx by some (not all) liberation theologians. One must be sensitive to the way some philosophies and practices can contain presuppositions and accompanying worldviews that if not challenged and questioned can turn 'inculturation' into uncritical assimilation. When this happens, as in the case of some forms of liberation theology, the Church can suddenly be viewed in primarily sociological categories of power rather than in sacramental terms. And with the use of some types of Eastern meditational practices by Christians, this might lead (but not at all necessarily) to pseudo-gnosticism which aims to liberate the soul from matter and body into a state of superior knowledge. It might also lead to 'Messalianism', named after the fourth-century charismatics who identified the redeeming

---

54 For example, Felix Wilfred, *Sunset in the East: Asian Challenges and Christian Involvement* (Madras: University of Madras Press, 1991).

grace of the Holy Spirit with the experiences of the Spirit's sustaining and enlivening presence in the soul. Both errors are in danger of attempting to overcome the distance separating creature from creator and to bypass the humanity of Christ and the sacraments of the Church. But these are only dangers, not intrinsic to proper inculturation, but that happen when uncritical syncretism or assimilation takes place.[55] To note these dangers is important, but they should in no way inhibit critical inculturation as affirmed in *LG*, as the Church's very catholicity is otherwise compromised.

In the future, who knows what the Indian Catholic Church might look like in its customs and rites and theology – and this organic growth, when done under the guidance of the bishops, can be understood as the Holy Spirit's uncovering ever anew the face of Christ. Christ's face is both known and unknown, but never seen in its fullness until we come to see Christ face to face in the eschaton. The Vatican called upon the Benedictine and Cistercian monastic orders, precisely those trained in meditation and prayer, to engage with Eastern religious traditions and communities to further this important quest for both better understanding of the 'Other' as well as deep learning through this process. The Monastic Interreligious Dialogue committee has developed its activities over many years and in many different countries.[56]

I should touch on one last issue before moving on, and that is the issue of prayer. If Judaism and Islam are involved with the real and living God, is interfaith prayer possible between Catholics and these religious traditions? Indeed, is interfaith prayer possible between Christianity and other theistic traditions such as Sikhism and strands of Hinduism? The formal teachings on this matter clarify three issues. First, authentic prayer is addressed to God as Trinity, is moved by the Holy Spirit, and draws us into an active and real

---

55 See the Congregation for the Doctrine of the Faith, *Letter to the Bishops of the Catholic Church on some Aspects of Christian Meditation*, 1989 (http://www.ewtn.com/library/curia/cdfmed.htm). The critical responses to this document sometimes fail to acknowledge that the document never restrains inculturation, but points to dangers in uncritical assimilation.

56 See: http://www.mid-gbi.com/index.html

relationship with the living God.[57] Second, the prayers of Israel in the Psalms are seen as authentic, even though they are not addressed explicitly to the trinitarian God. Third, as we see from point two, while not denying the 'authenticity' of some forms of non-Christian prayer, interfaith prayer is quite problematic because the explicit 'object' of prayer is different (Jews and Muslims, let alone Sikhs, do not pray to Father, Son and Spirit).

This last point is worth dwelling on, as the issue is addressed in *Redemptoris Missio, 29.* It is said that the prayers from other religions can arise from the movement of the Holy Spirit within a person's heart and be a genuine seeking after God. Pope John Paul II tried to clarify his presuppositions behind the Assisi meeting he convened in 1986 and again in 2002 after substantial concerns were expressed by some of the Roman curia, including the then Cardinal Ratzinger. In an address to the curia the Pope said:

> Every authentic prayer is under the influence of the Spirit 'who intercedes insistently for us' . . . , because we do not even know how to pray as we ought, but he prays in us 'with unutterable groaning' and 'the One who searches the heart knows what are the desires of the Spirit.' (See Rom. 8.26–7) We can indeed maintain that every authentic prayer is called forth by the Holy Spirit, who is mysteriously present in the heart of every person.[58]

This insight, slightly modified, has subsequently entered into an encyclical with teaching authority. In *Redemptoris Missio, 29* it is said that the

> Church's relationship with other religions is dictated by a twofold respect: 'Respect for man in his quest for answers to the deepest questions of his life, and respect for the action of the Spirit in man.' (*) Excluding any mistaken interpretation, the interreligious meeting held in Assisi was meant to confirm my

57 See John Paul II, *Redemptoris Missio*, 1991, 29; *The Catechism*, 2596; and my *The Meeting of Religions*, pp. 143–71.

58 In Address to Cardinals and the Roman Curia, 22 December 1986; published in *Bulletin* (Secretariat for Non-Christians), 64, 22, 1 (1987), pp. 54–62.

conviction that 'every authentic prayer is prompted by the Holy Spirit, who is mysteriously present in every human heart'.[59]

The action of the Holy Spirit in human hearts and cultures has now been repeated in a number of teaching documents, so in one sense, its application to prayer as one element of culture is unsurprising. But these prayers cannot be understood to be a full participation in the life of the triune God, but a form of participation that will find its fulfilment in trinitarian prayer and praise. Needless to say that the heart of the non-Christian might be more receptive and transformed (and thus their lives) in such prayer than that of a Christian who prays the Lord's Prayer without receptivity to the Spirit. The objective forms of beauty, reverence and solemnity such as the Muslim call to prayer properly recited, or the ecstatic joy and transformative rhythms of Sufi sung prayer, are remarkable. I have learnt greatly from both forms of prayer in their reverent and ecstatic witness, and have been deeply moved myself into prayer. I came to greatly appreciate the importance of communal public prayer and bodily movement in prayer, and also the importance of charismatic ecstatic prayer where we lose the security of a liturgy and leap into the abyss of the Spirit. I have met Muslims whose prayer life has caused me to feel shame for the lack of sincerity and regularity of my own prayer life. All this is of course a very different act from interfaith prayer, which while possibly legitimate in some limited cases,[60] cannot be possible as a regular practice given our deep differences in understanding God. I do not want to accentuate the intellectual dimension of prayer, but this aspect cannot be negotiated away either. Ratzinger makes a good case for deep respect and reverent witnessing to the prayers of others, but cannot see a strong case for interfaith prayer.[61]

---

59 The text then refers to the earlier papal speech given to the curia – see note above.

60 Such as a terrible public disaster within a community (like 9/11, or the tsunami in East Asia) or more intimately and inter-personally in hospital chaplaincies or interfaith marriages.

61 *Truth and Tolerance: Christian Belief and World Religions* (San Francisco: Ignatius Press, 2004), pp. 106–9.

Social justice

As we have seen, the relation between religions from a Catholic perspective has been profoundly oriented towards the common good. My own involvement with Hindus and Buddhists came precisely through this process in my Catholic commitment against nuclear weapons. While I was a doctoral student at Cambridge I was an active campaigner for the Campaign for Nuclear Disarmament (CND). Through CND I came to meet many Hindus and Buddhists (admittedly the majority were European converts to these religions), but found in their commitment to social justice a deep solidarity and a slowly growing friendship through our activities. At times I would despair that no one from my local Catholic community was involved in CND, while the religious commitment of my Hindu and Buddhist friends had led them to CND and a variety of other social justice networks. Some Catholics (including myself) are abysmally ignorant and inactive on the front of social justice despite the goldmine in the nearly one-century-long and constantly developing traditions of social justice.[62]

As has been made clear above a number of times, one of the major reasons given for interreligious dialogue is the service to the 'common good' which is enjoined upon all Catholics. Poverty, the environment, the arms race, the oppression of women and children all over the world are just some of the few horrendous crimes that cry out to God. Christians are called to address these problems in every way they can, and that includes working with those from other religions to bring about the 'common good'. These alliances can be grassroot communities working to build a well together, or groups to lobby politicians, or official bodies, like the Vatican and certain Muslim states coming together to put pressure on the United Nations regarding the issues of fertility. And of course, issues of social justice might also entail questioning and challenging

---

62 See the *Compendium of the Social Doctrine of the Church* (Vatican: Liberia Editrice Vaticana, 2004) and for the history of the social teaching, see Charles E. Curran, *Catholic Social Teaching 1891 – Present: A Historical, Theological and Ethical Analysis* (Washington: Georgetown University Press, 2002).

religious communities, including our own. For instance, the Vatican has made recent demands for reciprocal rights to be granted Christians in Muslim countries, such as Muslims enjoy in most western democracies. I think this is important, but we need to be careful here. It seems problematic to urge Muslim countries to be like western democracies (to be like us). There is surely more mileage in urging Muslim countries to follow the Qur'an more faithfully and show, if possible, that the Qur'an and *hadith* are capable of generating quite different views about religious freedoms within a Muslim society. I am not implying a type of relativism here, but simply following through my MacIntyrean form of argument: it is better to argue from within a tradition to a goal that one seeks. This type of intra-traditioned form of argument is more likely to convince a sincere Muslim. If that argument fails, then dialectical argument against the religion is required. If that fails, one might resort to international political pressure. If that fails, suffering must be undergone, for violence is not in my view a Christian option.

Conclusion

I want to commend the approach I have outlined above because it remains faithful to the ancient dogmatic teachings of the Christian Church, while applying and thinking them through in a very new context. It remains faithful to Christ and the revelation of the triune God, it remains faithful to Christ's founding of the Church as the means of salvation for all people, and yet without compromising these foundational tenets, it reaches out to other faiths and their adherents. In this reaching out there is a generous and joyful acknowledgement of the work of God in these religious cultures (in differentiated and nuanced ways) and a patient learning from these cultures. There should also be repentance for our many failures in these areas. In this reaching out there is a concern to join together to act for the common good and to help transform society and alleviate the suffering of the poor, to herald in the kingdom of God. In this reaching out there should be an acknowledgement that we can only 'reach out' as equals, seeking to learn how to love and serve and not dominate or denigrate. And in this reaching out, there is finally and foremost a call to be witnesses to Christ, to be missionaries of the gospel, and to call all peoples to baptism. Mission requires a delicate sensitivity to a plethora of issues, but it cannot be bypassed or ignored. Of course, the planting of church communities is the greatest witness, especially when those communities are marked by charity, love of the poor, and serving others out of the endless service of Christ to us. Learning to love involves an activity whereby only by being attentive to the triune God, the forsaken on the cross, can we learn that God's grace is to be found where we might expect it least.[63]

---

63 I am grateful for the use of some of this text from D'Costa, *The Catholic Church and the World Religions* (London; T&T Clark, 2011), pp. 1–33.

2

The Meeting of Religions: A Christian Debate

Paul F. Knitter

Theological method

The job description for theologians has been classically summarized as *fides quaerens intellectum* – faith seeking understanding.[1] That's what theology is. That, really, is what Christian life is all about – faith trying to make sense of itself within the world, the culture, the particular context of one's life. Faith naturally seeks understanding. And if it doesn't find it, it dwindles and disappears. After all, why believe something that doesn't make sense? Not even God would require that of us.

So to begin my section of this book, I'll try to lay out, as crisply and clearly as I can: (a) how theology works; (b) the role of language in theology; and (c) two of the most challenging issues that confront Christian faith and theology today.

Theology is an ongoing conversation

Let me offer this as a loose definition of theology: Theology is *a mutually clarifying and a mutually criticizing conversation between Christian experience and beliefs on the one side and ongoing human experience and understanding of self and the world on the other*

---

1 See Anselm of Canterbury, *Proslogion*, chs 1 and 2, in *Anselm: Basic Writings*, trans. Thomas Williams (Indianapolis, IN: Hackett, 2007).

side.[2] This is how 'faith seeks understanding' – by engaging in this honest and open-minded conversation between the two 'sources of theology' – that is, the 'text' of the Christian message and the 'context' of one's place in the world. It is a genuinely mutual conversation in which there are real questions and real answers on both sides. It's a conversation between what we believe God reveals particularly in Jesus the Christ and what God reveals universally in creation. God is speaking to us on both sides of the conversation, for while God has truly revealed something new and special in Jesus, God continues to 'speak' to us through the world. That's why we call this conversation 'mutually clarifying and criticizing'. What God has made known in and through Jesus helps us understand, clarify and correct our human experience. But our human experience and our human intelligence and conscience help us understand, clarify and correct our Christian beliefs. It's a two-way street.

I can hear the rumble of concern: does this mean that what God is revealing in my own experience and conscience is just as good as what God reveals in the Bible? Well, no, but also yes. Because the Bible – I'm talking especially about the New Testament – is the original witness, the primary source, for our knowledge of and contact with the particularly 'Good News' that God has offered in Jesus, it bears an authority that, one must say, is much more reliable than what I think God is making known through my own experience.

And yet – and yet – the truth and the authority of the Bible can become real and powerful for me only when it 'makes contact with' my own experience – only when it inspires me, or confounds me, with a truth that I can feel. This means that the truth that God has given us in the Bible is not, as it were, an apple that we can simply pick. It's more like a potato that we have to dig out. The Bible, in other words, has to be interpreted. And to interpret, we have to make connections between the 'sound waves' of the Bible and the

---

2 For an expanded description of the role of theology, see Brennan Hill, Paul F. Knitter and William Madges (eds), *Faith, Religion and Theology: A Contemporary Introduction* (Mystic, CT: Twenty-Third Publications, 1990), pt 3; also, Paul Tillich, *Systematic Theology*, vol. 1 (Chicago, IL: University of Chicago Press, 1951), Introduction.

'antennae' of our own lives. Or more simply, the Bible will speak to us only if we speak to it. Again, we're back to our image of theology as a give-and-take conversation.

Watch your language!

But the words that make up the conversation that is theology are a very special kind of words. They're special because their subject-matter is special. Theology, after all, literally means *theo-logia* – words about God. And if, as is commonly said, there are some things that are simply 'more than words can say', the reality of God has to be on the top of that list. In all the religions of the world, God or Ultimate Reality or *Brahman* or *Sunyata* is recognized as Mystery – that is, beyond human comprehension. And that means beyond human words. Therefore, if we ever think that our words or ideas are saying something about God in a final or full way, we are sadly, and dangerously, deluding ourselves. Augustine of Hippo's version of this truth should take the wind out of the sails of any theologian or Pope:

> If you have understood, then it is not God. If you were able to understand, then you understood something else instead of God. If you were able to understand partially, then you have deceived yourself with your own thoughts.[3]

Therefore, in my work as a theologian, and in my prayer as a Christian, I follow theologians like Paul Tillich and my teacher Karl Rahner in recognizing that all our 'God talk' is symbolic.[4] To speak about the Divine and things divine, we have to speak in symbols – that is, in metaphors, analogies, images. We should never think that our symbols or our notions capture all that can be said

---

3 Sermon 52, c. 1, n. 16.
4 Paul Tillich, 'Theology and Symbolism', in F. Ernest John (ed.), *Religious Symbolism* (New York: Harper, 1955), pp. 108–11; Karl Rahner, 'The Theology of the Symbol', in *Theological Investigations*, vol. 4 (Baltimore: Helicon Press, 1966), pp. 221–52.

about God. Yes, they say something. But they never say everything. The Buddhists have a symbolic image to make this point: when we try to speak about our deepest spiritual experiences – what they call Awakening or Nirvana – we must remember that our words, all our words, are 'fingers pointing to the moon'. Our words are never the moon itself. To identify our pointing fingers with the moon – or our language about God with God – is to make our fingers and our words into idols. That's what Augustine was worried about.

And if all our words are symbols, then, in general, they should not be taken literally. This is a tricky, disputed issue. Yes, the Bible or a church council are making what philosophers call 'truth claims', when they tell us that 'Jesus died on the cross and rose from the dead' or that 'the angel Gabriel appears to Mary'. They are announcing something that is really, actually true, something we can rely on. But there is always more to say, always a different way to say it. Religious language is much closer to poetry than to philosophy, more like a painting than a photograph. Therefore, the guideline for enabling religious language to 'work' for us is this: always take such language seriously; but be careful of taking it literally.

The two most pressing issues for Christian theology today

If theology is a conversation between 'what we are given to believe' and 'what is going on in our world', we have to be more precise about what is happening in today's world. For me, and for many Christians, the two most pressing questions that clamour for answers from my Christian beliefs are the many religions and the many poor. Yes, there have always been many religions and many poor people. But today, they are knocking on our door (sometimes literally!) and pushing themselves into our awareness as never before.

- Why, if Jesus is the only saviour and Christianity the only really true religion, has God allowed so many other religions to continue to prosper? And instead of competing and fighting

with each other, can the religions dialogue and co-operate together toward a world of greater peace and well-being?
• What can we do about the horrible reality of the millions of
people who cannot feed their children or provide a roof and
medicine for them? How address the glaring inequality of the
distribution of the goods of this world between the few who
have so much and the many who have so little? And of course,
when we talk of 'the many poor', that includes the impover-
ished earth, for the impoverishment of the earth, we are told,
and the impoverishment of peoples are intimately and murder-
ously related.[5]

Unless 'what I believe' helps me, if not answer, at least deal with
and struggle with such questions, it will not be a meaningful faith
for me. What is true must be meaningful. If it's not meaningful,
who cares if it's true?

Therefore, the two primary characteristics of the theology which
I will try to summarize in what follows – or the two criteria by
which I will evaluate whether a Christian theology is both meaningful for our contemporary world and faithful to the message of
Jesus – will be these: is it liberative and is it dialogical.[6]

• By liberative I mean, essentially, that it must be a theology that
shows how the message of Jesus and his Church enable us to
understand the causes of, and the solutions for, the widespread
suffering due to poverty and injustice.
• By dialogical I mean that it must be an understanding of Christian beliefs that both promotes and is informed by a dialogue
with other religions. Any theological interpretation of Christian belief that does not allow for and promote dialogue can't
be a responsible and orthodox interpretation. And once such

---

5 The Brundtland Report (1987) indicates that 'A world in which poverty
and inequality are endemic will always be prone to ecological and other crises.'
See World Commission on Environment and Development, *Our Common Future*, Oxford, Oxford University Press, 1987.

6 I try to lay out the necessity and possibilities of such a liberative dialogical engagement of religions in *One Earth, Many Religions: Multifaith Dialogue
and Global Responsibility* (Maryknoll: Orbis Books, 1995).

dialogue with other religions is embraced, it will in turn affect and inform the theological task of interpreting Jesus' message. In the pages that follow, I will try to make clear how much my dialogue with other religions, especially with Buddhism, has enabled me to understand more deeply and embrace more resolutely my own Christian faith.

These two essential characteristics of a relevant and orthodox Christian theology – that it be both liberative and dialogical – are vitally connected. With Hans Küng, I believe that only through a globally co-operative dialogue of religions can we achieve a world of global peace with justice.[7]

God/Trinity

Before I begin talking, or writing, about God, I need to post a reminder from my teacher, Karl Rahner: We experience God before we know God. All our 'talk' of the Divine is possible only because we have an inbuilt capacity to 'feel' the Divine. All the words we use for God are possible and meaningful only because they touch or give voice to what Rahner called the 'pre-thematic', or pre-verbal, experiences of the Divine that are as natural to our natures as a bee's bent to flowers.[8]

So where did I learn my 'God language'? From Jesus primarily. His ways of talking about the Mystery that held and guided his life – Abba, Spirit, Reign – confirm or clarify or correct the ways I have sensed this Mystery in my own interactions with people and the world. Certain Christian theologians – Rahner, Paul Tillich and, I should add, Raimon Panikkar[9] – have provided the broader philosophical framework for the deeper understanding

---

7 Hans Küng, *Global Responsibility: In Search of a New World Ethic* (New York: Crossroad, 1991), p. xv.

8 See Karl Rahner, *Foundations of Christian Faith: An Introduction to the Idea of Christianity* (New York: Seabury Press, 1978), pp. 126–33.

9 See Paul Tillich, *Systematic Theology*, vol. 1, pt 2; and vol. 3 (1963), pt 4; Raimon Panikkar, *The Trinity and the Religious Experience of Man* (London: Darton, Longman and Todd, 1973).

that my faith in Jesus seeks. And then there is Buddha. As I've tried to explain in a recent book, Gautama has helped me understand Jesus – or, the Dharma (Buddha's teachings) has enabled me to grasp the gospel – in such a profound, enlightening way that I can honestly say that *Without Buddha I Could Not Be a Christian*.[10] Like a growing number of Christians, I'm a 'double-belonger' – in this case, a 'Buddhist–Christian'.[11] Buddhist fingers, together with Rahner's and Tillich's and Panikkar's, have helped point me to the moon that guided Jesus' life and that he called 'Abba' or 'Dad'. I'll try to explain what I mean.

God as triune mystery

For Christians, to speak of the *one* God is not possible without speaking of the more-than-one God. The oneness of the divine Mystery does not exclude – indeed, it includes – the manyness of the divine Mystery. I know that sounds like polytheism (as my Muslim friends gently remind me). But it's not. Rather, it's a way of affirming and holding on to the Christian conviction that the unity that makes up the divine nature (and therefore the nature of the world) does not exclude – indeed, it absolutely requires – diversity. No diversity, no unity. No manyness, no oneness.

How do Christians know that? How can they dare to say anything about the inner nature of God? Rahner's answer is as simple as it is profound: the only way we can venture assertions about God's inner trinitarian nature (what he called the 'Trinity *ad intra*') is because that's how we experience God in our own lives and in the world (what he called the 'Trinity *ad extra*').[12] In other words: if this is how God seems to act in creation, we can assume that that's how God acts in the divine nature. The old theological slug makes common sense: '*agere sequitur esse*' – the way one acts flows from the way one is. We know what a person is like from the way

---

10 The title of my book (Oxford: Oneworld, 2009).

11 Catherine Cornille (ed.), *Many Mansions? Multiple Religious Belonging and Christian Identity* (Maryknoll: Orbis, 2002).

12 See Karl Rahner, *The Trinity* (London: Burns & Oates, 1970).

she interacts with us. If that doesn't apply also to God, we have no way of knowing anything about God. (This is what Catholic theologians call 'the analogy of being', and it forms the basis for all Catholic theology: finite being serves as a reflection pond for Infinite Being.)[13]

And after experiencing God in the way Jesus of Nazareth lived and died, in what he taught, and in the way his Spirit lived on in their communities after his death, the early Jesus-followers, through the course of the first four centuries after Jesus' death, came to conclude that the one God is also the triune God. Now there are different ways of 'unpacking' what it means to assert that 'three-ness' is part of God's oneness. Broadly and basically, we can put it this way: based on the way they encountered God through Jesus, Christians came to realize that God is a creating Mystery (therefore they used the symbol Father or Parent), a communicating Mystery (therefore the symbol of Word or Son/offspring), and an animating Mystery (thus, Spirit). The one divine Mystery acts, and therefore exists, in these three really different but essentially related ways.

The 'co-inhering' of God and world

This talk of God as triune may sound very abstract. But it contains very practical consequences for the way Christians understand and act in the finite world. To experience, and therefore to assert, that there is a divine power that creates, communicates and animates all that exists is to assert a mysterious immanence of God in the world – and of the world in God. The world is alive with the splendour and energy of the Divine. Within the very matter of the earth and within the complexities of human knowing and loving – God creates, communicates, and gives shape. As Paul in the Acts of the Apostles puts it: '*In God* we live and move and have our being' (Acts 17.28).

But if we really take the Trinity seriously, it also works the other way around: In the world, God lives and moves and has the divine

---

13 For 'the analogy of being', see Thomas Aquinas, *Summa Theologica* I, q. 4, a. 3.

being. This pervasive mutual indwelling of the infinite God and the finite world is what process theologians have called *panentheism*: it's not just that 'everything' (*pan*) participates in (*en*) God (*theos*), but God participates in everything. It's a two-way relationship: the world exists in God, but also, and just as truly, God exists in the world.[14] Here we are also touching on the powerful truth that Christians and Jews (I would also add Muslims) say is distinctive about their experience of God: theirs is a God of history: God does not just 'step into' or 'intervene' in history here and there. God expresses God's very self – we can say, that God takes shape – within the processes of history. (Here we're laying the groundwork for our next section on creation.)

My mentor and long-time friend, Raimon Panikkar, has expressed this profound co-inhering of God in the world and the world in God in the somewhat awkward but at the same time poetically powerful image of all reality as a *cosmotheandric* process. The universe as we know it (and there's admittedly a lot we don't know) is a dynamic, co-relational, and open-ended interacting of matter (*cosmos*), humanity (*aner*), and divinity (*theos*). They are all very different in their basic natures, and yet all of them are what they are by interacting with each other and giving life to each other. One cannot be reduced or boiled down to the other (a human being is more than a clump of primal mud, God is ever more than humanity). And yet, one, as it were, gives rise to the other, and then depends on what it has brought forth. Radical, irreducible difference. And yet radical, ineradicable inter-dependence.[15]

Paul Tillich has also helped me, as he has helped many Christians, come to a deeper awareness, both intellectual and experiential, of this profound immanence of God within all the world. He reminded Christians that what they mean by the symbol, 'God' (and he stressed that as soon as we open our mouth to speak about

---

14 See John B. Cobb, Jr, and Jeanyne B. Slettom (eds), *Process Perspective: Frequently Asked Questions about Process Theology* (St Louis: Chalice Press, 2003), ch. 1, 'God'.

15 Raimon Panikkar, *The Cosmotheandric Experience: Emerging Religious Consciousness* (Maryknoll: Orbis, 1993).

God, symbols, willy-nilly, are going to pour out) is not 'a being'. God, he stressed, is not a Being but rather, the 'Ground of Being', or 'the Power of Being'. Also, God is not a person, but rather the energy of love and freedom that makes us persons. Mixing poetry and philosophy, Tillich put it this way:

> The God who is a being is transcended by the God who is Being itself, the ground and abyss of every being. And the God who is a person is transcended by the God who is the Personal-Itself, the ground and abyss of every person.[16]

What Tillich and Panikkar and Rahner are labouring to express is a deep, pervasive and, yes, perceptible immanence or co-inhering of the Divine within the finite world. They are nudging, sometimes pushing, Christians to move beyond the 'God out there', the totally or primarily transcendent God. Philosophically, they are pursuing a more radical – really, a more mystical – non-duality between God and finite reality. For years, I have struggled, both in my thinking as a theologian and in my praying as a Christian, to come to a more satisfying understanding and feeling for what they were getting at. Or, to use the words of Jesus in John's Gospel, I have wanted to grasp, or be grasped by, what Jesus meant when he said, 'On that day you will know that I am in my Father, and you in me, and I in you' (John 14.20). This is where Buddha has helped.

God: the power of Inter-Being

My dialogue with Buddhism, and my practice of forms of Buddhist meditation, have enabled me, I believe, to come to a deeper, and more coherent, understanding of and feeling for this co-inhering of God and the world. One of the primary 'fingers' that Mahayana Buddhists use to point to what counts most for them is *Sunyata*. Contemporary Buddhists like Thich Nhat Hanh have translated its literal

---

16 Paul Tillich, *Biblical Religion and the Search for Ultimate Reality* (Chicago, IL: University of Chicago Press, 1955), pp. 82–3.

meaning, 'Emptiness', as Inter-Being. For Buddhists, Inter-Being is what gives reality and dynamism to all that exists. Inter-being is the ground and source or fundamental nature of everything – mineral, vegetable, animal. And every finite being is a form or expression of Inter-Being. That's what Mahayana Buddhists are getting at when they tease us with the pithy description of all reality: 'Emptiness is Form and Form is Emptiness.' Inter-Being is every single finite thing, and every single finite thing is Inter-Being.[17]

Inter-Being or *Sunyata* can serve us Christians, I believe, as another – and perhaps a more engaging and revealing – way of pointing to, or symbolizing, the triune God. Simply: the reality we call God *is* Inter-Being. Buddhism can help Christians, I believe, to comprehend and to feel the meaning of the only two texts in the New Testament that offer a 'definition' of God: 'God is Love' (1 John 4.8) and 'God is Spirit' (John 4.24). If God is love, what is love? It's the power, the creative dynamism that connects atoms, molecules, cells, species – and most marvellously, human beings who truly care about each other. When we feel the need to love, the power and beauty of love, the responsibility that love requires – we are experiencing God-as-Inter-Being.

We Christians have been given an engaging symbol for this God as Inter-Being: Spirit. Spirit is a symbol that points to the ever-present mystery, but at the same time the ever-present availability, of the Divine. As John's Gospel reminds us: 'The wind [or Spirit: *Pneuma*] blows where it chooses, and you hear the sound of it, but you do not know where it comes from or where it goes' (John 3.8). Indeed, we, usually without awareness, breathe in this Spirit and live by it just as we inhale and exhale air. It becomes us and we it. And it is the same Spirit that every living being is breathing in and out. By giving life and being to each, it is the Inter-Being of all. 'Spirit' (*Pneuma*) – the Christian symbol for God – and Inter-Being (*Sunyata*), the Buddhist symbol for what is ultimate – are symbols that can give life and deeper meaning to each other.

---

17 See Thich Nhat Hanh, *The Heart of Understanding: Commentaries on the Prajnaparamita Heart Sutra* (Berkeley, CA: Parallax Press, 1988), pp. 3–5; 15–18.

So Buddhism has enabled me and other Christians to comprehend and to find words and symbols for the profound, mysterious non-duality of God and all creation that I felt was truly present but not clearly affirmed in my own Christian tradition. To affirm 'a God of history' who truly acts in and through historical process, or even more profoundly, to affirm an incarnational God who is identified with human flesh and blood – that is to affirm a non-dual or mutual indwelling, or co-inhering, of the Infinite and the finite. Or as Panikkar likes to put it: God and the world – or more personally, God and I – are 'not two' (non-duality!). But that does not mean that they/we are one, that they are identical. God is both the 'totally Other' (*totaliter aliter*) but at the very same time, the 'not-Other' (the *Non-Aliud*)[18] What this really means, or how the Divine and the finite indwell or co-inhere with each other, can be known not through words but only through the experience that is called mystical.

Here we are touching the essential and the vital connection between theology and spirituality. Here we are full-circle with the opening sentence of this section: in order to know or think about God (theology), we first must experience or feel God (mysticism or spirituality). There are two primary ways, I suggest, by which we can and do become aware of the non-dual mystery of the indwelling Spirit that is always beyond all words: 'the mysticism of silence' and 'the mysticism of service'. We need both. To become aware of the Spirit breathing within us, we must withdraw from the daily demands of life into some form of regular meditational and prayerful silence. But we must also engage in the daily demands of life that come to us in the faces and the needs of others, for it is in the face of the *other* (human but also all sentient beings) that we feel the call and presence of the *Other*. In silence and in service, we will 'hear the sounds' of the Spirit, although we may not know 'where it comes from or where it is going'.

This non-dual reality of God as indwelling and inter-connecting Spirit is what Christians find present in and revealed by Jesus of Nazareth. But it was there *before* Jesus was born. It is the Mystery

---

18   This is the expression of Nicholas of Cusa. See *Nicholas of Cusa on God as Not-other* (Minneapolis: Arthur J. Banning Press, 1987).

that hovers within and comes to expression in very, very different ways beyond Jesus and Christianity. It is the Spirit that animates other religions as it animates Jesus and Christianity – in a diversity that, like the diversity of the triune God, enables ever greater unity among the religions but can never be reduced to only one religion.

Creation/Fall

The way we understand God determines the way we understand creation. So, if we take the image of God offered in the previous section – that is God as the dynamism of Inter-Being that creates, communicates with, and animates all that exists – then we will see and engage creation not as a product of God but as an outpouring of God. This is a crucial difference. As a product, the world, as it were, sits on God's work-bench having been put together by God, and then God tries to give it further shape by adding on here, subtracting there – all, of course, with due respect for human freedom. But if the world is an outpouring of God's very Inter-Being, then the divine creative Spirit forms the world from within as part of the world-processes. Again, this is a non-dualistic understanding of God–creation. It's not pantheism, which holds that God and creation are one and the same. But it's not dualism either, which holds that God and the world are two separately existing and functioning realities. A non-dualistic understanding of creation, which views the world as an outpouring of the Divine, tries to express the vital co-inhering and dynamic interaction between God and creation. Though profoundly different – as different as cause and effect – God and the world exist in and through and with each other.

A non-dualistic, co-inhering image of the God–world relationship both 'deconstructs' and 'reconstructs' traditional Christian understandings of creation.

Creation as free

Back in the first half of the 1960s, when I sat in the classrooms of the Gregorian University in Rome (during the same years when, down the street at the Vatican, the Second Vatican Council was shaking up the Catholic Church), I learned in my course on *De Creatione* that creation was an absolutely free act of God – that is, God didn't have to do it. God could have been just as happy all by God-self, without creating anything other than God. Actually, my professors went on, God wasn't really by God-self since God is tri-une and includes the diversity and the interactions of what theology call the 'three divine persons'. Since the 'oneness' of God includes the 'manyness' of the Trinity, God can never be alone.

Hmmm. The questions and doubts that nagged me then grew even more nagging over the years as I tried to connect these traditional understandings of creation with what I was learning from contemporary science and from other religions. But what I was forced to deconstruct, I was enabled to reconstruct. The reconstruction was based on this foundation: if we Christians want to be serious and consistent about our belief that 'God is love', then we also have to recognize that God *had to* create. Why? Because love, by its very nature, has to give of itself, it has to go out of itself, it has to enter into relationship – simply, it has to have something to love. To counter that God can satisfy this natural need by loving God's self in the Trinity is – well, to be honest, too neat, too easy; and to be even more honest, it sounds a little like the 'autoerotic spirituality' that Cardinal Josef Ratzinger once accused Buddhism of.[19]

But if God creates because God is love, there is nothing forced about such creation. This is what the traditional insistence on creation as a free act was worried about – God can't be forced. Right. But also, God cannot not love. God has to love because that's what God, in order to be God, does. If God cannot not love, God cannot not create. To say that God has to create is like saying that we have to breathe. Breathing is not a free choice; it's part of living. So is loving for God.

Therefore, there was never a time when God was not pouring out God's self in creation. This would mean that creation, like God, is eternal. That seems to contradict traditional teaching about

---

19 See Chapter 1, n. 36.

creation taking place 'in time'.[20] Not really. This creation, or the creation of this universe, took place in time – about 14 billion years ago, scientists tell us. But there may have been other creations, or other universes, before this one, just as there may be after this one. If the source of all reality is, as Christians affirm, a Mystery that can be symbolized as love, then that source and that God is, by nature, creative. In fact, as Gordon Kaufmann suggests, *Creativity* might be another appropriate name for God.[21]

Creation as evolution

This understanding of God as creating the world not from out-side (an efficient cause that produces) but from within (a formal cause that indwells) enables us to believe in God the Creator with-out denying Darwin the scientist. Creation is not a one-time event that took place at the very beginning of time. Rather, though it may have had a start, it's an ongoing process, the characteristics of which make it a messy and painful, but also a marvellous and open-ended, adventure. For if God creates not from above but from within, that means that God creates *together with*. If God is Cre-ator, we are co-creators.

And that 'we' includes not just us human beings, endowed with intelligence and free will, but also all the other animals and plants and elements endowed with in-built responses to the randomness of events. The growth or the evolution of the universe, and what we know of our earthly part of the universe, reveals, to the scien-tist and to the poet, on the one hand a bewildering mess of chance happenings (like genetic mutations) and complex connections and adjustments (like natural selection), and on the other hand, a cre-ativity or an ability to produce out of this mess surprisingly new creatures that weren't there in the beginning – atoms to molecules to cells to living beings. Within this mess of chance and competition

---

20 Ludwig Ott, *Fundamentals of Catholic Dogma*, trans. Patrick Lynch (St Louis: Herder, 1952), p.79.

21 See Gordon D. Kaufman, *In the Beginning . . . Creativity* (Minneapolis: Augsburg Fortress, 2000), ch. 3.

and co-operation, there is a Creativity that is utterly dependent on
the mess – but not limited by it. Indeed, the Creativity seems to
work in and through and with the mess that is chemistry, and biology, and humanity.

Pierre Teilhard de Chardin was one of the first theologians to
recognize that creation – and we can say, God as well – is evolutionary. From his experience as a scientist and a Jesuit, he proposed a
vision of the world as *The Divine Milieu*.[22] More recent theologians
like Sallie McFague have spoken about 'the world as God's body'.[23]
God is creating the world through the world! Process theologians
bring further clarity with their symbolism of the Divine Presence as
a 'creative lure' or a new possibility within the myriads of interactions (or 'actual occasions') taking place within every moment of
time. God can be imaged as a presence or energy within world processes that lures or invites to ever more relationships, ever greater
complexity, ever more pervasive unity – all of which means, ever
greater beauty. God is the artist of the world, able to work even
with ugliness and pain to create beauty and greater life.

Original sin and the fall

But there seems to be an awful lot of road-kill and ugliness on the zig-
zag path of evolution as well as in the life-span of every human being.
Christians have tried to wrestle with this reality through the symbols
of the fall and original sin. Like all doctrines, this one has gone through
an evolution of its own. Today, for most Christians, the meaning of
'the fall' is lost if taken as a one-time historical event because of which
we all enter the world with a blotch on our soul that has to be removed
through baptism before we can be admitted to heaven.

Rather, the truth of the story of Adam and Eve and of the serpent
and the apple lies not in its historicity but in its message that from

---

22 Pierre Teilhard de Chardin, *The Divine Milieu*, trans. Sion Cowell
(Brighton, and Portland, OR: Sussex Academic Press, 2004).

23 See Sallie McFague, *Life Abundant: Rethinking Theology and Economy
for a Planet in Peril* (Minneapolis, MN: Fortress Press, 2001), ch. 6, 'God and
the World'.

early on in the history of humanity, something went wrong. God didn't start it. Humans did. From the very get-go, we can say, human beings began to use – or better, abuse – their divinely endowed gift of freedom. And they did so mainly in decisions to use other human and sentient beings, as well as the earth itself, for the purpose of personal gain or self-aggrandizement. Selfishness seems to be at the heart of what went wrong.

And this selfishness has snow-balled throughout history and become social selfishness. We are born into a world which tells us that 'I' or 'we' are *numero uno* (that means everyone else is *numero dos* or even *tres*); in which for me to gain, you will have to lose (called zero-sum societies or economies); in which violence is the only way we can protect or maybe advance our well-being (called the 'myth of redemptive violence');[24] in which it is taken for granted that one class or nation or gender will have power over the other.[25] Original sin, therefore, is better understood as a corrupting social or cultural reality rather than as an individual blight that separates us from God. It bears enlightening resemblance to what contemporary Buddhists call *social karma*. Karmas tell us that what we are and what we have to deal with when we are born is determined by what happened before we were born. Both symbols – karma and original sin – remind us that we are born into the world that loads us down with a good bit of negative baggage. That's the 'bad news'. The good news is that it's the kind of baggage that we can unpack and replace.[26]

---

24 See Walter Wink, *Engaging the Powers: Discernment and Resistance in a World of Domination* (Minneapolis: Fortress Press, 1992), ch. 1, 'The Myth of the Domination System'.

25 Rosemary Radford Ruether sees patriarchy as a primary embodiment of original sin. See her *Sexism and God-talk: Toward a Feminist Theology* (Boston: Beacon Press, 1983), ch. 7.

26 For a Buddhist reflection on karma and justice, see Rita M. Gross, 'What Buddhists Could Learn from Christianity', in Rita M. Gross and Rosemary Radford Ruether, *Religious Feminism and the Future of the Planet: A Buddhist–Christian Conversation* (New York: Continuum, 2001), pp. 163–82; for Christian reflections on original sin as social sin, see Piet Schoonenberg, *Man and Sin: A Theological View* (Notre Dame, IN: University of Notre Dame Press, 1965).

But Buddhists, I suggest, can help us Christians clarify just what needs to be replaced. Although we agree that what Christians call 'sin' and Buddhists call 'suffering' is caused by 'selfishness', we differ on what makes us selfish. For Christians, we sin and act selfishly because we are 'fallen' – that is, broken down (the Protestant view) or deeply wounded (the Catholic). Buddhists see it differently: we act selfishly because of *avidya* – ignorance: we don't know what or who we really are. We think we are individual beings, but in reality we are 'inter-beings' who can find their personal happiness only by promoting the happiness of others. If we could really 'wake-up' or be 'enlightened' about that, our behaviour would begin to change; we would not act selfishly, not because it is sinful, but because it is silly.

Original blessing

I believe that Buddhists, in suggesting to Christians that their sinfulness is rooted in ignorance and not in corruption, can help Christians rediscover and start living the missed message of the Genesis story. It is a story not primarily of 'original sin' (that was an interpretation that came later, especially through Augustine of Hippo) but of 'original blessing'. We were created as God's children. That's our true nature. We've lost contact with that true nature not because we were corrupted by an action of the first human beings, but because we, like our first mythical parents, thought we knew better. We ate of 'the tree of the knowledge of good and evil' and got mixed up. But thanks to the help of people like Jesus and Buddha, we can clarify our vision and know who we really are; in Jesus' message, we remain God's children no matter what we have done. Divine love and divine grace are at our disposal. But before we can really know that and act on that, we may have to deal with the 'original sin' that is around us in a culture of selfishness. To change our hearts, we also have to change society.

And Jesus assures us that we can. The 'original blessing' is still the 'daily blessing'. Where there is sin and selfishness and ignorance, in ourselves and in our society, there is the possibility of even greater grace and love and change. That means that for Christians, evil – the suffering that we cause each other and ourselves because of our selfishness and ignorance – never need have the last word. 'Original blessing' is greater than 'original sin'. As Albert Nolan has put it: 'Anyone who thinks that evil will have the last word or that good and evil have a fifty–fifty chance is an atheist.'[27]

That, as we shall see in the next section, is the good news that Jesus delivered.

Jesus the Christ

The area of Christian belief that carries the lead, as well as the most threatened, voice in the new conversation with other religions is Christology. How to understand Jesus, his person and his work, in light of so many other religious founders and leaders? The question is loaded with both possibilities and perils. We want to proceed carefully, but also honestly. We're dealing with what makes Christians Christians.

To put all this in the terms and images of the previous sections: for people who call themselves Christians, Jesus is the decisive and transforming embodiment of the holy Mystery of love and Inter-Being that pervades all of creation. Jesus enables them to feel, to identify, and to trust the Spirit that is already present, truly but often ambiguously, at the core of human nature. As a recent book on Christology sums it up: for Christians, Jesus is indeed 'the Symbol of God'.[28] In more traditional language: the incarnation of God.

It all began some two millennia ago when a group of Jewish peasants in Galilee met one of their fellow peasants and soon realized that to meet this man was to meet God. The first accounts of these early meetings of Galilean peasants, the stories of what Jesus preached and did and how it all led to his execution under the occupying Roman army, the witness and interpretations of the early communities that grew up under the impact of his continued presence – all

27 Albert Nolan, *Jesus Before Christianity* (Maryknoll: Orbis, 1992), p. 103.

28 Roger Haight, *Jesus Symbol of God* (Maryknoll: Orbis, 1999).

this is contained in what is called 'the New Testament'. These 27 books are much more statements of faith than they are records of history. They speak more reliably about what Jesus meant to his followers and how he transformed their lives than about what Jesus actually said (his *ipsissima verba* or 'very words') and what he thought about himself. And yet, though not intending to be a history book, the New Testament offers us a trustworthy picture of what Jesus was about, what he preached, why it led to his state execution, why he so powerfully touched and transformed people's lives. The story of Jesus, as told in the books of the New Testament and as carried on in the life of his community called church, has proven, for millions, to be clear enough, powerful enough, reliable enough to recognize and follow Jesus as the presence, the Word, the incarnation of the Mystery they call God.[29]

Of all the marvellous things the early Jesus-followers said about him, of all the symbols and titles they applied to him (titles he never gave himself), I would like to focus on four claims that are both essential to Christian identity and, for many contemporaries, problematic for Christian belief: Jesus as Son of God, Jesus as saviour of the world, Jesus as raised from the dead, and 'there is no other name under heaven given among mortals by which we must be saved' (Acts 4.12). Again, I want to proceed as carefully as I can in both critiquing and reclaiming how these beliefs can be affirmed meaningfully and coherently in a world of religious pluralism.

Jesus the Son of God

The proclamation that Jesus is the Son of God is the foundational and the distinguishing belief of Christianity. It is also a symbolic statement. In saying that, I certainly don't mean that it is not true. I

---

29   Recent Christologies that have helped me: Jon Sobrino, *Jesus the Liberator: A Historical-Theological Reading of Jesus of Nazareth* (Maryknoll: Orbis, 1993); John Dominic Crossan, *Jesus: A Revolutionary Biography* (San Francisco: HarperSanFrancisco, 1994); Marcus J. Borg, *Meeting Jesus Again for the First Time: The Historical Jesus and the Heart of Contemporary Faith* (San Francisco: HarperSanFrancisco, 1994).

mean that its truth is in its power as a symbol. It cannot be taken as a literal statement, for as the Muslims remind us, God does not generate offspring as animals, both rational and otherwise, do. When the early Christians first proclaimed, to themselves and to the world, that Jesus was the Son of God, they were trying to express how Jesus had affected their lives and why he was able to do so. They called him the Son of God not because he told them to, but because their experience of him led them to this conclusion. When they looked for words to express their experience of him, they found suitable images in the language of their own Jewish or Greek cultures – a language that spoke about human beings as 'sons and daughters' of God. Yes, such language, such images, captured what they felt, what Jesus meant for them. He was God's son par excellence – more than, different from, all other sons or daughters of God.[30]

To designate 'Son of God' a symbol is, as I said, not to deny its truth. But it is to challenge us not just to assert its truth with our minds but to feel its truth with our whole being. What I'm trying to say is contained in Paul Tillich's and Karl Rahner's understanding of what a symbol really is. For both these theologians, symbols are necessary to communicate or express realities that are beyond ordinary words. Symbols enable us to see things we would otherwise not be able to see. Symbols participate in that which they symbolize but cannot be identified with what they symbolize. A wedding ring, in the eternity of its circularity and in the preciousness of its material, truly participates in the love that it expresses; yet that love is so much greater than this little, but so important, ring.[31]

So when the first Jesus-followers called Jesus the Son of God, they were using a symbol that expressed for them the experience that to meet Jesus was to meet God. It was a symbol that communicated

---

30   Haight, *Jesus Symbol of God*, ch. 15, 'The Divinity of Jesus Christ'; Edward Schillebeecckx, *Christ: The Experience of Jesus as Lord* (New York: Seabury Press, 1980), pp. 427–32; and *Jesus: An Experiment in Christology* (New York: Seabury Press, 1979), pp. 256–69 and 480–99.

31   Karl Rahner, 'The Theology of the Symbol' and 'The Word and the Eucharist', in *Theological Investigations* (Baltimore: Helicon Press, 1966), vol. 4, pp. 221–52, 253–86; Paul Tillich, *The Dynamics of Faith* (New York: Harper & Row, 1957), ch. 3, 'Symbol of Faith'.

a closeness between Jesus and God, a relationship, a participation that was as tight, as intimate, as they could imagine. For them, 'Jesus' and 'God' were almost the same thing. But they weren't the same thing! Jesus as symbol participated fully in the divine reality he symbolized; yet he was not the fullness of that reality, for as he reminded his disciples in John's Gospel, 'the Father is greater than I' (John 14.28b). For these early Christians, all of Jesus symbolized God; but they knew that Jesus did not symbolize all of God. There's more to God than the God that is Jesus.

But how can a human being symbolize God? For Rahner, that's really not such a difficult question. With thunderous simplicity (it was thunderous for me the first time I read it back in the 1960s) he wrote that to say that Jesus is divine is to say that in this human being, human nature achieved its full potential! When God wanted to fully communicate God's self, Rahner tells us, God created (through an evolutionary process) human beings; human nature becomes fully alive when it is attuned to divine nature – when it responds to the Spirit given to all of us.[32]

Given this understanding of what it means to call Jesus the Son of God, the question that presses is not how Jesus was the Son of God, but why he is the only Son (or Daughter) of God. If we understand Jesus' divinity as the fulfilment of his humanity, it would make sense, so it seems, that others have also achieved this fulfilment so that they, too, can serve as symbols for the majority of us struggling to figure out who we really are.

Jesus: saviour of the world

After Jesus' death, and after their experience of his continued presence, the first Jesus-followers knew that he 'saved' them – that is, that he enabled them, as John's Gospel puts it, to 'have life, and have it abundantly' (John 10.10b). But they couldn't agree on just

---

32 Tillich, *Systematic Theology*, vol. 2, pp. 94–6; Rahner, *Foundations of Christian Faith*, pp. 212–27.

how. There are a variety of 'soteriologies' in the New Testament – efforts to explain why and how Jesus is saviour.[33]

Risking precision for clarity, I identify two quite different paths that the early Church followed in trying to explain how Jesus, in his teachings and in his life and death, saves us. Both are rooted in the New Testament, but one of them became, from the Middle Ages on, much more popular. This 'soteriology' has been called the Atonement or the Satisfaction model. Essentially, it understands the death of Jesus as fixing something that was broken. Because of original sin and the fall (understood rather literally), the relationship between God and humanity had been broken; there's a gap between God's love and humanity's fallen state. Jesus, especially on the cross, repairs that gap and that relationship. By satisfying the divine justice, Jesus at-ones the loving God and all human beings who believe and trust in Jesus' atoning death. For many Christians, this understanding of Jesus' death as the washing away of sins still works, as is evident to anyone in the United States who flips through the radio or television stations on Sunday mornings. For other Christians – and I'm one of them – a God who sacrifices his own Son in order to satisfy his sense of justice looks a lot like a petulant and even an abusive father.[34]

The other way of explaining and responding to how Jesus saves can be called the Sacramental model. In this view, Jesus doesn't fix anything, because there's nothing to be fixed. Yes, we humans have created a mess by acting ignorantly and selfishly; but that has not changed the reality of the ineradicable presence and power of God's love. Our problem is that either we have lost touch with the ever-present, loving and creating God; or we are afraid to trust that such a divine presence is real. Jesus makes a difference by revealing, by embodying and making known this God whom he called 'Abba' or Father. This, according to Catholic sacramental theology,

---

33 Stephen Finlan, *Options on Atonement in Christian Thought* (Collegeville, MN: Liturgical Press, 2007).

34 Dolores Williams, *Sisters in the Wilderness: The Challenge of Womanist God-Talk* (Maryknoll: Orbis, 1993).

is what sacraments do: they make known and make real what is already there and available but not seen or trusted. And by making it known in such a powerful way, they make it real for us. So Jesus, in the way he makes God's love powerfully present for us and in the way he calls us to be ready, as he was, to lay down our lives – not to satisfy an offended God but for each other – in this way, Jesus is God's *primary Sacrament* for Christians.

There is a further advantage to this model. Besides being more meaningful for many Christians, it also makes room for others, for other saviours in other religions. If salvation is understood as a matter of fixing what is broken, then there can be only one fixer. Once something is repaired, especially if the repairer is divine, it doesn't need to be fixed again. But if salvation comes through a re-vealer of something that is already to be found within creation, then there is not only room, there is also the need, for other revealers for other cultures and other historical periods. Jesus as the Sacrament of salvation is open to other sacraments.

Jesus the risen one

Throughout this section, I've often referred to 'the continued pres-ence' of Jesus after his execution. What kind of presence? How did it come about? We're asking about the resurrection, another of the much debated issues of contemporary Christology.

Again, in a bold attempt to unravel a tangle of viewpoints, I be-lieve there are three contrasting viewpoints on what the resurrection was. The historical fact, which no one can deny, is that a group of Jesus' disciples, in a matter of a few days, were transformed from a state of despondency after his execution to renewed commitment to his cause. Something must have happened to them. What was it?

1 *A physical event.* The traditional view holds that Jesus stood in front of them in a physical, tangible body.
2 *A psychological event.* This more radical view holds that the resurrection is fundamentally a subjective event in the psyches of the disciples. Despite their despondence, they gathered up their courage and continued to believe in Jesus and his cause.

3 *A spiritual event.* Proponents of this perspective recognize that the resurrection was a subjective experience in the disciples' faith, but they also recognize that this experience had to have an *objective* cause. It was not self-generated. As the apostle Paul tells us, it was the still-living 'Spirit of Christ' that they encountered after his death (Rom. 8.9–11; 12.12–13; Phil. 1.19).[35]

For me, the data of the New Testament leads me to endorse the third interpretation – the resurrection as a genuine encounter with the living spirit of Jesus (probably in the context of breaking bread and remembering him), which the New Testament authors described as various appearances (some very physical, as when Jesus asks for something to eat (Luke 24.41–3), and others not physical at all, as when all Paul hears is a voice and those with him don't even hear the voice (Acts 9.1–8)).[36]

But, honestly, I don't want to argue about it. What I want to insist on, loudly and clearly, is that no matter how you understand 'what actually happened' at the resurrection, if Jesus is not a continuing presence in your life right now, if the Spirit of Jesus is not living in the Christian community as his 'mystical body' right now, then so what if he physically stepped out of the tomb. The best proof that Jesus rose from the dead is that he continues to live in the lives of his followers and in the Church.

But to be fully honest, there is a further reason why I prefer an understanding of the resurrection as a historical and continuing encounter with the still-alive Spirit of Jesus: it makes room for others. It doesn't put Jesus on an unreachable pedestal above all other religious founders or figures. Indeed, though Buddhists and Hindus do not speak of resurrection, they do affirm, in different ways, the

---

35 For an overview of interpretations of the resurrection: John Dominic Crossan and N. T. Wright, *The Resurrection of Jesus: The Crossan–Wright Dialogue* (Minneapolis: Fortress Press, 2006); Gavin D'Costa (ed.), *Resurrection Reconsidered* (Oxford: OneWorld, 1996).

36 For me one of the best summaries of the discussion is offered by Edward Schillebeeckx, *Interim Report on the Books Jesus and Christ* (New York: Crossroad, 1981). Also, Haight, *Jesus Symbol of God*, ch. 5, 'Jesus' Resurrection'.

continued power and presence of Buddha or Krishna in the lives of their devotees.

The 'uniqueness' of Jesus

So, is Jesus unique? If so, how so? We'll touch on this more in the next section, but for the moment let me try to say succinctly what I have laid out more elaborately elsewhere: With a growing number of Christians, I continue to affirm that Jesus of Nazareth is truly the Son of God, truly saviour – but I do not feel the need of insisting that he is the only Son of God and saviour.[37] By holding to 'truly', without claiming 'only', Christians can, I believe, remain faithful to the intent of the New Testament witness: they can continue to be disciples of Jesus, experiencing his presence and living his message in their own lives and witnessing it to others.

So I am questioning Jesus' uniqueness only if it means 'only'. I am not questioning it if it means 'distinctive'. By holding to 'truly', I am affirming that both the person and the work of Jesus are distinct, for they contain something that is not found elsewhere in the same way, to the same degree, with the same focus. There are many ingredients in the message of Jesus for which all the 'one and only' language of the New Testament can make sense. No other saviour saves like Jesus. But there may be other saviours, who may bring people 'to have life and have it more abundantly' in different ways. In holding to the distinctiveness of Jesus, Christians can be open to the distinctiveness of Buddha or Muhammad or Confucius. God may be revealing other 'distinctive' and universally relevant truths in other religions, and these religions might enhance or clarify or correct the way we have understood the message of Jesus. Whether that is the case can be known only if we engage those other religions in authentic dialogue and co-operation.

---

37 See my *Jesus and the Other Names: Christian Mission and Global Responsibility* (Maryknoll: Orbis, 1995). Also, Leonard Swidler and Paul Mojzes (eds), *The Uniqueness of Jesus: A Dialogue with Paul Knitter* (Maryknoll: Orbis, 1997).

Salvation and justice

If, as I've just tried to explain, it is much more engaging for many Christians to relate to Jesus as a Sacrament rather than a Satisfier – as one who makes known what is really true rather than fixes what is radically broken – how can we describe what Jesus makes known? And how can we do that in a way that both makes sense for and does not exclude people of other religions?

If Rahner helped me get a better hold on how Jesus saves, it is liberation theologians like Aloysius Pieris, Jon Sobrino and Gustavo Gutierrez who have helped me grasp what salvation is – that is, what it feels like and what it looks like. Christian salvation, briefly but I think accurately, is both a mystical and a prophetic experience. I've found that trying to explain what that means elicits the interest and the response of my other-religious friends.

A mystical experience of 'being in Christ'

If one were to ask the apostle Paul to give a one-sentence summary of what it means to be saved by Jesus Christ, I bet his response would have been: 'To be saved means *to be in Christ Jesus.*' That phrase comes up over a hundred times throughout his authentic epistles.[38] For Paul, to be a Christian is, in his original Greek, '*en Christo einai*' – to be, to live, to act, to see the world 'in Christ'. What Paul is trying to describe is what we would today call a mystical experience – an experience of transformation by unification, of finding oneself by finding a larger Reality that embraces oneself, of finding one's own identity beyond one's own identity, an experience of being empowered by a Power that is both beyond and within oneself. For Paul, that Power, that Presence was 'Christ Jesus' or 'the Spirit of Christ'.

Salvation as being in Christ brings further light to what was meant in the previous section when I suggested that Jesus saves by making

---

38 Marcus J. Borg and John Dominic Crossan, *The First Paul: Reclaiming the Radical Visionary behind the Church's Conservative Icon* (New York: HarperOne, 2009), pp. 185–213.

known. What is made known is not a body of knowledge such as a professor might communicate to her students. It's not knowledge that stays in the head. Rather, it seeps through one's entire being to enlighten and empower one's heart and feelings. This is what the medieval theologians meant when they told us: 'sacraments *cause* by *symbolizing*' (*symbolizando causant*). What they make known through symbolizing is not just knowledge but power (or, empowering knowledge) that brings forth something new, something that wasn't there before: a transformed life – or better, a life in the process of transformation. When I really encounter Jesus the Sacrament of God, I can say not only that I know something new but that I am something new. As Paul Tillich used to put it, Jesus embodies and communicates New Being.[39]

This New Being is lived out as an embodiment and continuation of the way Jesus of Nazareth lived his identity with the Christ–Spirit. In other words, to be in Christ is to be the 'body' in which Jesus continues to do his thing, to carry on his mission. We Christians, individually and collectively, are all Christ's body, animated by his Spirit, trusting in the same Abba, working to realize this Abba's Reign.

The classical text in which Paul summarizes what it means to be a Christian is Galatians 2.20: 'It is no longer I who live, but it is Christ who lives in me.'

This understanding of what it means to be saved will have some salutary repercussions on how we come across to persons of other faiths. If being saved means first and foremost living our lives 'in Christ Jesus', the most important and the most defining thing about being a Christian will not be to praise Jesus, but to follow him. (That, of course, does not exclude praise.) Our primary concern, throughout our Christian lives, but also in the way we interact with other believers, will not be to announce that Jesus is superior over all other religious figures; it will not be to insist that 'our saviour is better than your saviour'. Rather, it will be to be Christ and to follow Jesus. And that means following his 'greatest commandment' – to love, respect, learn from, challenge, co-operate with

---

39   Tillich, *Systematic Theology*, vol. 2, pp. 118–38.

our neighbours, even or especially when those neighbours follow other religious paths. Compared to this greatest commandment to love and dialogue, questions concerning whose saviour is bigger, or whether there is only one or many saviours are secondary. Saviours are meant to be followed, not bragged about. For Christians, it's important to 'be in Christ Jesus'. Let others see that, and then draw their own conclusions.

The prophetic experience of seeking the reign of God

If the heart of Paul's message was 'to be in Christ Jesus', the heart of Jesus' message was 'the kingdom of God has come near' (Mark 1.15). Different though they are, both messages are vitally linked to each other. Both make up, if I may extend the image, the 'bicameral heart' of Christian belief and practice. The mystical experience of being in Christ is lived out as the prophetic experience of working toward the Reign of God. Such prophetic work, in turn, calls for and gives further depth to the mystical experience of being nurtured and motivated by one's union with Christ.

If there's anything that can unify the often dissonant chorus of scripture scholars, it's the centrality that the *Basileia tou Theou* – the Reign of God – played in the spirituality and in the preaching of Jesus. Before he was identified as the Son of God or saviour, he was seen as a Jewish prophet. And Jewish prophets have a long history of measuring fidelity to Yahweh by a concern for social justice. To know God is to do justice, they proclaim (Jer. 22.13–16). Jesus was a part of this tradition (in fact, some experts hold that he considered himself the last in the line-up of Jewish prophets).

As Jon Sobrino has pointed out, we're missing something crucial if we think that the focus of Jesus' mission was faith in the Abba-God. That's true. But it's also incomplete. Jesus' controlling concern was God's Reign. 'God' without 'Reign' was for Jesus a false, or at least a limping, God. If he would have preached only about God, he wouldn't have ended up on the cross. What got him into trouble with the Roman and Jewish authorities was the Reign part of his preaching – especially that aspect of the Reign that Christians pray for every day: 'may thy Reign come on earth as it is in heaven'. Jesus truly believed that if people could really get in touch with the God he called Abba (through mystical experience), they would also believe in and work towards a different way of organizing society and politics right here in this world – a new world order.[40]

It would be a social and a political order based on compassion and justice. Such values, clearly, were not foundational for Roman politics (and if one looks at the impoverishing economic disparity in today's world, nor for today's global politics). Jesus grew up in Galilee, one of the poorest and most exploited regions of the Roman colony of Palestine. His notion of the Reign of God was a prophetic protest. That's why, as with most prophets, he had to be silenced.

The distinctiveness of Christian salvation

This brings us to what makes for the distinctiveness of Christian salvation. Note, by 'distinctiveness', I don't mean superiority. I mean that which gives something its particular identity, that without which it would not be what it is. So what makes Christian salvation distinct? What gives it its particular identity and therefore its universal meaning for others? Such a question cannot receive a 'once and for all' answer. The distinctiveness of what Christians call salvation will be grasped differently at different stages of history or in different cultures.

But today, given what scripture scholars tell us about the message of Jesus and given the needs of our world (back to our theological method in the first section!) we can say that one of the most distinctive contents of Jesus' saving message is what liberation theologians have called 'the preferential option for the poor'. In the way he preached, and more so in the way he worked toward, the Reign of God, Jesus called his followers to work for a more

40 John Dominic Crossan, *God and Empire: Jesus Against Rome, Then and Now* (San Francisco: HarperSanFrancisco, 2007); Richard A. Horsley, *Jesus and Empire: The Kingdom of God and the New World Disorder* (Minneapolis, MN: Fortress Press, 2003).

compassionate and just world order by starting with a particular concern for those who have been pushed aside, marginalized, stepped on, exploited by 'the powers that be'. That doesn't mean that the powers that be – whose power is based on having more money or more weapons – are themselves to be pushed aside or not-loved. Jesus preached both compassion and justice. This means compassion also for the powerful holders of wealth. An option for the oppressed is not necessarily an option against the oppressors.

But it does mean that the needs, the experience, the voice of the 'little ones' or of the people who 'don't really count' must be given priority. The God of Jesus loves everyone, but this God has a more pressing concern for people who want to but can't feed their children. The followers of Jesus have to stand with and stand for the marginalized of this world – even if it costs them their jobs, their own families, their lives. That's a pretty distinctive message.

As Aloysius Pieris puts it, with intentional provocation, Jesus is 'God's defence pact with the poor'. He admits that this is right in line with all the Jewish prophets. But in the prophet Jesus it takes on a particular depth and power. As Pieris goes on, given the intimacy of God and creation (see the section above), we shouldn't really be surprised that 'God became human' (or 'is revealed as human') in the incarnation in Jesus. After all, Pieris comments, God could incarnate God's self in a flower as well. But what is really surprising, especially for those in power, is that in Jesus God became or is embodied as a poor person, a peasant, a *campesino*, a carpenter. With Mary and Joseph (and his siblings, the Bible tells us) he was a Galilean peasant who couldn't make ends meet because of a horrible burden of taxation from the Roman and the temple authorities. As Elizabeth Johnson concludes, the fact that Christians claim that they find God in a Galilean peasant 'reveals the creator God to be freely on the underside of history, identified as a source of hope with those ground down by oppression and death'.[41]

Now, Pieris, in his dialogue with friends from other religions (and I can confirm this in my own experience), has found that when

---

41 See Elizabeth A. Johnson, 'Galilee: A Critical Matrix for Marian Studies', *Theological Studies* 70:2 (2009), p. 340.

he speaks of 'the distinctiveness' or the 'uniqueness' of Christ and Christianity in this way, people listen; they do not hear this as 'our saviour is better than yours'. Rather, this is an approach that calls on Christians to state forthrightly what they believe is distinctive and urgent in their understanding of 'salvation', at the same time calling upon Christians to listen openly to what is distinctive in the experience of other religious traditions.[42]

This is the message that Christians humbly but resolutely bring to the interreligious dialogue: If you are not tending to the marginalized, the oppressed, the pushed-aside of this earth, you are not yet in touch with the fullness of the Mystery we call God. Your mystical experience of the Divine may be profound (and we Christians may have much to learn from you in that regard); but if mystical experience does not also include a prophetic commitment to the oppressed, something is drastically missing.

Only if Christians are trying to live this 'distinctiveness' can they credibly announce it to others.

Church/mission/dialogue

I place these three pieces of the mosaic of Christian beliefs together – church, mission, dialogue – because one defines the other; or, you can't have one without the other. The Church is mission; mission is dialogue. And if they're all held together, and lived together in the practice of Christian life, they make for what can be called 'a dialogical ecclesiology' – an understanding of the Church in which, as the bishops of Asia have phrased it, 'dialogue is a new way of being church'.[43] – Let me try to unpack that simple but powerful declaration.

---

42 Aloysius Pieris, 'Christ beyond Dogma: Doing Christology in the Context of the Religions and the Poor', *Louvain Studies* 25 (2000), pp. 187–231.

43 Gaudencio B. Rosales DD and C. G. Arévalo (eds), *For All the Peoples of Asia: Federation of Asian Bishops' Conferences Documents from 1970–1991* (Maryknoll: Orbis, 1992), pt III.

The Church is mission

'As the Father has sent me, so I send you' (John 20.21b). There you have the foundation of the Christian Church. If, as theologians and New Testament scholars remind us, Jesus cannot be called 'the founder' of the Church – in the sense of laying out its basic, unchanging structure of Pope, bishops, priests, seven sacraments – he certainly laid its foundation.[44] And that foundation is itself rooted in Jesus' conviction that he was 'on a mission'. Even after his bloody execution, even after the Roman authorities made him into a *desaparecido*' (a 'disappeared one', as the churches of El Salvador speak of their martyrs), his disciples came to know and be convinced that he was still alive, still carrying on his mission – but now *in them*.

And for Jesus to carry on his mission in them, they had to come together, consolidate their community, carry on already familiar rituals such as baptism and the 'Lord's Supper', determine how to organize leadership and the various roles or 'offices' within the group (a very complicated process that took a particular shape of bishops–priests–laity but is open to taking on new shapes).[45] Like creation, the founding of the Church had a beginning, but it is ongoing. And all the different 'shapes' that the Church has taken over the centuries, especially since the much-needed Reformation of the sixteenth century, all of the 'externals' of ritual and organization and preaching and teaching – all of this has one central purpose: to carry on the mission of Jesus.

Therefore, we can and we must recognize that the Church doesn't *have* a mission but the church *is* a mission. The Christian Church is not a community with a mission. Rather, the Church is a mission that needs a community. These distinctions are not just theological niceties. They make for life-orienting differences in why one chooses to be a Christian and a member of the Church. The rock-bottom

---

44 Richard P. McBrien, *The Church: The Evolution of Catholicism* (New York: HarperOne, 2008), pp. 29–31.

45 See Edward Schillebeeckx, *Ministry: Leadership in the Community of Jesus Christ* (New York: Crossroad, 1981). Also, McBrien, *The Church*, pp. 285–321.

reason why one chooses to be part of the Church is *not* to save one's soul! Certainly, the Church will help one do that. But as the Catholic Church has officially taught since the Council of Trent in the sixteenth century and more clearly in the Vatican Council of the 1960s, you don't have to be a member of the Christian Church in order to save your soul.[46] That you can do elsewhere as well. But to carry on the mission of Jesus in the world, if that's your desire, then you choose to join a community with whom you can work and struggle and believe. You need a Church.

To understand and live in the Church-as-mission means that the life and dynamic of this community is centrifugal rather than centripetal. Its fundamental dynamism is to move out into the world, rather than to retreat from or find refuge from the world. Certainly, however, before one can 'move out', one has to 'move in'. Before we can carry out the mission, we ourselves have to have imbibed and been transformed by the mission of Jesus. The inner life of the Church – prayer, liturgy, community – building and – sustaining – are absolutely essential for its life. But all that Christians do to build their own communities is never an end in itself. Its purpose is to form disciples who know who they are, who can draw on their 'being in Christ', who will have the courage and the stamina to 'hang in there', even when they face the prospect, like Jesus, of being hung.

But all this may sound a bit grandiose – as if only the Church, only Christians, can 'save the world'. This is where we need to take seriously the reminder of contemporary missiologists (missiology = the theology of mission): the mission of the Church, like the mission of Jesus, is part of the *missio Dei* – the mission of God. That means that it is only one part – surely a central, essential part, but still only one – of a broader movement: the movement of the divine Spirit (that we described in the sections on God and creation) as it permeates and continually creates, transforms, and so 'saves' all of creation.[47] While Christians affirm that Jesus is a distinctive and universally

---

46   The clearest statement of this is found in Vatican II's Constitution on the Church, *Gaudium et Spes*, 16.

47   David J. Bosch, *Transforming Mission: Paradigm Shifts in Theology of Mission* (Maryknoll: Orbis, 1999), pp. 389–93.

powerful incarnation of the *missio Dei*, that mission is bigger than Jesus and the Church. It has multiple expressions, throughout history, especially in the religious traditions of the world.

The Church of God and the Reign of God

But Christians give the symbol of the 'mission of God' greater specificity and concreteness. They describe this mission in terms that Jesus used: the mission of God is the promotion of the Reign of God. In specifying 'mission' as 'Reign', we get an even clearer picture of the role of the Church: the Church is always a means to an end, never an end in itself. That end is the Reign of God – the gradual, incremental growth of a 'new world order' which some theologians call 'the Commonwealth of God'[48] – a new way of organizing society, national politics, globalization on the basis of justice and compassion instead of greed and domination. That's the primary and the ultimate goal of the Church – as philosophers might put it, the Church's *raison d'être* or reason for existing: to foster, to insist on, never to give up hope for, what Jesus called the Reign or the Commonwealth of God.

The Church, essentially and fundamentally, is a servant of the Reign of God. That means that as this Christian community gathers together to nurture its own life (centripetal) and as it makes its missionary movement into the world (centrifugal), its primary intent is not to promote itself but to promote the Reign of God. More precisely, and perhaps uncomfortably, the first and really determinative goal of the Church's mission and of the Church's missionaries is not conversions to the Church but transformation of society. It's not to make the Church bigger but the world better. This seems pretty clear in the way the Gospel of Luke describes one of the first missionary mandates that Jesus gave his disciples: 'Then Jesus called the twelve together and gave them power and

---

48 David Ray Griffin, John B. Cobb, Jr, Richard A. Falk and Catherine Keller, *The American Empire and the Commonwealth of God: A Political, Economic, Religious Statement* (Louisville, KY: Westminster John Knox Press, 2006).

authority over all demons and to cure diseases, and he sent them
out to proclaim the kingdom of God and to heal' (Luke 9.1–2). He
sent them to proclaim the Reign of God, which meant first of all
to cure diseases, to heal, to cast out demons. He doesn't mention
making them into new disciples for his little community. I suggest
we Christians keep this first missionary mandate in mind when we
try to understand the 'last mandate' in Matthew's Gospel (Matt.
28.16–20). To 'make disciples of all nations' means, first of all,
calling them to heal, cast out demons of selfishness, transform the
world. That's the primary definition of a 'disciple'. Baptism into the
Church of Christ can be a next step. But it's not a necessary step. A
disciple, understood as someone who heals and cures the sufferings
of the world, can also be a disciple of Buddha.

But don't get me wrong. In claiming that the primary mission
of the Church is to promote the Reign not the Church, or to call
people to discipleship in the Reign not baptism into the Church, I
am not at all suggesting that the Church should disregard conversions and baptism into the Christian community. The community
of Jesus-followers, announcing Jesus' distinctive message of the
Reign of God, needs to grow, to continue, and that means to take
on new cultural forms beyond those of the Graeco-Roman world
(now the Euro-American world) in which it has found its dominant
cultural expression.[49] When people decide to 'convert' and join the
community called Church, Christians will rejoice and welcome
them warmly. But such conversions are not the primary goal, the
dominant concern, of missionary work. To paraphrase Jesus: 'Seek
first the Reign of God, and everything else, including conversions,
will be added' (Matt. 6.33).

Mission = prophetic dialogue

All these calls that I've been making to my fellow Christians to
'go forth' and build the Reign of God might come across as – or

---

49 But not the only cultural expression: see Philip Jenkins, *The Lost History of Christianity* (Oxford: Lion Hudson, 2008).

actually become – rather imperialistic. We're no longer going forth to establish Church; but we are trying to establish the Reign. And the very real danger in this is that we will impose on others our understanding of the new world order implied in this Reign. It is here, therefore, that we have to add the third ingredient in the title of this section: if the Church is mission, mission is dialogue.

I'd like to suggest a simple, but perhaps demanding, solution to the contemporary controversy among theologians on how to reconcile dialogue and mission.[50] There is no need to reconcile them, for they are essentially the same thing. The problem lies in what are really the restricted understandings of dialogue and mission. Mission has been understood as announcing, and dialogue has been understood as listening. Really, though, both these dynamics – speaking and listening, or teaching and learning – are essential to what we understand dialogue to be: both partners in a dialogue have to listen to each other, but both also have to state loudly and clearly what they believe. Otherwise, there's really nothing to listen to!

And this is basically the expanded understanding of mission that theologians are talking about nowadays (at least in many mainline churches): mission is proclaiming or teaching, but it is also, just as much, listening or learning. Missionaries both give witness and accept witness. But that's the definition of dialogue. Dialogue is a synonym for mission. Missionaries are dialoguers – both teachers and learners. As teachers and announcers, they will be bringing something to the other religions that will challenge and fulfil these other traditions. But as listeners and learners, missionaries will enrich the Church with challenges from other religions that will fulfil the Christian churches.[51]

But Christian missionaries or dialoguers, if they want to represent and be faithful to Jesus the Christ, will bring to the dialogue with other religions a specific content and challenge. It has to do with the distinctiveness of Jesus that we explored in the previous

50   This controversy is addressed in the Vatican's statement: *Dialogue and Proclamation*.

51   For more on this notion of mission = dialogue, see my *Jesus and the Other Names*, pp. 136–64.

section. Jesus not only announced his vision of the Reign of God and of the possibility and necessity of fashioning a world of greater co-operation and well-being for all; he also stressed that to do this we must give particular attention to the plight and needs of those who have been pushed aside. This central, co-ordinating concern for justice, especially and primarily for those who have been treated unjustly and have been taken advantage of – this is what makes the Christian part of the dialogue with others prophetic. Jesus' and the Church's understanding of God's demand for justice and preferred concern for the poor and marginalized will come as a challenge and often a threat to those who hold power. Power is gained and held by subordinating some people to other people. That was the case with the Roman empire, the British empire, the American empire.

So the Christian mission will be understood as prophetic dialogue. Christians will go forth into the world and enter into relationships and conversations with other religious believers, as well as with secular humanists, convinced that they have much to learn. But they will also deliver the prophetic message of Jesus that justice with compassion, for all people but especially for the marginalized, is essential for building a better world, a world closer to what Jesus envisioned as the Commonwealth of God.

In carrying out such a mission-as-prophetic-dialogue, Christians will be contributing to an encounter of religions in which religious believers, in general, will not change their religious affiliation; but they will deepen, clarify and fulfil their own spiritual identities. Christian mission will make Christians better Christians and their dialogue partners better Hindus, Muslims, Buddhists or Jews. The world stands in dire need of all religions sending such missionaries to each other.

Eschatology – the last things

'Eschatology' is a big word theologians use to try to answer an even bigger question: Where is it all going? What comes at the end of it all – the end of my life, this planet, the universe? In trying to answer such questions, one thing is certain: no one knows for sure. Here, perhaps more than elsewhere, Christians have to be careful about taking their language too literally or too assuredly. Granted such caveats, in trying to outline a Christian eschatology for a religiously plural world, I believe that Christians have a lot to contribute to the religious dialogue, but also a lot (maybe even a little more) to learn.

There's 'something going on' in history

It's generally said that there are contradictory differences in the way monotheistic and Asian religions understand time. For Jews, Christians and Muslims, time moves forward linearly; for Hindus, Buddhists and Taoists it goes around in a circle.

First, then, to summarize the Christian view of time: it's one of hope.

Because Christians have, for the most part, learned well from their Jewish mother, they believe in, and try to live in sync with, a God who is up to something in history. As we saw in the section on creation: the Holy Mystery that Christians call God is intimately engaged in creation; the incarnation of this God in Jesus is a symbol or a revelation of what is happening throughout history: God is expressing Godself in the stuff of matter and humanity. And in the section on Jesus, we learned that what God is up to in history can succinctly be described in the symbol of the Reign or the Common-wealth of God. Followers of this Jesus believe that in and through human agency – that means in and through human intelligence and free will – the Divine is seeking to bring the planet a little closer to a new world order based on compassion and justice.

That means that history – world history and your personal history – is going somewhere. Or more accurately, it *can* go some-where. The potential is there. No matter what happens, no matter how much humans mess up and misuse their free will, no matter the inconceivable evils of the Holocaust, of slavery, of patriarchy, of the decimation of indigenous peoples – no matter what, there is always the possibility of turning things around, of making things better, even of using what clearly looks like 'evil' as an occasion for a greater good. Why? Because the inter-connecting Spirit is working within history and through human beings. Humans are never left to their own resources, even though their own resources are necessary for changing things. So in situations that look utterly hopeless (a broken marriage, the death of a child, the war in Iraq), Christians have to say 'looks are deceiving'. Though it may take a while to recoup and gather one's emotions and strength, there is always hope.

The end of the world?

But Christian symbolism about the end of the world and the 'Second Coming of Jesus' imply not only that history can move forward but that it will reach an end point, a grand finale. Heaven is envisioned in many Christian imaginations as a 'beatific vision' which comes after this material world is totally dissolved, and in which we will enjoy the vision of God forever. Buddhism has been for me the occasion to ask whether such a view of 'the end' is the only or most enriching way to understand the symbol of heaven and the second coming. For Buddhists, there are no final ends – for the simple reason that everything changes. Nothing, absolutely nothing, stays the way it is. There is always change – because there is always Inter-Being, ongoing life through relationships.

So my dialogue with Asian religions has prompted me to ask whether we western Christians, in the way we have understood our eschatological symbols, have ended up imposing human categories on the Divine. More precisely, what we think is final for us may not be final for God. The end of this world, for example, may not be the end of all worlds. And if what we said in the section on creation about God having-to-create because of having-to-love is correct, then there have to be other worlds, other creations, other universes. The end of this world will then be the beginning of another world. I guess I'm proposing an open-ended eschatology – an eschatology of ends that are beginnings. There's never a really final end.

The future is nowhere else but now-here

With such an open-ended eschatology, Christians are basically and incorrigibly optimists about the future. They can believe that progress is possible, that this world of selfishness, violence, domination of the weak by the strong does not have to stay the way it is. Christians are oriented toward the future, toward a 'better world'.

But there are dangers in such a commitment to the future. Buddhists have helped me become aware of such dangers, for they don't like to talk about the future at all. In fact, they see dangers in hoping too much.[52] They insist on 'being here now'. Don't worry about or be distracted by plans or hopes for the future, Buddhism admonishes. Rather, give your full attention and energies to the present moment. Whatever the future might be is all contained in the present moment.

Here the Buddhists are nudging us Christians to take more seriously what New Testament scholars have been reminding us of over the past few decades: for Jesus, the 'Reign of God' was both *already* and *not yet*.[53] At this very moment – for Jesus then and for us now – the Reign of God is both truly present in all its power and inspiration, and at the very same time, it is still coming, still to be realized. There's a powerful eschatological paradox bursting the seams of Jesus' message, a paradox that I, and many Christians, perhaps miss. The already/not-yet quality of the Reign does not mean simply that we're not there yet. Rather – and here is where Buddhism pushes us to look more deeply – the Reign of God is already fully present right now, right in this situation; but we have not yet awakened to it in order to real-ize it – that is, to make it real.

This still sounds too theoretical, too philosophical. To wake up to and to real-ize the 'not yet' aspect of the Reign of God, we have to be fully present to, fully responsive to – or as the Buddhists put

52 Pema Chodron, *When Things Fall Apart: Heartfelt Advice for Difficult Times* (Boston: Shambhala, 1997), pp. 38–45.

53 Crossan, *Jesus: A Revolutionary Biography*, ch. 3, 'A Kingdom of Nuisances and Nobodies'; Marcus J. Borg, *The Heart of Christianity: Rediscovering a Life of Faith* (San Francisco: Harper San Francisco, 2003), ch. 7, 'The Kingdom of God: The Heart of Justice'.

it, fully mindful of – the 'already' aspect of the Reign. To resort back to the terminology of our section on God, there is a *nonduality* between the not-yet Reign and the already Reign – a co-inhering of the future and the present. So the only way to realize or bring about the future is to be truly mindful of, and responsive to, and ready to learn from the present moment. Don't let our plans for what the future must be like distract us from what's going on in the present moment. If we are so distracted, we may miss the future by imposing our plans on it! So the sub-heading of this section is an admonition and an inspiration: the future is nowhere else but now-here. Everything we need for the future is given to us in the present. To know that and to live that is an act of faith, an act of trust – a mystical experience of the Spirit, who is already present but not yet fully realized.

Personal immortality: heaven? hell?

So far we've explored Christian eschatology in cosmic terms (the end of this world is the beginning of another) and in earthly terms (history is going somewhere). But Christian belief in 'the final things' also attempts to answer the question: 'What about me?' Personal immortality. And the sobering response – as terrifying as it can be inspiring – has been: You're going to end up in either hell or heaven (maybe with a stint in purgatory before heaven). How can such symbols be understood in our religiously plural and dialogical world?

Regarding hell, like many of my fellow Christians, I don't have a big problem with the noun; my difficulties are stirred up by the adjective that is usually placed before the noun: *eternal*. Hell may be an important symbol in Christian belief. But it has been literalized to the point of standing in blatant contradiction to other, and more pivotal, doctrines. Its importance lies in its admonition to take our free-will very seriously, for our decisions can have drastically harmful consequences, for us and for others, during our lifetimes and after we've left the scene. Like the Buddhist teachings on karma, hell warns us that we can mess up and mess up profoundly.

But to take the adjective 'eternal' – which, we should remember, is attached only twice to the 15 times that 'hell' is mentioned in the Gospels – literally and absolutely and to conclude that God decrees, or just allows, God's children to suffer infinitely and eternally for the finite and context-conditioned selfish choices they made – such a conclusion and such a doctrine not only offends common sense and sensitivity, it contradicts the teachings of Jesus that God is Abba, a loving parent. For human parents to allow their children to suffer the often painful consequences of their foolishness is understandable. For a human parent to allow their children to suffer forever and ever and ever – that is a sign of a sick parent. I cannot avoid the conclusion that the same would apply, even more so, to a divine parent.

The symbol of hell warns us that the effects of our 'evil' and selfish decisions are hellishly painful, lasting, able to reach beyond our individual selves and lifetime. But given the image of a God who is incorrigibly loving and patiently persistent, evil never has the last word. Nor does hell. How the Spirit will overcome and save us and the world from our selfish choices is a mystery that we cannot comprehend but that we are intimately involved in.

But how will we, as individuals, be involved in the mystery that carries on after our death? Over the past decades theologians – especially process theologians – have been exploring, with significant controversy, just what kind of immortality followers of Jesus should expect: subjective or objective?[54] Will we enjoy 'eternal life' as individuals with the same self-consciousness we have now, or will it be an existence that transcends individuality?

The dialogue with Buddhism can, I suggest, offer Christians some inspiring help with this question. Buddha taught that our true nature as human beings is to be 'not-selves' (*anattas*); to discover who we really are, we have to move beyond our own ego-awareness and

---

54 For Christian views of afterlife as beyond personality, see Schubert M. Ogden, 'The Meaning of Christian Hope', in Henry James Cargas and Bernard Lee (eds), *Religious Experience and Process Theology* (New York: Paulist Press, 1976), pp. 195–214; Marjorie Suchocki, *The End of Evil: Process Eschatology in Historical Context* (Albany: State University of New York Press, 1988), pp. 81–96.

ego-needs; only then can we realize that our 'true self' is to be a 'not-self' in the web of Inter-Being. Is this what Jesus was getting at when he said that we have to lose our life in order to find it (Matt. 10.39; 16.25)? Or what Paul meant when he proclaimed that he no longer lives because Christ lives as him (Gal. 2.20)? These are calls to transcend individuality in this life. And what we strive for as Christians in this life will be, we hope and expect, even more radically realized 'in heaven'. We will live on, not in our body-bound individuality but in the limitlessness of the divine life of Inter-Being.

I know that such an image of afterlife leaves a lot of questions unanswered – mainly, 'Who am I after I am no longer me?' Such a question, I suggest, should not be answered because it cannot be answered. It's mystery. I prefer to cherish the mystery and not to cloud it with too many words. All I can and want to do is trust that 'what I am' will be transformed into 'what continues to be'. Just trust. The older I get, the more that makes sense. Cherish the mystery.[55]

---

55   If you want a few more words on this mystery, see Paul F. Knitter, *Without Buddha I Could Not Be a Christian* (Oxford: Oneworld, 2010), ch. 4.

3

Perilous Exchange, Precious Good News: A Reformed 'Subversive Fulfilment' Interpretation of Other Religions

Daniel Strange

Indeed their rock is not like our Rock.[1]

This apprehension of the essential 'otherness' of the world of divine realities revealed in Jesus Christ from the atmosphere of religion as we know it in the history of the race, cannot be grasped merely by way of investigation and reasoning. Only an attentive study of the Bible can open the eyes to the fact that Christ, 'the power of God' and 'the wisdom of God' stands in contradiction to the power and wisdom of man. Perhaps in some respects it is proper to speak of contradictive or subversive fulfillment.[2]

Introduction

'Be prepared!' In the interests of pastoral health and safety, both authors and audience would do well to heed the universally recognized Scouting motto, and brace themselves for what I imagine we may well witness in this volume; the 'whiteknuckle' experience of

---

[1] Deut. 32.31. Unless otherwise indicated, biblical references are from the New Revised Standard Version.

[2] Hendrik Kraemer, 'Continuity or Discontinuity', in *The Authority of Faith: International Missionary Council Meeting at Tambaram, Madras*, vol. 1 (London: Oxford University Press, 1939), p. 5.

what happens when hermetically sealed, and often incommensurable theological worlds, not only come into contact with each other, but are seen to be on a trajectory for head-on collision. Such 'pioneering' can be exciting and constructive, helpfully prising us out of our own unquestioning confessional comfort zones. However, these encounters are not for the temperamentally faint-hearted or easily offended, nor are they for those who simply want to undertake theological experimentation in a sterile academic test tube. Ultimately, what is at stake here in this ensuing dialogue is the self-understanding of the worldwide Christian Church, her beliefs, her boundaries and her mission. So, 'Be prepared!'[3]

Speaking from my own tradition-specific perspective, and knowing the Christian 'theology of religions' I am about to both describe and prescribe, I am contextually self-aware enough to know the enormity of the apologetic task ahead of me. For in what follows I will seek to interpret other religions from within a particular confessional tradition which might be labelled 'Protestant Reformed orthodoxy' or 'conservative evangelical'. Both methodologically and substantially the doctrinal 'grammar' from which I will be articulating a Christian interpretation of religion seeks to be faithful to

---

3 I would like to add an appreciative note here that both my Roman Catholic co-authors are experienced practitioners of such intra-Christian understanding and dialogue. Not only has Paul Knitter acknowledged my 'evangelical' tradition (for example 'to ignore, or downplay, the strength, importance, and challenge of Fundamentalists and Evangelicals within contemporary Christianity is to cut off, or do injustice to, a large part of the Christian family', *Theologies of Religions* (Maryknoll: Orbis, 2002), p. 19), and interacted with other evangelical Christians (such as Leonard Swidler and Paul Mojzes (eds), *The Uniqueness of Jesus: A Dialogue with Paul Knitter* (Maryknoll: Orbis, 1997)), but his 1972 Marburg doctoral dissertation (the first Roman Catholic to receive a doctorate from this Protestant faculty), was an important study of certain Protestant scholars within the theology of religions, and which was later published (ironically in the year of this author's birth!): *Towards a Protestant Theology of Religions: A Case Study of Paul Althaus and Contemporary Attitudes* (Marburg: N. G. Elwert, 1974). D'Costa is well aware of my own tradition and has made reference to this in his work (for example *Christianity and World Religions: Disputed Questions in the Theology of Religions* (Chichester: Wiley-Blackwell, 2009), pp. 25–33). I should note also that I have personal knowledge of D'Costa as he supervised my own doctoral research.

biblical revelation (supremely), but also the ecumenical creeds,[4] the five *solas* of the Reformation,[5] the creedal affirmations of Reformed orthodoxy,[6] and several pan-evangelical statements and covenants that have appeared in the last forty years.[7] In particular I need to note my indebtedness to the thinking of the Dutch Reformed missiologist J. H. Bavinck (1895–1964).[8] I make no apologies for my dependence on his work in this area.

My 'theology of religions' can be summarized as follows: from the presupposition of an epistemologically authoritative biblical revelation (itself presupposed on the self-contained ontological triune God who speaks authoritatively), I will argue that non-Christian religions are essentially an idolatrous refashioning of divine revelation, which are antithetical and yet parasitic on Christian truth, and of which the gospel of Jesus Christ is this 'subversive fulfilment'. Such an interpretation has a number of soteriological and missiological implications which I will also outline.

Now it is fairly uncontroversial that the weight of Christian history has supported a position with strong family resemblances to

---

4   The Apostle's Creed (third to fourth century), the Nicene Creed (381), the Athanasian Creed (fourth to fifth century), and the Creed of Chalcedon (451).

5   *Sola Scriptura, solus Christus, sola fide, sola gratia, soli Deo Gloria.*

6   The 39 Articles (1571, Anglican); the Westminster Confession of Faith (1643–6, Presbyterian); the so-called 'Three Forms of Unity' which consist of the continental creeds (the Heidelberg Catechism (1563), the Belgic Confession (1561), and the Canons of Dordrecht (1618–19)); and the New Hampshire Baptist Confession (1833, Baptist).

7   Particularly significant here are the Frankfurt Declaration (1970), the Lausanne Covenant (1974) (the fruit of the International Congress on World Evangelization, originally initiated by Billy Graham), and the Manila Manifesto (1989). For details and commentaries on these documents see John Stott (ed.), *Making Christ Known: Historical Mission Documents from the Lausanne Movement 1974–1989* (Carlisle: Paternoster, 1996).

8   J. H. Bavinck occupied the Chair of Mission at the Free University in Amsterdam from 1939 to 1965. Prior to this he was a missionary in Indonesia. For more details of his life and work, see Paul J. Visser, *Heart for the Gospel, Heart for the World* (Eugene: Wipf & Stock, 2003). I am especially indebted to Visser as his book contains many quotations from Bavinck's work that have yet to be translated into English.

the one just summarized.[9] It can also be argued (albeit less uncontroversially) that the continuing growth of Christianity in the world is largely occurring in confessional communities that would again historically espouse a position similar to my own.[10]

However, within the context of liberal western culture generally, and more specifically within the western theological/religious-studies academy, there exists a deep implausibility structure regarding a position like my own, with 'defeaters' being legion.[11] I have no doubt that for some I will be perceived as a culpable historical relic because in 2011 we are no longer in the times of ignorance and infancy when Christians did not know any better because they did not know the religious Other any better. More importantly I may be seen as an apologetic embarrassment in communicating Christian truth to its late modern cultured despisers. For despite strong sociological support which testifies worldwide to the withering of secularization and the flourishing of sacralization,[12] the catch-all term 'religion' continues to be seen by many (at the level both of popular conversation and of academic discourse) not as the solution, but as the problem.[13] In such a climate, where the world we are told we all want is one of human dignity, tolerance, inclusivity, justice and peace, a Christian 'theology of religions' that continues to stress uniqueness, particularity and difference will be seen, by those inside and outside the Church, as exacerbating misunderstanding, marginalization and oppression. However, it will be my contention that *only* in the 'scandal of particularity', and the uniqueness of the

---

9   See my brief historical survey in 'Exclusivisms', in Alan Race and Paul M. Hedges (eds), *Christian Approaches to Other Faiths* (London: SCM Press, 2008), pp. 37–45.

10   A bold claim, I admit. However, there is evidence to suggest that growth of Christianity in the world is occurring in theologically conservative denominations. See Philip Jenkins, *The Next Christendom* (Oxford: Oxford University Press, 2002).

11   A 'defeater belief' is a philosophical term to say that if belief A is true belief B *cannot* be true.

12   See, perhaps most famously, Peter Berger (ed.), *The Desecularization of the World: Resurgent Religion and World Politics* (Grand Rapids: Eerdmans, 1999).

13   Note, for example, the rise of the 'new atheism' associated with writers such as Richard Dawkins, Christopher Hitchens and Philip Pullman.

Christian message can such laudable hopes be realized and justified, and where peace with the living God and consequently with each other will be found.

Before describing this approach in more detail, I would like to make two further introductory remarks. First is what could be called a ground-clearing exercise, or perhaps more polemically, a 'levelling of the playing field' exercise. This concerns the much discussed issue of 'typologies' within the theology of religions and consequently the categorization of a position such as my own. Concerning typology, debate continues to revolve around the validity or otherwise of the 'classic' tripolar model of exclusivism, inclusivism and pluralism.[14] To adopt an infamous analogy, some scholars still believe it worth retaining this Ptolemaic model, helpfully noting qualifications, limitations and adding various new epicycles.[15] Others believe the time has come for a Copernican revolution or paradigm shift, with the need for a new typological map which offers greater detail and clarity concerning the questions that the theology of religions asks, and the answers that various Christian traditions offer.[16] This debate continues.

Although recently I have described and defended my own position under the 'exclusivist' label,[17] I have deliberately chosen not to use it here for two reasons, both of which are apologetic in nature and which also give an early indication as to the trajectory of my argument. First, and more defensively, I remain sensitive as to how many perceive the classical typology with 'exclusivism' often portrayed in overly emotive and sensationalistic terms (intolerant, arrogant, 'fundamentalist'), and pluralism (and to a lesser extent

---

14 Originally used by Alan Race in *Christians and Religious Pluralism* (London: SCM Press, 1983).

15 See, for example, Paul M. Hedges, 'A Reflection on Typologies: Negotiating a Fast Moving Discussion', in Race and Hedges (eds), *Christian Approaches*, pp. 17–35. Hedges wishes to retain this typology, adding a fourth position called 'particularities', and seeing all the positions as 'fluid categories with permeable membranes' (p. 27).

16 See, for example, Gavin D'Costa, *Christianity and World Religions: Disputed Questions in the Theology of Religions* (Oxford: Wiley-Blackwell, 2009), pp. 34–7.

17 'Exclusivisms' in Race & Hedges (eds), *Christian Approaches*, pp. 36–62.

inclusivism) portrayed as more benign, enlightened and tolerant. Alvin Plantinga deals not with the truth of exclusivism but rather the propriety or rightness of exclusivism against claims that such a position 'is irrational, or egotistical and unjustified, or intellectually arrogant, or elitist, or a manifestation of harmful pride, or even oppressive and imperialistic'.[18] Concerning moral objections, Plantinga shows that these common objections to exclusivism are not necessary objections and even if they are valid then they equally apply to other positions with the result that so-called non-exclusive positions become guilty of a self-referential incoherence. All positions that claim to be true and privileged are 'exclusive'.

Second, and more in the manner of an offensive pre-emptive strike, I believe that the classical tripolar model has unhelpfully encouraged, particularly in pluralism, a concealment of crucial metaphysical, epistemological and ethical presuppositions that urgently demand explanation and justification. When unmasked, such construals are not only unable to claim epistemological neutrality or humility, but worse, are not distinctively 'Christian'. Concerning one of the most celebrated 'pluralist' illustrations based on the ancient fable of the blind men and elephant,[19] Newbigin writes:

In the famous story of the blind men and the elephant, so often quoted in the interest of religious agnosticism, the real point of the story is constantly overlooked. The story is told from the point of view of the king and his courtiers, who are not blind but can see that the blind men are unable to grasp the full reality of the elephant and are only able to get a hold of part of the truth. The story is constantly told in order to neutralise the affirmation of the great religions, to suggest that they learn more humility and recognise that none of them can have more than one aspect of the truth. But of course, the real point of the story is exactly the opposite. If the king were also blind there would be no story.

---

18 Alvin Plantinga, 'Pluralism: A Defense of Religious Exclusivism', in Thomas D. Senor (ed.), *The Rationality of Belief and the Plurality of Faith* (London: Cornell University Press, 1995), p. 194.

19 John Hick uses the illustration in *God and the Universe of Faiths* (Oxford: Oneworld, 1973), p. 140.

The story is told by the king, and it is the immensely arrogant claim of one who sees the full truth which all the world's religions are only groping after. It embodies the claim to know the full reality which relativizes all the claims of the religions.[20]

D'Costa names this king, more despotic than benign, as a Kantian exclusive modernity, 'a mastercode within which all the religions are positioned and neutered'.[21] His conclusion is that as a slave to this master, 'pluralism' becomes something other than Christian.

Given that the justification of authority and theological presuppositions (ontological, epistemological and ethical) are vital, not only in my own construction of a theology of religions, but also in my deconstruction of the religious Other (including pluralism), it seems appropriate to reiterate the tradition-specific nature of all positions together with their ultimate confessional commitments.

Finally, having stressed both the importance and the inevitability of a tradition-specific stance on these issues, it would be remiss of me not to say a few words about my own personal journey as it pertains to the theology of religions. I put my faith in the Lord Jesus Christ at the age of 16 but brought with me lots of questions arising from my own family background. Although my English mother was a Christian, my late Indo-Guyanese father was not. Indeed my grandmother, who is still alive, is a Hindu believer. Such a personal history generated various questions of a 'theology of religions' nature and eventually led me to studying Theology and Religious Studies at Bristol University, where I had the opportunity to study under and interact with various tutors of other faiths,[22] and to come into contact with a number of important scholars including Ursula King, John Hick and Ninian Smart. While at Bristol, the courses that made the greatest impact upon me personally, and that further whetted my appetite for further questioning and research, were the

---

20   Lesslie Newbigin, *The Gospel in a Pluralistic Age* (Grand Rapids: Eerdmans, 1989), pp. 9–10.
21   Gavin D'Costa, *The Meeting of Religions and the Trinity* (Maryknoll: Orbis, 2000), p. 91.
22   Including my Buddhist lecturer Professor Paul Williams, who has since converted to Catholicism.

'theology of religions' modules brilliantly and graciously taught by Gavin D'Costa, who later encouraged me to undertake doctoral studies with him on evangelical approaches to the question of the fate of those who never hear about Jesus Christ. Five years of university student ministry and now five years of teaching and training at Oak Hill Theological College in north London, as well as leadership in local church ministry, has further fuelled my passion and sense of urgency in reflecting upon the nature and status of other religions in light of the gospel of Jesus Christ.

The elephant speaks: theological method

In your light we see light. (Ps. 36.9)

As well as modelling sound pedagogical practice, an explanation of my method and 'workings' is especially relevant for my own theology of religions as time and again I will be wanting to concentrate our focus on foundational theological prolegomena and presuppositions, which cannot simply be assumed but must be justified; hence my sensitivity concerning the concealing of such foundations in the above discussion on typology.

Having voiced disquiet towards those who would align themselves with the king in the story of the blind men and the elephant, I recognize that I now have to reveal my *pou stō* (place to stand):[23] the ultimate authority upon which I base and build my theology of religions. Fundamental to my position is a doctrine of revelation, an 'extracosmic base for knowledge and meaning'.[24] To continue our illustration, knowledge of the elephant is only possible because the elephant speaks and tells us who he is. Without this self-disclosure, we may speculate, guess or dream, but we have no secure starting point for knowledge; we remain blind.

---

23   Archimedes' looking for a base outside the world for his lever's fulcrum, 'Give me a place where I may stand and I will move the world.'
24   Robert Reymond, *A New Systematic Theology of the Christian Faith* (Nashville: Thomas Nelson, 1998), p. 111, n. 1.

Without entering into unnecessary detail here, a number of clarificatory notes must be made. First, although it might appear otherwise, and thoroughly counter-Kantian, revelation implies that ontology precedes epistemology for 'before there can be revelation, there must be something to be revealed and someone or something to reveal it. Revelation can never be first, as if we or God depended on it. It always depends on God.'[25] While we will expound further the nature and actions of God shortly, we note here that both the self-attesting, personal and ultimate authority of divine revelation is what it is solely because it is derived from a God who is self-attesting, personal and absolute.

Second, given this metaphysics of knowledge, one can steer a safe passage without being devoured by the Scylla of modern and hubristic rationalism (which in reality always leads to scepticism[26]) or sucked into the Charybdis of postmodern and despairing irrationalism (which in reality is always made on a rationalistic basis[27]). The nature of human knowledge is a reflection of the creature's metaphysical total dependence upon, and distinction from, a totally independent Creator. It is neither 'univocal' knowledge, nor 'equivocal' knowledge, but 'analogous' in the sense of being a 'finite replica', image or reflection: 'We think God's thoughts after him, without presuming to think God's thoughts.'[28]

Third, although God's revelation of himself comes to us through various media (nature, history, word, person),[29] all of which is

25   James Sire, *Naming the Elephant* (Downers Grove: InterVarsity Press, 2004), p. 68.

26   For the finite human mind is not a stable starting point for knowledge and is certainly not omniscient.

27   The 'confidence' that we know that we don't know and that we can rationally communicate that we know we don't know.

28   Michael Horton, 'Consistently Reformed: The Inheritance and Legacy of Van Til's Apologetic', in K. Scott Oliphint and Lane G. Tipton (eds), *Revelation and Reason: New Essays in Reformed Theology* (Phillipsburg: P&R, 2007), p. 132. For more on this 'analogical' understanding of religious language see John Frame, *Cornelius Van Til: An Analysis of his Thought* (Phillipsburg: P&R, 1995), pp. 89–96.

29   Theologians often organize these various media into two categories, general revelation and special revelation.

authoritative and consistent, 'the Bible has a unique role in the organism of revelation'[30] as both a verbal and a written revelation are understood to be necessary. As I will elucidate, given the universal suppression and distortion of God's revelation, the gospel message, now exclusively revealed in the Bible (for Jesus has ascended and the apostles have died) is necessary to 'correct' our vision:

> Just as old or bleary-eyed men and those with weak vision, if you thrust them before a most beautiful volume, even if they recognise it to be some sort of writing, yet can scarcely construe two words, but with the aid of spectacles will begin to read distinctly; so Scripture, gathering up the otherwise confused knowledge of God, having dispersed our dullness, clearly shows us the true God.[31]

That this revelation is *verbal* is again necessary, given the specificity of the message contained within: 'The reality of the Trinity, and the purpose of the incarnation, crucifixion, resurrection and ascension are sufficiently complex that they cannot be mimed, or communicated through a religious impulse or sensation; they need to be spoken.'[32] That it is *written* is necessary, not only given the need for it to be preserved and propagated, but given the Bible's 'covenantal' and constitutional nature.[33]

Fourth, in adopting the Reformation slogan of *sola Scriptura*, we are not 'divinizing' the Bible, distracting from Christ, nor dismissing the role of the 'rule of faith'. Ward is helpful here. To the first charge,

---

30   John Frame, *The Doctrine of the Christian Life* (Phillipsburg: P&R, 2008), p. 141.

31   John Calvin, *Institutes of the Christian Religion*, Library of Christian Classics, vols. 20–21, ed. John T. McNeill, trans. Ford Lewis Battles (Philadelphia: Westminster, 1960), 1.6.1.

32   Timothy Ward, *Words of Life: Scripture as the Living and Active Word of God* (Nottingham: InterVarsity Press, 2009), p. 106.

33   Ward, *Words of Life*, writes: 'It is in line with the very nature of the covenant that God has established and revealed progressively through time that its stipulations and history, as witness to God's faithfulness to it, be written down. It was not an absolute necessity that it was, but it is highly appropriate to the nature of his chosen form of revelation and salvation that God ensured it was' (p. 107).

Ward uses the discourse of 'speech act theory', to argue that God is 'semantically present' in the Bible: 'there is, then, a complex but real relationship between God and his actions, expressed and performed, as they are, through God's words. In philosophical terms, there is an ontological relationship between God and his words. It seems that God's action including his verbal actions, are a kind of extension of him.'[34] To the second charge, and while noting important distinctions, Ward can affirm both Christ and the Bible as the 'word of God' because 'the speech acts related in Scripture are the means by which Christ continues to present himself as a knowable person in the world'.[35] Hence *solus Christus* is not compromised but enhanced in *sola Scriptura*: all of scripture points to him, he is fulfilment and climax of all God's promises. To the third charge, Ward, along with others, is keen to distinguish *sola Scriptura* from 'solo *scriptura*', or 'nuda *scriptura*:' 'The Reformers' conviction of *sola Scriptura* is the conviction that Scripture is the only *infallible* authority, the only supreme authority. Yet it is not the *only* authority, for the creeds and the church's teaching function as important subordinate authorities, under the authority of Scripture.'[36]

Finally, given that the authority of scripture is shorthand for 'the authority of God as he speaks through Scripture', so the Bible is the Christian's ultimate authority in all metaphysical, epistemological, ethical and soteriological issues, and is totally trustworthy and consistent because it has been inspired (or better 'breathed out') by

---

34 Ward, *Words of Life*, p. 33.

35 Ward, *Words of Life*, p. 75.

36 Ward, *Words of Life*, p. 149. Ward here is indebted to Keith A. Mathison's important study, *The Shape of Sola Scriptura* (Moscow, ID: Canon Press, 2001), which is a detailed study carefully distinguishing between different understandings of the authority of scripture and using Heiko Oberman's categories of Tradition, tradition and traditions in *The Dawn of the Reformation* (Edinburgh: T&T Clark, 1986). 'Tradition I' is a one-source theory that sees scripture and tradition as identical; 'Tradition II' is a two-source theory that sees scripture and tradition as equally authoritative sources of revelation; 'Tradition III' understands the real source of revelation to be the living magisterium of the church; 'Tradition 0' 'exalts the individual's interpretation of Scripture over and against that of corporate interpretation of past generation of Christians', Ward, *Words of Life*, p. 150. In this chapter I am defending 'Tradition I'.

a totally trustworthy and consistent God.[37] In terms of justification, the Bible is self-attesting because God is self-attesting, being ultimate and self-contained.[38] Philosophically such self-attestation is not fallaciously circular, for all *ultimate* commitments (Enlightenment rationalism included) must be self-attesting if they are not to be self-referentially incoherent.

As I come now to expound my theology of religions, and given the above methodological sketch, it will come as no surprise that I seek to construct my position from the biblical revelation and those creeds and confessions that are a faithful summary of biblical revelation. Two introductory points are to be noted. First, although the structure of this outline will be primarily thematic and systematic, I will strive to give consideration to the fact that the Bible is a metanarrative,[39] written in a variety of literary genres, by different writers at different times, but with a unified and distinct plot-line (and with particular turning points and climaxes, and so forth). These redemptive historical features should not be flattened out. Second, given the creedal 'richness' of my own tradition, I am aware of both the simplicity and brevity in approaching these doctrinal loci as they pertain to the theology of religions. In the footnotes I have attempted to reference fuller doctrinal and creedal formulations.

YHWH's transcendent uniqueness: God and Trinity

The God who made the world and everything in it, he who is Lord of heaven and earth, does not live in shrines made by

---

37 For contemporary defences of an evangelical doctrine of scripture see, Ward, *Words of Life*; Peter Jensen, *The Revelation of God* (Leicester: InterVarsity Press, 2002); D. A. Carson and John D. Woodbridge (eds), *Scripture and Truth* (Leicester: InterVarsity Press, 1983); and *Hermeneutics, Authority and Canon* (Leicester: InterVarsity Press, 1986); Mathison, *The Shape of Sola Scriptura*.

38 See below for more on this description of God. Biblically, we see an example of this in Hebrews 6.13, where God swears an oath by himself for there is no greater authority to swear an oath by.

39 Indeed *the* metanarrative which includes and 'out-narrates' all other metanarratives.

human hands, nor is he served by human hands, as though he needed anything, since he himself gives to all mortals life and breath and all things . . . though indeed he is not far from each one of us. For 'In him we live and move and have our being' . . . (Acts 17. 24–8)

The apostle Paul's address to the Areopagus is an appropriate starting point as we attempt the seemingly impossible task of summarizing the doctrine of God in a few pages. The following points can be made.

First, the 'religious' setting in which Paul gives this thumbnail portrait of God is a familiar one in redemptive history and therefore significant. From Genesis to Revelation and the corresponding history it encompasses, the surrounding context of the people of God was, like our own today, one of philosophical and religious diversity, not just a factual pluralism but often a cherished pluralism, be it henotheism, polytheism, or syncretism.[40] This makes any claims to Christian uniqueness all the more self-conscious and stark.

Second, Paul's own understanding of God is not a novel formulation, but is steeped in his Jewish background and worldview, albeit now 'fulfilled' (or 'filled in') in the coming of Christ. Paul names God as Lord. This personal name is God's own self-description of himself in Exodus 3.14, 'I AM WHAT I AM', the name he wants to be known by for all generations, and subsequently the 'fundamental confession of the people of God in the Old Testament'.[41] There is a long theological tradition grounding description of God in the name YHWH; 'that was the name that described his essence par excellence. God is the Existent One. His whole identity is wrapped

---

40 See, for example, Richard S. Hess, 'Yahweh and His Asherah? Epigraphic Evidence for Religious Pluralism in Old Testament Times', in Andrew D. Clarke and Bruce W. Winter (eds), *One God, One Lord: Christianity in a World of Religious Pluralism* (Cambridge: Tyndale House, 1991), pp. 5–33; Bruce Winter, 'In Public and in Private: Early Christians and Religious Pluralism', in Clarke and Winter (eds), *One God, One Lord*, pp. 125–48.

41 John Frame, *Salvation Belongs to the Lord: An Introduction to Systematic Theology* (Phillipsburg: P&R, 2006), p. 7.

up in the name: "I will be what I will be". All God's other perfections are derived from this name.'[42]

What must be noted here is that the Christian God is distinctively a personal absolute and absolute personality. He is both transcendent (but not 'wholly other' to creation) in that he 'does not need anything' and immanent (but not identical to creation) in that 'he is not far from each one of us'.[43] We have already alluded to the personal nature of God in our comments on revelation: the Living God 'speaks' and is one with whom creatures can have a covenantal I–Thou relationship. The Bible is replete with personal names, personal descriptions and personal actions of this God. While, of course, we note the analogous and anthropomorphic nature of all such statements, it is significant that ultimate reality is not impersonal matter, principle or fate but a personal and living God, involved in the world and especially with his people.

Not only is the Lord personal, but he is absolute, or self-sufficient. Vos comments that the name YHWH 'gives expression to the self-determination, the independence of God, that which, especially in soteric associations, we are accustomed to call his sovereignty . . . The name . . . signifies primarily that in all that God does for his people, He is from-within-determined, not moved upon by outside influences.'[44]

With the help of the Reformed theologian and apologist Cornelius Van Til, it is worth dwelling a little more on God's 'self-existence' or aseity, for again in this description of God we are saying something *sui generis* about the Christian God. God can be described as the 'self-contained ontological Trinity', 'God is in no

---

42   Herman Bavinck, *Reformed Dogmatics*, vol. 2: *God and Creation*, ed. John Bolt, trans. John Vriend (Grand Rapids: Baker, 2004), p. 151.

43   John Frame in *The Doctrine of the Knowledge of God* (Phillipsburg: P&R, 1987), points out the epistemological problems if God is either 'wholly other' or 'wholly revealed': 'If God is "wholly other", then how can we say or know that He is "wholly other"? . . . And if God is indistinguishable from the world, why should the theologian even speak about God? Why not simply speak of the world? Is it faith that validates such talk? Faith based on what? Can such a faith be more than an irrational leap in the dark?' (p. 14).

44   Geerhardus Vos, *Biblical Theology* (Grand Rapids: Eerdmans, 1948), p. 134, quoted in Reymond, *A New Systematic*, p. 158.

sense correlative to or dependent upon anything besides his own being. God is the source of his own being, or rather the term source cannot be applied to God. God is *absolute*. He is sufficient unto himself.'[45] From this Van Til connects and extrapolates a number of other descriptions and characteristics of God. For example, God's unity:

> Theologians traditionally distinguish God's unity of singularity (there is only one God) from his unity of simplicity (that he is not made up of parts or aspects that are intelligible in themselves, apart from the divine being as a whole) . . . If there is only one God, then there is nothing 'in' him that is independent of him. God's goodness, for example, is not something in his mind to which he brings himself into conformity. If it were, that goodness, an abstract quality, would be a second deity coordinate with God himself. Thus, denial of God's unity of simplicity violates God's unity of singularity.[46]

God's simplicity complements what we stated regarding God's personal nature in that God is not subject or subordinate to impersonal principles outside of himself, he *is* goodness, holiness, righteousness etc. This also implies God's sovereignty: 'It is edifying to observe that only a personal God can be sovereign and only a sovereign God can be an absolute person. That is to say, only a personal being can make choices and carry them out, and only a sovereign God can avoid being subject, ultimately, to impersonal principles.'[47]

Even more significant is the inextricable link made between God being self-contained and God's triunity. God is not dependent on or correlative to the world, but a conception of God as 'abstract oneness' always is. As Frame explains:

> Now orthodox Trinitarianism renounces such correlativism. On the orthodox view, God's unity is correlative only to himself, to

---

45 Cornelius Van Til, *The Defense of the Faith*, rev. edn (Phillipsburg: P&R, 1964), p. 9.

46 Frame, *Cornelius Van Til*, p. 56.

47 Frame, *Cornelius Van Til*, p. 60.

the complexities and pluralities of his own being. The world also is a unity and a diversity, because God made it that way. Consider love, as an attribute of God. If God is a mere unity without Trinity, then what is the object of God's eternal love? Himself? But love in the fullest biblical sense by its very nature reaches out to another, not merely to the self. The world? Then God's eternal attribute of love depends on the world; it needs the world. On a Trinitarian basis, however, God's love is both interpersonal and self-contained: God's love is the love among Father, Son, and Spirit for one another and it is not dependent on the world . . . The Trinity guards aseity, for without it, God is relative to the world. The Trinity also guards the personality of God: he is not a blank unity, which would be impersonal. Rather, he is unity of persons.[48]

What are the implications of this description of God for our theology of religions? First, and as Wright and Bauckham point out, a constant theme throughout the history of Israel and in the founding of the Christian Church, is not merely the relative claim of 'no other' meaning 'no other' God for Israel, or 'no other' God for Christians, but rather both the incomparability (none like him) and transcendent uniqueness (no other God)[49] of YHWH and of Jesus Christ who is God incarnate and Lord. As Bauckham explains:

> The essential element in what I have called Jewish monotheism, the element that makes it a kind of monotheism, is not the denial of the existence of other 'gods,' but an understanding of the uniqueness of YHWH that puts him in a class of his own, a wholly different class from any other heavenly or supernatural beings, even if these are called 'gods'. I call this YHWH's transcendent uniqueness (Mere 'uniqueness' can be what distinguishes one member of a class from other members of it. By 'transcendent uniqueness' I mean a form of uniqueness that puts

---

48   Frame, *Cornelius Van Til*, p. 65.
49   See Christopher J. H Wright, *The Mission of God: Unlocking the Bible's Grand Narrative* (Nottingham: Apollos, 2006), p. 82.

YHWH in a class of his own). Especially important for identifying this transcendent uniqueness are statements that distinguish YHWH by means of a unique relationship to the whole of reality: YHWH alone is Creator of all things, whereas all other things are created by him; and YHWH alone is the sovereign Lord of all things, whereas all other things serve or are subject to his universal lordship.[50]

And commenting on 1 Kings 8.60, 'so that all the peoples of the earth may know that LORD is God; there is no other,' he writes: 'It can surely not mean that all the peoples of the earth will know that YHWH is the only god *for Israel*. What they will recognize is that YHWH alone is "the God". They need not deny that there are other gods, but they will recognize the uniqueness of YHWH as the only one who can be called "the God". It is in this category that "there is no other".'[51]

Concerning first, who the triune God is (in terms of metaphysics); second, what the triune God says (in terms of epistemology and revelation); and third, what the triune God does (in terms of his sovereignty over both creation and redemption), there is no-one like Him. We are not defending bare theism, impersonal Being or non-absolute personal beings. *The* God *is* the Living God of the Bible, the self-revealing, self-contained ontological Trinity: YHWH. There is no ultimate reality behind this God. It is this God, or no god. As we will see shortly, there is either the worship of the Christian God, or the worship of idols which are nothing at all.[52]

---

50 Richard Bauckham, 'Biblical Theology and the Problems of Monotheism', in Craig Bartholomew et al. (eds), *Out of Egypt: Biblical Theology and Biblical Interpretation* (Grand Rapids: Zondervan, 2004), p. 211, quoted in Wright, *The Mission of God*, pp. 81f.

51 Bauckham, 'Biblical Theology', p. 195, quoted in Wright, *The Mission of God*, p. 83.

52 Wright, *The Mission of God*, pp. 39f., makes the important point that in comparison to YHWH, idols are nothing but to their followers they are something. He also notes another important theme, picked up strongly in the NT, that behind idols lie demons (cf. Deut. 32.17; 1 Cor. 10.20).

Second, there is a recurring theme throughout scripture that the LORD is rightly jealous of his own name, and acts for the sake of his name and reputation, because his name is inextricably linked with his glory – the recognition of God as he truly is in all his perfections:[53]

I am the LORD, that is my name; my glory I give to no other, nor my praise to idols. (Isa. 42.8)

Therefore say to the house of Israel, Thus says the Lord GOD: It is not for your sake, O house of Israel, that I am about to act, but for the sake of my holy name, which you have profaned among the nations to which you came. I will sanctify my great name, which has been profaned among the nations, and which you have profaned among them; and the nations shall know that I am the LORD, says the Lord GOD, when through you I display my holiness before their eyes. (Ezek. 36.22–3)

Teleologically, all proximate ends serve this ultimate end, and the Reformation slogan *soli Deo Gloria* is acknowledgement of this.

Third, and anticipating subsequent sections, a consequence of the transcendent uniqueness of God, comes a secondary affirmation of the incomparability and uniqueness of both Israel and the Church. There is no other covenant community like them, and there is no other community with a history like theirs because the incomparable and unique God has covenanted with them alone and intervened salvifically on their behalf alone. Crucially however, with such strong default themes of particularity also come complementary themes of

---

53 Bauckham, *The Bible and Mission* (Carlisle: Paternoster, 2003) writes, 'We may have difficulty with this picture of God desiring and achieving fame for himself, something we would regard as self-seeking vanity and ambition if it were said of a human being. But this is surely one of those human analogies which is actually appropriate uniquely to God. The good of God's human creatures requires that he be known to them as God. There is no vanity, only revelation of truth, in God's demonstrating his deity to the nations' (p. 37). To this we must add that there is no narcissism here as God's triune and self-contained nature means that the persons of the Trinity seek the others' glory from eternity.

universality, inclusion, diversity and tolerance.[54] Such exclusivity should never lead to vainglory or malice, for both Israel and the Church are chosen by the sheer grace of God to display his glory, and have a unique responsibility and calling to be a light for the nations in both word and deed. To neglect and abuse such a calling is an abuse of this delegated authority and power and leads to greater culpability.[55]

The perilous exchange: creation and fall

. . . For though they knew God, they did not honour him as God or give thanks to him, but they became futile in their thinking, and their senseless minds were darkened. (Rom. 1.21)

Although historically the 'theology of religions' has often preoccupied itself with questions of soteriology, another, more basic question should perhaps take precedence: If as Christians we are to think God's thoughts after him, what is 'human religion in God's sight'?[56] Under the loci of creation and fall, we are able to describe the complex phenomena of non-Christian religions as essentially *an idolatrous refashioning of divine revelation*, arguing that 'Religion is the human answer to divine, or at least allegedly divine, revelation . . . Religion is never a soliloquy, a dialogue of a man with himself.'[57] Under this definition, we are also able to affirm *both* a principial discontinuity/dissimilarity between Christianity

---

54   Such as attitudes towards the alien and stranger; attitudes towards ethnic diversity, including the eschatological hope of Christians being drawn from all nations and languages; God's universal care and sustenance of creation; the universal scope of the gospel and the universal mandate to take the gospel to the nations; etc.

55   See, for example, Wright, *The Mission of God*, pp. 90–2; Walter C. Kaiser, Jr, *Mission in the Old Testament: Israel as a Light to the Nations* (Grand Rapids: Baker, 2000).

56   The title of one of J. H. Bavinck's chapters in his posthumous, *The Church Between Temple and Mosque* (Grand Rapids, Eerdmans, 1966).

57   Bavinck, *The Church*, p. 18.

and other religions *and* a practical continuity/similarity. From this understanding of other religions, we will be able to describe the salvation offered only in Jesus Christ as the 'subversive fulfilment' of other religions.

We start this account where we left off in the previous section, with God's total self-sufficiency, as opposed to our finite dependence. Through this prism, we can summarize the cornerstone of the Christian doctrine of creation as the preservation of the Creator–creature distinction. Metaphysically although we can never become God, nor can God lose his deity, we are made in God's image, built with the purpose of worshipping and glorifying the one who made us and built for speaking and making under the authority of the ultimate Speaker and Maker. Epistemologically we were created to depend upon and obey God's authoritative and benevolent revelation, both given in the medium of 'works' and 'words'.

Similarly, summarizing the doctrine of the fall in the archetypal account in Genesis 3, we can say that this involves a blurring of the Creator–Creature relationship, a de-creation, whereby we pull God down to the level of the creature and push ourselves up to the level of Creator. The consequences here are shattering:

> How shallow, then, is the oft-heard mockery of the whole situation in Genesis 3 that ascribes to God a 'temper tantrum' merely because someone committed the picayunish [insignificant] act of 'eating a piece of apple'. The transgression of Adam was far more than that; it was at its core the creature's deliberate rejection of God's authority and an act of wilful rebellion against the Creator. It was man claiming the stance of autonomy and freedom from God. It was man believing he had the right to determine for himself what he would be *metaphysically* ('You will be like God'), what he would know *epistemologically* ('like God, knowing good and evil'), and how he would behave *ethically* ('she took and ate . . . her husband ate'). It was heeding Satan's call to worship the creature rather than the Creator. Authority was the issue at stake, and man decided against God and in his own favour.[58]

---

58 Reymond, *Systematic Theology*, p. 445.

The Reformed scholastic Turretin describes what happens here as an act of 'false faith',[59] for although God has shown himself in Genesis 1 and 2 to be a God who blesses (benevolent and good), and a God who is truthful and effective (he speaks and it is so), Adam and Eve disbelieve the truth about God, accepting he is not good (actuated by envy), and not truthful (we will not die). We therefore believe lies about him, but these lies about him are 'leaps of faith'.[60] At this point we are able to connect the 'fall' and 'sin' to the pervasive and seminal biblical category of idolatry. Far from being an anachronistic and 'blunt' concept, idolatry is a sophisticated analytical tool with which we can understand non-Christian religions. Understanding idolatry as 'false faith' means an inclusive definition of both physical and mental creations, not just displacements of the triune God, but also distortions and even denials. As Ovey notes:

This reversal of relationship involves idolatry as telling a 'story' about God, but a fictitious one. The 'making' is a 'making up'. The Bible strongly develops this motif that idolatry is human fiction as 'lie' (Isaiah 44.20). The idol lies about God by likening something to the unique uncreated God. Thus Isaiah 40−55 insists the 'nations' are idolatrous and proclaims God is incomparable to anything within the created order. This contrasts with depicting him as a golden bull, something created (Exodus 32.4). But idolatry equally lies about God by asserting what is not true of him − for example that he requires human sacrifice. Alternatively the fiction may attribute divine characteristics to something we create . . . The first and second commandments reflect these forms of fiction (no *other* gods, and no *made thing* to be worshipped, even if it allegedly represents Yahweh).[61]

---

59 Francis Turretin, *Institutes of Elenctic Theology*, ed. J. T. Dennison, trans. G. M. Giger (Phillipsburg: P&R, 1992), Topic 9. Q. 6. IX.

60 On this Ovey notes that sincerity is not the issue: 'the truth or falsehood of the faith turns not on whether the person who has faith is sincere or not, but on whether the belief that person holds is true to the reality of the person of whom he or she believes it', 'The Cross, Creation and the Human Predicament', in David Peterson (ed.), *Where Wrath and Mercy Meet: Proclaiming the Atonement Today* (Carlisle: Paternoster, 2001), p. 109.

61 Mike Ovey, 'Idolatry and Spiritual Parody: Counterfeit Faiths', *Cambridge Papers* 11:1 (March 2002), p. 3.

It is under the category of 'idolatry' that we are to interpret all beliefs/worldviews (both those demarcated as 'religious' and those not) that do not cohere with God's own revelation of himself, including all 'other religions'.

To expand a little more on the anatomy of idolatry and its relationship to other religions, we turn to the *locus classicus* of Romans 1.18–32, in which Paul gives us a microcosm of the universal human predicament. Here our guide is the Dutch Reformed missiologist J. H. Bavinck, who exegetes this passage within the larger context of his expertise within the theology of religions and a life spent studying and interacting with the religious other on the mission field.[62] First, Bavinck notes that in the created order there is true and objective knowledge of 'God's eternal power and divine nature' and stresses its dynamic, personal and relational character:

If we wish to use the expression 'general revelation' we must not do so in the sense that one can conclude God's existence from it. This may be logically possible, but it only leads to a philosophical notion of God as the first cause. But that is not the biblical idea of general revelation. When the Bible speaks of general revelation it means something quite different. There it has a much more personal nature. It is divine concern for men collectively and individually. God's deity and eternal power are evident; they overwhelm man; they strike him suddenly, in moments when he thought they were far away. They creep up on him; they do not let go of him, even though man does his best to escape them.[63]

Second, Bavinck moves onto mankind's subjective reaction to this revelation. The first thing to note is that there is a reaction; general revelation 'does not simply slide off man ineffectually like a raindrop glides off a waxy tree leaf'.[64] Visser comments:

---

62 See Bavinck, *The Church*; also *An Introduction to the Science of Missions* (Grand Rapids, MI: Baker, 1960); and 'General Revelation and the Non-Christian Religions', *Free University Quarterly* 4 (1944), pp. 43–55.
63 Bavinck, *The Church*, p. 124.
64 Visser, *Heart for the Gospel*, p. 142.

In Bavinck's view, when God manifests himself to man through general revelation, man becomes knowledgeable in a *de jure* (juridical) sense but proves, in that revelatory encounter with God, to be so profoundly sinful that *de facto* (actual) attainment of knowledge does not occur. Man 'is a knower who does not know, a perceiver who does not perceive.'[65]

Here Bavinck focuses on Paul's use of the word 'suppression' (*katechein*) and 'exchange' (*allasso/met'allasso*). Here again it is important to note the dynamic nature of what is going on. Suppression carries with it the sense of violently holding down. The sinner constantly suppresses general revelation and is therefore without excuse. The illustration might be that of a child playing with an inflatable ball in the water. She tries to push the ball under the water with all her might and thinks she has succeeded, but the ball always pops up to the surface again for the child to try again and so on. Here is the 'game' between revelation and suppression. Bavinck notes, 'this repression occurs so immediately, so spontaneously, so simultaneously with understanding a perception that at the very same moment he sees, he no longer sees, at the very moment he knows, he no longer knows'.[66] As well as suppression comes substitution, what Bavinck calls 'a perilous exchange'.[67] General revelation is not obliterated totally but rather perverted, twisted and distorted: 'the sparse, totally decontextualized elements deriving from it that do manage to stick in the conscious mind form nuclei around which complexes of a totally deviant nature crystallize'.[68] Thus, like Calvin, Bavinck describes human nature as a 'perpetual factory of idols'.[69]

---

65 Visser, *Heart for the Gospel*, p. 144. He is quoting Bavinck from *Religiieus besef en christelijk geloof* (*Religious Consciousness and Christian Faith*) (Kampen, 1949).

66 Bavinck, *Religiieus besef*, p. 172, quoted in Visser, *Heart for the Gospel*, p. 145.

67 Bavinck, *The Church*, p. 122.

68 Bavinck, *Religiieus besef*, p. 179, quoted in Visser, *Heart for the Gospel*, p. 146.

69 Bavinck, *The Church*, p. 122. cf. Calvin, *Institutes*, 1.11.8.

Finally in his exposition, Bavinck adds a crucial nuance to his argument. While all humanity is guilty of suppression and substitution, there is no uniformity but a great variety in the depth of suppression and substitution. The reason for such variation is not the 'goodness' of man but rather the restraining grace of God through the operation of the Holy Spirit:

> We always encounter the powers of repression and exchange, but that does not mean they are always of the same nature and strength. We meet figures in the history of the non-Christian religions of whom we feel that God wrestled with them in a particular way. We still notice traces of that process of suppression and substitution in the way they responded, but occasionally we observe a far greater influence of God there than in many other human religions. The history of religion is not always and everywhere the same; it does not present a monotonous picture of only folly and degeneration. There are culminating points in it, not because human beings are much better than others, but because every now and then divine compassion interferes, compassion which keeps man from suppressing and substituting the truth completely.[70]

Let us now synthesize the above insights into a more systematic whole. The relationship between Christianity and other religions is one of *both* principial discontinuity *and* practical continuity. Let us explore this seemingly contradictory statement.

Scripture often attests to an extreme opposition or 'antithesis'[71] between true faith and 'false faith', light and dark, death and life, those who are blind and those who can see, covenant keepers and covenant breakers, those in Adam and those in Christ. As Jesus says, 'Whoever is not with me is against me, and whoever does not gather with me scatters' (Matt. 12.30), and 'No one can serve two masters . . . ' (Matt. 6.24). We might say that despite the plethora of

---

70 Bavinck, *The Church*, p. 126.

71 The term 'antithesis' as used here does not refer to Hegelian thinking but is rather a technical theological term associated with Reformed theology and referring to the difference between believer and unbeliever.

worldviews and religions that exist in the world, in reality there are only two: those rooted and built up in Christ, and those founded on 'philosophy and empty deceit, according to human tradition, according to the elemental spirits of the world, and not according to Christ' (Col. 2.6–10).

In terms of our analysis, the antithesis can be seen between those who worship YHWH, the self-contained ontological Trinity of the Bible, and those who worship idols. The worship of the created rather than the Creator is a definition of human sin and fallenness.[72] As we saw, YHWH is jealous for his own name and will not share his glory with another. By worshipping idols God is deprived of his glory and humans are deprived of their God:

> Such idolatrous lies falsify a person, obscuring and distorting who the person is. The lie destroys true relationship as humans stop relating to God as he knows himself to be, instead treating him as they have fashioned him. Idolatry strongly expresses human sovereignty, but sovereignty at the expense of true relationship. God is treated not as a person we encounter (a 'Thou' in Martin Buber's terms), but as an object (an 'It'), indeed a plastic, malleable one. Buber writes 'The *Thou* meets me.' Imposing identities on other persons risks not 'meeting' them – preventing them being a 'Thou'. The biblical God reveals he is not infinitely plastic and malleable. To treat him as that involves counterfeit, not true, relationship, with him. The price for being makers of God, albeit attractive, is that the God we make is not real. The true God is hidden, because we attempt to reduce him to an 'It' of our choosing. Buber notes: 'This selfhood . . . steps in between and shuts off from us the light of heaven.'[73]

---

72 For example, Tertullian writes, 'The principle crime of the human race, the highest guilt charged upon the world, the whole procuring cause of judgement, is idolatry. For although each single fault retains its own proper feature, . . . yet it is marked off under the general account of idolatry.' *On Idolatry* (Whitefish, MT: Kessinger, 2004), p. 3.

73 Ovey, 'Idolatry', p. 3. The Buber quotations are taken from *I and Thou*, 2nd edn (Edinburgh: T&T Clark, 1958), p. 11; and *The Eclipse of God* (Atlantic Highlands: Humanities Press International, 1952), p. 129.

It is because of these 'lies' being told about him, that God's holy and righteous wrath is kindled and is 'being revealed' from heaven,[74] a foretaste and warning of God's unrestrained wrath to come. Idols, and the religious traditions built on them, do not save but only lead to divine judgement. Idol worship also leads to human disintegration:

> *Idolatry is radical self-harm.* It is also radically, terribly ironic. In trying to be as God, we have ended up less human. The principle affirmed in several places in the Bible that you become like the object of your worship (e.g., Ps. 115:8; Is. 41:24; 44:9) is very apparent. If you worship that which is not *God*, you reduce the image of God in yourself. If you worship that which is not even *human*, you reduce your humanity still further.[75]

Finally idols deceive, and no-one stops to consider this deception.[76] As counterfeits, they promise much and mimic divine attributes and actions, but ultimately they only bring disappointment, disillusionment and destruction:

> Has a nation changed its gods,
> 　　even though they are no gods?
> But my people have changed their glory
> 　　for something that does not profit.
> Be appalled, O heavens, at this,
> 　　be shocked, be utterly desolate, says the LORD,

> for my people have committed two evils:

> 　　they have forsaken me,
> the fountain of living water,
> 　　and dug out cisterns for themselves,
> cracked cisterns
> 　　that can hold no water. (Jer. 2.11–13)

---

74 Romans 1.18; 'being revealed' here is a present passive.
75 Wright, *The Mission of God*, p. 173.
76 This is Isaiah's complaint in his vicious satire of idol worship in Isa. 44.19.

The above analysis means that we must be cautious of speaking about 'truth' in other religions. With Kraemer we affirm the 'radical difference' between Christianity and other religions with every religion being 'an indivisible unity of existential apprehension'.[77] Phenomenologically religions are hermetically sealed interpretations of reality (worldviews) and as such are incommensurable, defying superficial comparison. Bavinck is helpful once more here, again highlighting the dynamic nature of religions' refashioning of revelation:

> The residues of revelation never lie hidden as petrified fossils in the soil of pseudo religion. False religion always presents itself as, and in actual fact invariably constitutes, a monolithic aggregate. Consequently, all ideas it absorbs become amalgamated with and deformed by the whole. In other words, it is not possible for isolated elements of verity, sparks of divine truth to exist in the midst of falsehood and error – in fact, if such sparks were present, they would lead to friction in and destruction of the very essence of pseudo religions.[78]

The picture I have sketched so far is stark, and bleak, as the antithesis must be. It is also extremely counter-intuitive, for a posteriori within our own religiously plural context, we do experience similarity and commonality between various religious traditions. Adherents of other religions often appear to do 'good' works, can have a belief system like those of the Christian, and aspire to common human goals and values. How are we theologically to explain these things, while still upholding the principle of the antithesis? That is to say, within an overarching pattern of discontinuity between Christianity and other faiths, can there be elements of continuity also?

First, is what might be called an anthropological complexity. The antithesis between Christianity and other religious traditions is what one might call its 'pure' state or consistent state. In terms of 'principle' that is 'principially', the antithesis between Christianity and other religions

77 Hendrik Kraemer, *The Christian Message in a Non-Christian World* (London: Edinburgh House), p. 135.
78 Visser, *Heart for the Gospel*, p. 172.

is total. However, only to emphasize the antithesis is simplistic, lacking theological sophistication. In practice, religious worldviews often show internal inconsistency. This is often noted by critics of Christianity but of course it is a profound theological truth. Principally Christians are described as new creations, rooted in Christ, and yet daily they struggle with indwelling sin.[79] Similarly there are various reasons why those who are not Christians are inconsistent in their unbelief:

> The natural man, 'sins against' his own essentially Satanic principle. As the Christian has the incubus of his 'old man' weighing him down and therefore keeping him from realizing the 'life of Christ' within, so the natural man has the incubus of the sense of Deity weighing him down and keeping him from realizing the life of Satan within. The actual situation is therefore always a mix of truth with error. Being 'without God in the world' the natural man yet knows God, and, in spite of himself, to some extent recognizes God. By virtue of their creation in God's image, by virtue of the ineradicable sense of deity within them and by virtue of God's restraining general grace, those who hate God, yet in a restricted sense know God, and do good.[80]

We equate here the 'natural man' with those in other religious traditions. As Van Til notes, there are several theological factors that cause such inconsistency. First, is the Reformed doctrine of 'common grace'.[81] This variegated non-salvific work of the Holy Spirit restrains sin and the consequences of sin in the non-Christian and excites non-Christians to perform acts of 'civic righteousness' and culture-building. Second are implications arising from our doctrine of creation. While the non-Christian desires epistemological autonomy from God, metaphysically all humanity relies on the triune God for their very being. Despite ethically rebelling against their Creator, all humans are made in the image of the triune God, a

---

79 Cf. Gal. 5.7.
80 Cornelius Van Til, *An Introduction to Systematic Theology*, ed. William Edgar (Phillipsburg: P&R, 2007), p. 65.
81 See John Murray, 'Common Grace', in John Murray, *Collected Writings*, vol. 2: *Systematic Theology* (Edinburgh: Banner of Truth, 1977), pp. 93–122.

finite replica built to worship its Creator. Such an image can never be erased and is there as a constant reminder of the true God to be worshipped. Calvin famously called this a *sensus divinitatis*, and a *semen religionis*.[82] This universal religious consciousness accounts for the religiosity of human beings, and all other religious traditions. Following Witte,[83] Bavinck helpfully calls this the *'thatness'* to humanity's religious quest, delineating 'five magnetic' points that humanity cannot evade, questions that humanity has always asked and that provide a 'unity of mankind' and 'anthropological structure' that he cannot outgrow:[84] 'If only man could shed his self-being, his individuality, his sense of royalty, if only he could let himself sink down in this world to the level of a plant or an animal without norms or morals! But he cannot do that. He is man, bearer of a name at once unutterably noble and desperately pathetic.'[85]

For Bavinck, even though the 'thatness' of a universal religious consciousness is almost immediately 'filled' by the 'whatness' of the sinful suppression and substitution of this knowledge of God, 'thatness' is still missiologically essential:

> Sometimes people cannot resist God's approach and are over-whelmed by it: 'We may say that by the grace of God repression and substitution does not always succeed. Time and again we notice things in the history of religion which show that God has

---

82 Calvin, *Institutes*, 1.3.1–2.

83 J. Witte, *Die Christus-Botschaft und die Religionen* (Göttingen, 1936), pp. 37ff., quoted in Visser, *Heart for the Gospel*, p. 171.

84 Bavinck expounds these in *The Church Between Temple and Mosque*:
  1 'I and the cosmos.' A sense of belonging to the whole.
  2 'I and the norm.' A sense of transcendent norms.
  3 'I and the riddle of my existence.' A sense of the governance of existence by a providential or destining power.
  4 'I and salvation.' A recognition of the need for redemption.
  5 'I and the Supreme Power.' A sense of relatedness to a Superior or Supreme power.
These points can be organized into three questions with which one can analyse other religions: What have you done with God? What are your standards? How do you deal with suffering and guilt?

85 Bavinck, *Religiieus besef*, p. 166, quoted in Visser, *Heart for the Gospel*, pp. 157f.

really concerned Himself with 'people of other faiths', and 'we may thankfully state *that* they believe in God.' Why this matter of gratitude? Because without this 'thatness', this objective fact of religious consciousness . . . missionary communication would be 'utterly impossible'.[86]

Ironically, understanding other religions in terms of idolatry supports a structural or formal 'commonality' between Christianity and other religions. Idols are not created *ex nihilo*, for they are created things made to replace the Creator: 'To speak of an idol in the biblical sense assumes that there is a true God of whom the idol is a counterfeit.'[87] As worshipping beings, we must worship someone or something, but what we worship are self-refuting distortions and perversions of the unique triune God (a personal absolute and absolute personality); his unique attributes (a God who is both transcendent and immanent); and his unique actions (in providing salvation not on the basis of works but by grace). Idols are parasitic. So, for example, all religions and worldviews will have their own *a se* ultimate explanation of everything, but this is often impersonal rather than personal. Panentheistic religions counterfeit God's immanence at the expense of his transcendence; pantheistic religions do the opposite as well as denying the Creator–creature distinction. Dualistic religions counterfeit this Creator–creature distinction, but at the expense of God's accessibility. Even the media of authentic revelation are mimicked: 'In false theophanies, prophecies and miracles, we have an indication of man's deepest needs. Christianity stands, to be sure in antithetical relation to the religions of the world, but it also offers itself as the fulfilment of that of which the nations have unwittingly had some faint desire.'[88]

Second, we might add an historical or phenomenological complexity. I have defined other religions as the idolatrous refashioning of revelation, but there is a great variation in the 'type' of revelation

---

86 Visser, *Heart for the Gospel*, p. 172.

87 Richard Keyes, 'The Idol Factory', in Os Guinness and John Seel (eds), *No God But God: Breaking With the Idols of Our Age* (Chicago: Moody Press, 1992), pp. 37–48.

88 Van Til, *Introduction*, pp. 204f.

that other religions use in their religious constructions – revelation in nature, in history and in words, often categorized as general revelation and special revelation. Both the early fathers and theologians like Jonathan Edwards talked about the *prisca theologia*, that is, special revelation present from the creation of man, which has been passed from Adam and his progeny down through generations, perverted and distorted yes, but still an echo of true knowledge. Bavinck calls this 'proto-word' revelation.[89] Added to this is what can be called the 'radiation or inflow of special revelation' into another religious tradition, for example Plato being influenced by the prophets, Thomas preaching in India, Nestorian influence in China,[90] to which I would add the strong possibility that Muhammad came into contact with some form of Christianity.[91] On similar lines, Leithart makes a plausible case that moral consensus between Christians and non-Christians does not originate in general revelation, as is often assumed, but rather originates in a mixture of general and special revelation.[92] Religions are dynamic and constantly in flux and development, with one needing to take into account both intrareligious and interreligious change.

Finally we note a personal complexity. As I have tried to indicate, revelation is both dynamic and personal. While understanding religious traditions *qua* traditions is important, God through his Spirit does not strive with religious traditions and systems but with individuals made in his image. This person-variable nature of the religious consciousness will avoid blunt generalization and superficiality when encountering those in other religious traditions.

---

89 Bavinck, 'General Revelation', p. 51. See also Gerald McDermott, *Jonathan Edwards Confronts the Gods: Christian Theology, Enlightenment Religion and Non-Christian Faiths* (Oxford: Oxford University Press, 2000), pp. 93–5.

90 Bavinck, 'General Revelation', p. 52.

91 See Peter J. Leithart, 'Mirror of Christendom', http://www.marshillaudio.org/resources/pdf/Leithart.pdf.

92 Peter J. Leithart, 'Did Plato Read Moses? Middle Grace and Moral Consensus', *Biblical Horizons Occasional Paper 23* (Florida: Biblical Horizons, 1995).

The precious 'good news': Christ and salvation

This Jesus is 'the stone that was rejected by you, the builders; it has become the cornerstone.' There is salvation in no one else, for there is no other name under heaven given among mortals by which we must be saved. (Acts 4.11–12)

In the person and work of Jesus Christ we reach the 'Omega' point not only of the biblical revelation and redemptive history, but of the Reformed tradition, where the great 'solas' coalesce most explicitly. The question posed by Jesus himself, 'Who do people say I am?'[93] remains also the crux for the theology of religions.

Given my tradition-specific context and presuppositions, together with my definition of God as the 'self-contained ontological Trinity', it is predictable that I wish to defend and promote a 'high' constitutive Chalcedonian Christology.[94] It might also be predictable as to some of the general themes and specific texts in the New Testament I might refer to, for even a pluralist like Race in his seminal book on the theology of religions writes, 'Not even the most detached reader of the New Testament can fail to gain the impression that the overall picture of Christian faith which it presents is intended to be absolute and final.'[95]

However, and with much of the groundwork now complete, I wish to articulate the relevance of such a Christology within the context of the themes I have been developing already in this chapter and why 'there is no other name under heaven by which we must be saved'. First, concerning Christ's person, I wish to highlight the New Testament writers' conscious and deliberate equating of the identity and action of the historical Jesus of Nazareth with *the* God

---

93 Mark 8.27.

94 'High' here meaning an affirmation of Jesus' divinity; 'constitutive' meaning that Jesus' life, death and resurrection ontologically 'constitute' salvation as opposed to merely 'representing' salvation; 'Chalcedonian' referring to the classic Christological statement of 451.

95 Race, *Christians*, p. 10.

of Israel, YHWH. Jesus Christ is LORD. Citing example after example, Wright concludes:

> YHWH stood *sui generis*, entirely in a class of his own as *the* God, the sole Creator of the universe, and Ruler, Judge and Saviour of the nations. And the New Testament repeatedly makes the same affirmation about Jesus of Nazareth, putting him in the same exclusively singular, transcendent framework and frequently quoting the same texts to do so.[96]

> Jesus then, according to the consistent witness of many strands in the New Testament documents, shares the identity of YHWH, the Lord God of Israel, and performs functions that were uniquely and exclusively the prerogative of YHWH in the Old Testament. These include especially God's role as Creator and owner of the universe, Ruler of history, Judge of all nations and Saviour of all who turn to him. In all of these dimensions of God's identity and activity, New Testament believers saw the face of Jesus, spoke of him in exactly the same terms and worshiped him accordingly.[97]

This identical association is part of what can be called a 'Christology from within', which focuses on Jesus as the person who brings fulfilment. Jesus is the antitype to the many Old Testament types.[98] All the scriptures are about him (John 5.39), he is a 'yes' to God's promises (2 Cor. 1.20), 'Jesus is not merely the agent through whom the knowledge of God is communicated (as any messenger might be) He himself is the very content of the communication.'[99]

Second, and concerning Christ and our universal human predicament, we return to Turretin's description of sin as being ethically unjustifiable 'false faith'. Commenting on John 3.36, 'Whoever *believes* in the Son has eternal life; whoever *disobeys* the Son will not see life, but must endure God's wrath', Ovey notes examples of 'false faith' and lies told about Jesus that mirror Genesis 3:

---

96 Wright, *The Mission of God*, p. 131.
97 Wright, *The Mission of God*, p. 122.
98 Calvin focuses on Jesus fulfilling the roles of prophet, priest and king (*triplex munus*).
99 Wright, *The Mission of God*, p. 123.

For he is the creative Word (Jn 1:1–3), yet the world sees him as untruthful. For example, in Jn 5:18 his claims to be God's Son are treated as blasphemy, while in John 7:12 some say he is a false teacher. In Genesis 3 God's word is seen as ineffective: as Son he claims to have life within him (Jn. 5:26) and to be the one who will rise from the dead (Jn. 2:19). Yet the tone of the mockery at the crucifixion (e.g. Mt. 27:39–44) shows a dismissal of Jesus' words as ineffective. Further in Genesis 3, God's goodness is implicitly denied, while in the New Testament Jesus is seen as morally wrong. Finally, of course, in Genesis 3, God's rightful claims are defied, while in Jesus humanity crucifies its king ('Pilate asked them, "Shall I crucify your King?" The chief priests answered, "We have no king but the emperor,"' Jn. 19:15).[100]

Not to recognize the risen and ascended LORD Jesus for who he truly is, is an act of idolatry and again provokes divine wrath, a wrath that will be most intensely revealed on that day when everyone will call on mountains and rocks, 'Fall on us and hide us from the face of the one seated on the throne, and from the wrath of the Lamb; for the great day of their wrath has come, and who is able to stand?' (Rev. 6.16–17). For all the many personal and societal, spiritual and physical implications of fallenness and sin, it is this theocentric perspective that is the hub from which we understand our dilemma.

Third, concerning Christ's saving work, if divine wrath lies at the heart of the human predicament, then the 'good news' of the gospel is that in Christ's life, death and resurrection, this wrath has been dealt with for his people, that 'Jesus Christ our Lord, moved by a love that was determined to do everything to save us, endured and exhausted the destructive divine judgement for which we were inescapably destined, and so won us forgiveness, adoption and glory.'[101] It is to be remembered here that this 'propitiatory' substitutionary work is both theocentric and triune in nature:

---

100   Ovey, 'The Cross', pp. 110f.

101   James Packer, *What did the Cross Achieve: The Logic of Penal Substitution* (Leicester: RTSF, 2002), p. 35.

It is God himself who in holy wrath needs to be propitiated, God himself who in holy love undertook to do the propitiating, and God himself who in the person of his Son died for the propitiation of our sins. Thus God took his own loving initiative to appease his own righteous anger by bearing it his own self in his own Son when he took our place and died for us.[102]

As before, although there are multiple perspectives concerning the benefits of Christ's work,[103] it is this Godward reference that must be considered both 'linchpin' and hermeneutical 'key'.

Fourth, and because of the above, we return full circle to the necessity of God's verbal revelation to hear this good news. Although authoritative, God's revelation of himself through his 'works' lacks the specificity of his disclosure through his words, and the Word. God's words have always been needed to interpret, supplement and therefore complement God's works, these two modes of revelation were never meant to be separated from one another or to work independently of each other.

This objective epistemological insufficiency of natural revelation becomes more acute after the fall with the universal suppression and substitution of God's revelation. As Van Til notes:

It is accordingly no easier for sinners to accept God's revelation in nature than to accept God's revelation in Scripture. They are no more ready of themselves to do the one than to do the other. From the point of the view of the sinner, theism is as objectionable as Christianity. Theism that is worthy of the name is Christian theism. Christ said that no man can come to the Father but by him. No one can become a theist unless he becomes a Christian. Any God that is not the Father of our Lord Jesus Christ is not God but an idol. It is therefore the Holy Spirit bearing witness by and with the Word in our hearts that alone effects the

---

102   John Stott, *The Cross of Christ* (Leicester: InterVarsity Press, 1986), p. 175.

103   See Daniel Strange, 'The Many-Splendoured Cross: Atonement, Controversy and Victory', *Foundations* (Autumn 2005), pp. 5–22.

required Copernican revolution and makes us both Christians and theists.[104]

After the fall what sinners need is spiritual illumination, the regenerating power of the gospel to know God as Creator and Redeemer, and general revelation is an inappropriate vehicle because knowledge of the gospel of our Lord Jesus Christ is not contained in it: 'Man the sinner, as Calvin puts it, through the testimony of the Spirit receives a new power of sight by which he can appreciate the new light given in Scripture. The new light and the new power of sight imply one another. The one is fruitless for salvation without the other.'[105] Johnson echoes this:

Special revelation is needed because special grace is needed. An intense knowledge of one's own unworthiness and a determination to do better, even *with* the gospel is not salvific. Faith must be consciously placed in the gospel of Jesus. The difference here is the difference between knowing the standard for which man was made and receiving God's provision for the standard breaker. It is the difference between law and gospel.[106]

Unlike special revelation, general revelation simply does not contain the truth content necessary for saving faith and so is not an appropriate vehicle for the Spirit's saving work of regeneration.[107] Faith cannot maintain its fully orbed character of *notitia, fiducia* and *assensus*[108] if the object changes from Christ to God (or even Reality), as it is a knowledge of who Christ is and what he has done

---

104 Cornelius Van Til, 'Nature and Scripture', in N. B. Stonehouse and Paul Woolley (eds), *The Infallible Word: A Symposium* (Phillipsburg: P&R, 1946), p. 280.

105 Van Til, 'Nature and Scripture', p. 281.

106 Greg Johnson, 'The Inadequacy of General Revelation for the Salvation of the Nations', http://gregscouch.homestead.com/files/Generalrev.html.

107 John Murray, *Redemption Accomplished and Applied* (Grand Rapids, MI: Eerdmans, 1961), p. 112.

108 The knowledge of our minds of; assent of our wills to; and trust in our hearts in, Jesus Christ.

that defines saving faith. Looking outside ourselves to the objective work of Christ, tells us also something of the role of faith and its efficacy. As John Murray writes:

> It is to be remembered that the efficacy of faith does not reside in itself. Faith is not something that merits the favour of God. All the efficacy unto salvation resides in the Saviour . . . , it is not faith that saves but faith in Jesus Christ; strictly speaking, it is not even faith in Christ that saves but Christ that saves through faith. Faith unites us to Christ in the bonds of abiding attachment and entrustment and it is this union which ensures that the saving power, grace, and virtue of the Saviour become operative in the believer. The specific character of faith is that it looks away from itself and finds its whole interest and object in Christ. He is the absorbing preoccupation of faith.[109]

Naturally there is a plethora of outstanding questions concerning soteriology, which cannot be entered into here and which I have attempted to answer in detail elsewhere.[110] However, two pressing issues can be mentioned. Concerning the principle of *fides ex auditu*, can we posit multiple modalities both pre-mortem and post-mortem, through which the gospel can be heard? Here I think we must be extremely cautious. First, there is scant exegetical evidence for a post-mortem opportunity to respond to Christ, and strong evidence that eternal destinies are fixed pre-mortem. Second, with regard to proto-word revelation, oral tradition and the inflow of special revelation into other traditions, I have already indicated the sinful human propensity to pervert and distort

---

109   Murray, *Redemption*, p. 112.

110   See Daniel Strange, *The Possibility of Salvation Among the Unevangelised: An Analysis of Inclusivism in Recent Evangelical Theology* (Carlisle: Paternoster, 2001); 'General Revelation: Sufficient or Insufficient', in Christopher W. Morgan and Robert A. Peterson (eds), *Faith Comes By Hearing: A Response to Inclusivism* (Nottingham: Apollos, 2008), pp. 40–77; 'A Calvinist's Response to Talbott's Universalism', in Robin Parry and Christopher Partridge (eds), *Universal Salvation: The Current Debate* (Carlisle: Paternoster, 2003), pp. 145–68.

the truth of God's revelation which becomes a basis for further judgement rather than a *praeparatio evangelica*. Third, in all the biblical accounts of conversion, it appears that at some point all people come into contact with a human messenger. Is missionary contact normative or exclusively necessary for salvation? The whole tenor of the book of Acts and the sending of the Church into the world seems to strongly prioritize the modality of the human messenger although I might tentatively suggest that if God does use other modalities then they can be seen as providentially pre-evangelistic and part of God's wonderful sovereignty in calling his people to himself.[111]

Concerning the distributive justice of God and the question of those who never hear of Christ 'through no fault of their own', we must say that Romans 1.20 is clear that enough revelation is given to all humanity, 'so they are without excuse'. Given the holiness and justice of God, and the universal sinfulness of mankind, both of which are constants, salvation, or even the offer of salvation, is not a universally accessible human right but a gracious gift. That God saves anyone is an act of sheer grace and mercy.

Finally, we are now in a position to describe the overall relationship between the Christian gospel of Jesus Christ and non-Christian religions as that of 'subversive fulfilment,' a complex and almost paradoxical relationship but the only description that does justice to a fully orbed biblical interpretation of other religions.

On the one hand the gospel is an antithetical confrontation to all other religions. The universal sinful suppression and substitution of our knowledge of God, the *'whatness'* of religion, means that even the most contextualized communication of the gospel (such as Acts 17) must issue in a call for repentance (17.30), a turning from idols to the living and true God.[112] As Bavinck states:

Such altars, dedicated to the 'unknown god' are the cries of distress of a heart torn loose from God, a heart with no inner

111   See Strange, 'General Revelation', pp. 69–77.
112   1 Thess. 1.9.

resting. Such manifestations are not to be understood as in any way pointing to the real Christ. The real Christ differs radically from the so-called saviours conjured up by the religions of man. His gospel is not the answer to man's inquiry, but in a deep and profound sense the gospel of Christ is rather a condemnation of all such human fancy and speculation. Consequently, if we begin with the ideas of those we would convert, a point will be reached when the breach between our view and theirs is clearly evident. There is no direct uninterrupted path from the darkness of paganism to the light of the gospel. Pagan systems of thought can be examined and humanly speaking, their beauty, inner consistency, scope, and systematic character can even be admired to a degree, but somewhere along the line, we must pause to point out our tremendous differences. Without that, our garment is not finished and it may even be dangerous and misleading. There is no detour that can bridge the gap; the transition from paganism to Christianity is not continuous and smooth, and it would be dishonest and unfaithful to Christ if it were to try to camouflage the gulf separating the two.[113]

However, on the other hand the gospel is both an appeal, and appealing. Because we are metaphysically all made in God's image, because of God's variegated common grace which restrains the depth of our suppression and substitution, because idols are parasites and counterfeits of *the* God, YHWH, there is a *'thatness'* to our humanity. Perennial metaphysical, epistemological, and ethical questions which other religions cannot ultimately answer are answered by the self-contained ontological triune Creator and saviour. Philosophically speaking, Christianity is true because of the impossibility of the contrary. Biblically speaking, the cracked cisterns of idolatry that bring only disillusionment, despair and unfulfilled desires are wonderfully fulfilled and surpassed in the fount of living water, Jesus Christ the LORD. There is always a point of contact, 'this is the only chink in the Goliath armour of pseudo-religion, where the

---

113   Bavinck, *Introduction*, pp. 136f.

shepherd boy with his stone – if God guides his hand – can hit people.'[114]

Let the nations be glad: the Church, mission and eschatology

... concerning his Son, who was descended from David according to the flesh and was declared to be the Son of God with power
according to the Spirit of holiness by resurrection from the dead,
Jesus Christ our LORD, through whom we have received grace
and apostleship to bring about the obedience of faith among all
the Gentiles for the sake of his name ... (Rom. 1.4–5)

In a recent address, itself an example of the gospel's 'subversive
fulfilment' of cherished pluralism, the Reformed New York pastor Timothy Keller argues that it is precisely the *unique* aspects of
Christianity that should provide the lasting reconciliation and peace
that our world cries out for – and all these flow from the unique
person and work of Christ. [115] Focusing on 1 John 4, he mentions
first the *origin* of Jesus' salvation: unlike the human founders of
many of the world religions, Jesus Christ has come 'from God'
(v. 2). Jesus Christ is God incarnate. Second, he mentions the *purpose* of Jesus' salvation: unlike many other religions, which seek
liberation or escape from creation and the physical world, Jesus

---

114   J. H. Bavinck, *Het problem van de pseudo-religie en de algemene open-
baring* (*The Problem of Pseudo-Religion and General Revelation*) (n.d., n.p.),
quoted in Visser, *Heart for the Gospel*, p. 266. Bavinck prefers to speak of
a 'point of attack' (*aangrijpingspunt*) rather than a 'point of contact' (*aan-
knopingspunt*). 'The point of attack signifies for us the awareness of need, poverty, and inability, which we frequently encounter in non-Christian nations, as
well as in our own surroundings. This universal feeling of need or of anxiety is
not in itself a thirsting for Christ, but we can use it in our preaching to bring to
light the deeper need of man, the need for God.' *Introduction*, pp. 140f.
115   See his audio talk, 'How Can There Be Just One Religion?' http://
www.bethinking.org/truth-tolerance/intermediate/exclusivity-how-can-there-
be-just-one-true-religion.htm.

has 'come in the flesh' (v. 2). Christianity says that in the incarnation God added to himself a human nature and in the resurrection we see that salvation is not about escaping creation but redeeming and transforming creation, transforming 'this world'. Christianity gives hope for 'this' world. Third he mentions the *method* of grace: unlike other religions in which you have to perform in certain ways to be saved – love God, love neighbour, and so forth – the gospel says the opposite: 'In this is love, not that we loved God but that he loved us and sent his Son to be the atoning sacrifice for our sins' (v. 10). Jesus is not mainly a teacher, but a wonderful saviour.

Why are these unique distinctives so important? Keller argues that it is these doctrinal distinctives that are the foundation for truly loving behaviour. Without these unique foundations, a concept like 'love' can lose its meaning and quickly becomes self-righteous and intolerant. However, because of the *method* of grace, Christians know they are not saved because of their performance, so they are to be humble not self-righteous; because of the *purpose* of Jesus' salvation, Christians know they are to serve others in their communities, because the resurrection shows us that God's creation matters, 'this world' matters; finally, because of the *origin* of Jesus' salvation, Christians know that a self-sacrificing God must lead to self-sacrificing followers, not self-righteous followers.

Although Keller's argument is incredibly 'broad-brushstroke', it helpfully highlights both the substance and sentiment of Christian mission as it pertains to other religions. In this final section I note several missiological implications and applications of the 'theology of religions' that I have described in this chapter.

First is the motivation and 'vision' of Christian mission. In keeping with the themes of this chapter, we echo Stott's comments on Romans 1.5:

The highest of missionary motives is neither obedience to the Great Commission (important as that is), nor love for sinners who are alienated and perishing (strong as that incentive is, especially when we contemplate the wrath of God . . .), but rather zeal – burning and passionate zeal – for the glory of Jesus Christ . . . Only one imperialism is Christian . . . and that is concern for His Imperial Majesty Jesus Christ, and for the glory of his empire.[116]

This empire is eschatologically inaugurated, that is to say, our present situation in redemptive history is that between the 'already' of Christ's life, death, resurrection and ascension, and the 'not yet' of the consummation of the kingdom and final judgement. This entails both continuity and discontinuity between the earth now and the new heaven and the new earth to come. Even though we recognize the pattern of discipleship given to us by Christ of suffering followed by glory, we still note the inexorable growth of the kingdom:

> The Calvinist and Reformed concept of the commonwealth is linked to the doctrine of the kingdom of God by being the kingdom's slowly realised, still imperfect, but proleptic expression. In the end at the last judgment, Jesus Christ the Lord completely 'restores' and 'renews' the whole world. He restores a completely 'just order'. The kingdom of God or Christ is cosmic in scope and utterly invincible. All things *will* be made new. With a Marxist-like paradox of zeal for the inevitable, the church serves as a witness to the new order, as agent for it, and as first model or exemplar of it. For the decisive turn has already been taken in the work of Christ.[117]

Second, concerning the Christian content of mission, we advocate a holistic, transformative or integral approach to mission that recognizes, on the one hand, the spiritual and social dimensions of sin and idolatry and, on the other, the scope of the gospel and its entailments to transform individuals, communities and cultures, spiritually, socially, economically, politically, and so on.[118] As Christians we are to take every thought captive for Christ (2 Cor. 10.5).

---

116 John Stott, *Romans: God's Good News for the World* (Downers Grove: InterVarsity Press, 1994), p. 53.

117 Cornelius Plantinga, Jr, 'The Concern of the Church in the Socio-Political World: A Calvinist and Reformed Perspective', *Calvin Theological Journal* 28:2 (1983), p. 203.

118 On this see, for example, Udo Middelmann, *Christianity versus Fatalistic Religions in the War Against Poverty* (Colorado: Paternoster, 2007).

In order to further this mission, and in terms of interreligious socio-political involvement, it is possible that there may be times when a strategic 'co-belligerence' between Christians and those from non-Christian religions might be appropriate. For although there is a principal antithetical relationship between the two, because of the inconsistency of non-Christian worldviews (due to God's common grace and the *imago Dei*), other faiths may agree with a Christian stance on a certain ethical or political issue, because they are using the 'borrowed capital' of the Christian worldview.[119] However, such co-belligerence must be conducted with discernment and can only be temporary:

> Christians must realise that there is a difference between being a co-belligerent and being an ally. At times we will seem to be saying exactly the same things as those without a Christian base are saying . . . We must say what the Bible says when it causes us *to seem to be saying* what others are saying, such as Justice or Stop the meaningless bombings. But we must never forget that this is only a passing co-belligerency and not an alliance.[120]

We must be careful that in our co-belligerence we do not communicate the possibility of religious neutrality or the dilution of the exclusivity of Christ and the gospel.

Third, although in terms of God's sovereignty there is a sense in which the whole universe is God's kingdom,

> in the New Testament the word more commonly refers to that invasive aspect of his sovereignty under which there is eternal life. Everyone is under the kingdom in the first sense, whether they like it or not; only those who have passed from the kingdom of darkness to the kingdom of God's dear Son (Col. 1.13), those

---

119   The important apologetic point here, and the heart of what is known as 'presuppositional apologetics', is not whether those in non-Christian religions argue for a similar position to Christians – they can and do – but whether they can give a justification for their position based on their own religious presuppositions. This 'common' ground is not 'neutral' ground but 'Christian' ground.

120   Francis Schaeffer, 'The Church at the End of the Twentieth Century', in *The Complete Works of Francis A. Schaeffer*, vol. 4 (Wheaton: Crossway, 1982), p. 30.

who have been born from above (John 3.3, 5), are under or in the kingdom in the second sense.[121]

Given that eternal life is only to be found in the gospel of Christ, and that normatively this comes through the human messenger in this life, in terms of missionary activity, we must speak about the ultimacy of evangelism, that is, the verbal proclamation of the gospel message with the call for faith and repentance in Christ.

Fourth, our interpretation of other religions shapes our approach to matters of contextualization. Once again Bavinck is helpful here. First is the recognition that 'each time the gospel is preached in a different language, to a different people, it has to transmute a variety of words, as it were and give them new content. The Gospel does not find anywhere in the world a ready language that fits completely and absolutely like a garment.'[122] Second is the recognition that in communicating the gospel, 'The missionary exhales many pagan ideas with every word he speaks. He cannot do otherwise, since he has no other vocabulary at his disposal, but he will shudder at times when he is conscious of what he is doing.'[123] Therefore, 'we must never lost sight of the dangers involved, and we must endeavor to purify terms we have borrowed from their pagan connotations. This is what the apostles did with concepts such as salvation, redemption, "logos", and many others, which undoubtedly could easily have led to a world of misunderstanding.'[124] Third, in terms of living the gospel or better, ecclesial theologizing, Bavinck speaks of '*possessio*' rather than accommodation:

'Accommodation' connotes something of a denial, of a mutilation. We would, therefore prefer to use the term *possessio*, to take in possession. The Christian life does not accommodate or adapt

---

121 Don Carson, *The Gagging of God: Christianity Confronts Pluralism* (Leicester: Apollos, 1996), p. 410.

122 J. H. Bavinck, *Christus en de mystiek van het Oosten* (*Christ and Eastern Mysticism*) (Kampen, 1934), p. 109, quoted in Visser, *Heart for the Gospel*, p. 286.

123 Bavinck, *Introduction*, p. 138.

124 Bavinck, *Introduction*, p. 140.

itself to heathen forms of life, but it takes the latter in possession and thereby makes them new. Whoever is in Christ is a new creature. Within the framework of the non-Christian life, customs and practices serve idolatrous tendencies and drive a person away from God. The Christian life takes them in hand and turns them in an entirely different direction; they acquire an entirely different content . . . Such is neither 'adaptation' nor 'accommodation'; it is in essence the legitimate taking possession of something by him to whom all power is given in heaven and on earth. [125]

Finally, given our *a priori* approach, which sees all non-Christian religions in an antithetical relationship with Christianity, one might be surprised to see a desire to engage in both interreligious dialogue and the phenomenological study of religions. Both these activities are necessary providing they are understood within the discipline of missionary apologetics, historically known as 'elenctics'.[126] Elenctics is the convicting work of the Holy Spirit as described in John 16.8:

The Holy Spirit will convince the world of sin. The Holy Spirit is actually the only conceivable action of the verb, for the conviction of sin exceeds all human ability. Only the Holy Spirit can do this, even though he can and will use us as instruments in his hand. Taken in this sense, elenctics is the science which is concerned with the conviction of sin. In a special sense then it is the science which unmasks all false religion as sin against God and calls people to the knowledge of the one, true God.[127]

Elenctics is a trialogue in which the Christian enters into the already existing dialogue between the non-Christian and the Holy Spirit, a dialogue already described as that dynamic relationship

---

125 Bavinck, *Introduction*, p. 179.

126 See Cornelius J. Haak, 'The Missional Approach: Reconsidering Elenctics', *Calvin Theological Journal* 44:1 (2009), pp. 37–48. Elenctics means 'to convict' or 'to rebuke'.

127 Bavinck, *Introduction*, p. 222. See also Brian DeVries, 'The Evangelistic Trialogue: Gospel Communication and the Holy Spirit', *Calvin Theological Journal* 44:1 (2009), pp. 49–73.

of objective divine revealing and subjective human suppressed and substitution. As Bavinck notes, 'we do not open the discussion, but we need only to make it clear that the God who has revealed his eternal power and Godhead to them, now addressed them in a new way, through our words'.[128] In such a trialogue it is essential that the Christian takes time to compassionately listen and understand the religious other to discover what they have done with God. To achieve this goal, one needs to be familiar with both a general 'scientific awareness' of other religions (historically, psychologically, philosophically and phenomenologically), and a more particular 'living approach' which appreciates the individualistic nature of religious consciousness.

In all our missionary endeavours, and in conclusion, there always must be gentleness and respect, and there can be no self-righteous superiority, 'for at each moment the person knows the weapons which he turns against another have wounded himself':[129]

The practice of elenctics is evidence of God's love for unbelievers. Why does the evangelist proclaim this love? Because he or she knows all too well his or her own sinful condition apart from Christ, standing condemned before God's throne *if he himself does not take shelter with Jesus Christ*. Knowing this, he reaches out to the unbeliever, aiming to protect him from God's wrath. Indeed elenctics is combat. However, it is not combat to kill but to rescue. Satan attacks to 'kill'. The divine struggle is driven by God's love and is inspired by the wonderful sacrifice of Christ; a sacrifice that was made out of love for all humanity. The coming judgement at the end of times is real. Let, then, the messengers of the gospel, the soldiers of peace, go into the world to rescue and heal.[130]

---

128   J. H. Bavinck, *The Impact of Christianity on the Non-Christian World* (Grand Rapids: Eerdmans, 1948), p. 109.
129   Bavinck, *Introduction*, p. 272.
130   Haak, 'The Missional Approach', p. 48.

PART TWO

The Dialogue Begins

4

Gavin D'Costa Responds to Paul Knitter and Daniel Strange

Response to Paul Knitter

Paul says various things with which I happily agree, and there is much to admire and learn from his characteristically open-minded essay. There are three particular aspects that I would highlight for praise. First, I join Paul in his deep commitment to the poor, suffering and marginalized and his concern that the gospel is an incisive challenge as to the shape of our lives. He prophetically challenges all religions, including Christianity, on what he calls 'kingdom' values, such that all religions stand under judgement; and also, hopefully, might stand together in our troubled world practising these values. Second, Paul exudes a spirit of respect towards other religions and the persons who make up such 'traditions', especially Buddhism, from which he has so learnt so much. There is a genuine openness, a humility to learn, a willingness to listen patiently, and to discern and celebrate the possible work of the Spirit. Third, Paul's essay testifies to the restless theological rethinking of the Christian tradition in the light of his experience of other religions, especially Buddhism.

My basic objection to Paul is that he unnecessarily throws out the 'baby with the bath water', or to put it theologically: he revises and changes the fundamental doctrines of the Christian faith to make them compatible with *his* notion of interreligious dialogue. His goal is a universal social just order in which religions can be primary instigators of this order and work together without arrogance, disdain or superiority towards each other. His means to this goal is to relativize doctrinal truth claims, excepting political-social-justice truth claims. Hence, ironically, to achieve interreligious harmony he ends up by relativizing all orthodox religions, including Christianity, whereby harmony is attained through a pact between liberal liberationists. I have argued elsewhere that this coalition is based on 'universal modern liberalism', the master discourse of interpretation.[1] Here Paul dangerously moves outside the bounds of orthodox Christianity because his master discourse is located in the Enlightenment tradition of modernity. The double irony is that Paul's noble goals can be best achieved within orthodox Catholicism, as I hope to have shown in my opening essay, without the large scale revisionism that departs so problematically from what Dan has rightly called a constitutive Chalcedonian Christology.

Why Paul's revisionism is problematic

Over the years Paul cannot see a fit between orthodox Catholicism and the goals of interreligious dialogue for two main reasons. The first has methodological and substantitive aspects; the second is a psychological argument. First, Paul does not like exclusive truth claims because they are allegedly inimical to dialogue. Methodologically, he excludes 'any theological interpretation of Christian belief that does not allow for and promote dialogue' because such interpretations 'can't be a responsible and orthodox interpretation' (p. 51). Substantitively, Paul excludes exclusive claims, especially the core exclusive claim regarding Christ: that Jesus is the *only* Son of God or the only true self-revelation of the triune God (p. 70). Paul reinterprets this classic claim so that there can be other sons, 'saviours', and revelations (p. 70), while he holds at the subjective level that Jesus is his saviour and the saviour for millions of Christians. This move relativizes the truth claims made by orthodox Christians to one of subjective preference, a personal commitment, rather than a preference and commitment to the truth of who God is, as Trinity, as revealed in Christ.

---

1 Gavin D'Costa, *The Meeting of Religions and the Trinity* (Maryknoll: Orbis, 2000), pp. 30–40, which include references to Paul's corpus regarding my claims.

Second, Paul employs what I call a psychological argument. He equates arrogance and superiority with making exclusive claims. Such superiority is allegedly inimical to interreligious dialogue (taking us back to his methodological rule). Thus, Paul's entire project is an attempt to recast Christianity so that all its doctrinal claims are inclusive and all its ethical claims mirror modern liberal agendas (which are also 'inclusive'). This works for Paul on the doctrinal level through his use of a theory of symbolic language. Thus 'literal' language is seen to be problematic in making truth claims about the nature of the world, whereas symbolic understanding renders religious language as fundamentally expressive of an attitude or an outlook without definitive metaphysical or ontological claims.[2] Whether this is actually Rahner's theory of 'symbol' is debatable, but Paul's assumptions about language allow him to deconstruct all exclusive religious claims through an implicit refusal of their metaphysical force. This becomes clear whenever he turns to central doctrinal claims regarding eschatology, the doctrine of God, and the hypostatic union.

What can be said about this? First, to make a truth claim that has ontological purchase should not be (and is not) inimical to dialogue unless it is employed with social power threatening the 'other'. This threat has clearly been the case during certain periods of history and Christians today should eschew all such forms of coercive 'mission'. The truth of Christianity must be grasped entirely for its own sake, not for social power, advancement, or status. Vatican II's Declaration on Religious Freedom (1965) reiterates this: men and women 'should act on their own judgment, enjoying and making use of a responsible freedom, not driven by coercion but motivated by a sense of duty' (1). Methodologically we should be suspicious of Paul's rule that only theological interpretations that allow for and promote dialogue are acceptable and 'orthodox'. The apostle Paul (in Tarsus, not New York!) was keen to convert Jewish contemporaries and realized that his preaching was a scandal to both Jews and Greeks. On Knitter's criterion Saint Paul's theological interpretations are problematic for

---

2 George Lindbeck, *The Nature of Doctrine: Religion and Theology in a Postliberal Age* (London: SPCK, 1984), pp. 46–63 sees this theory operative in Rahner and Hick.

they created disharmony among Jewish congregations, scandal to gentiles (and Muslims), and claimed something remarkably exclusive: that men and women need to be baptized in the name of the Father, Son and Spirit to enter into full fellowship with God.

Paul, from New York, says he accepts 'mission', but subtly turns mission into social action, rather than the gospel's primary call to baptism which then results in social action. Indeed, Matthew 28.16–20, cited by Paul to support his point, tells the disciples to baptize the nations (v. 19), 'teaching them to obey everything that I have commanded you' (v. 20). Men and women are not saved by works as such, but by a faith that leads to works of charity and mercy. Without the latter, faith is empty, but faith is central and issues in the gifts of the Spirit. This does not exclude mission as prophetic witness, nor mission as social service, but Paul simply obscures a central plank of Catholic teaching over thousands of years: mission involves the 'necessity' of baptism (which does not uncritically involve the loss of one's cultural and religious heritage, although it has sadly sometimes meant this).

Is Paul's methodological rule sensible: should we only hold doctrines that are conducive to interreligious dialogue? I think not. I meet Muslims and Buddhists and others who make exclusive claims in order to be good Muslims and Buddhists. I respect this. I also understand that what follows from these claims might logically, but not always necessarily, call into question the truthfulness of my most cherished beliefs. Muslims just cannot accept the claim of the incarnation (expressed in Chalcedon) that in Jesus Christ there came together without confusion or identity, a human and a divine nature in the divine person of Jesus Christ. Of course, 'nature' and 'person' and 'hypostasis' all require unpacking, especially to avoid idolatry (*shirk* – confusion of the divine and the human). But my Muslim friend still cannot accept my claims about Jesus based on her reading of the Qur'an, which determines Jesus' (Isa's) identity as a prophet who is a forerunner to Muhammad. Hence, respectfully, she thinks my claims are false. This is not a problem, for it seems to me dialogue is only interesting if we are in pursuit of truth; and we must argue for, debate and defend what we take as truth, until we discover otherwise. Or to take Buddhism, the tradition with which Paul engages (at least with its more modern western manifestations). Elsewhere, I have shown that the Dalai Lama makes rigorously exclusivist truth claims which require one to be a *dGe lugs* Buddhist monk as a precondition of final release.[3] The Dalai Lama does not push this point in a missionary fashion because of the doctrine of reincarnation. One can wait for thousands of lives. But the point still holds: nirvana can only be attained by a *dGe lugs* monk. Will Paul tell the Dalai Lama that his language is only symbolic and that Nagarjuna and the Mahayana tradition are plain wrong in this ancient claim? Would that be problematic for interreligious dialogue on Paul's own criterion?

Second, the claims regarding Jesus in Paul's approach are problematic. They are unorthodox in failing to meet the objective claims advanced by the Bible, classical orthodox creeds, and tradition (as exemplified recently in *Dominus Iesus* and in *Dei Verbum*, two Catholic documents with differing levels of regulative and normative force). Paul does include elements of subjective claims about Jesus from the orthodox tradition (such as: I find salvation in Jesus, he is God for me, and so on). But the ontological force of these claims is undermined. Technically speaking, Paul advances a degree Christology (Jesus is different in degree from us, not in kind – see p. 72) and an exemplary atonement Christology (Christ's death is not constitutive for salvation, but rather exemplifies his faithfulness to his vocation even at the cost of death). There are three ways of responding to Paul's Christological picture. First, one might say, as I do, that they do not meet what is required by the canons of orthodoxy. That is important to me as a Catholic theologian. Second, what are the authorities that we can invoke in our debate? Can I say: Paul, as a Catholic, your position does not conform to *Dominus Iesus* and thus you need to rethink? Can I say: Paul, your position does not make sense of the New Testament, for example the Hebrews Christology of Christ as high priest or John's high Christology which holds that Jesus 'was' God and 'was with' God (John 1.1)? Can I say: Paul, your Christology departs from the classical Christological creedal confessions; surely this is unacceptable? It is not clear to me what the guiding authorities are in Paul's theological work,

---

3 See my study of this matter with textual justification in *The Meeting of Religions*, pp. 72–95.

except a sort of eclectic synthesis of views that he has found helpful. I do not mean this disrespectfully, but methodologically it means I'm not clear how to proceed in challenging his views. What are the authorities to which his position is subject: the necessity of interreligious dialogue, or fidelity to scripture and tradition? In my longer analysis of his work, I isolate those authorities as liberal modernity.

Third, is the Christological choice really an either/or between a low-degree exemplary Christology advanced by Paul or a 'petulant and even an abusive' God the Father who sadomasochistically 'sacrifices' his own Son (p. 69)? For Paul, this is what the traditional atonement doctrine seems to amount to. There can be no question that the traditional doctrine of atonement requires careful explication to avoid all sorts of dangerous pitfalls: that God 'owes' the devil ransom; that Jesus 'had to' merit/satisfy for sins by his cross; that the penal substitution invokes a fiction that God treats Christ 'as if' he were guilty of sin; that God wills pain and suffering upon an innocent human. However, there are numerous rehabilitations (*not* revisions) that continue what *The Catechism of the Catholic Church* sees as central to the faith (606–18): that 'Our salvation flows from God's initiative for us, because "he loved us and sent his Son to be the expiation for ours sins" (1 John 4.10). "God was in Christ reconciling the world to himself." (2 Cor. 5.19)' (620).[4]

Christ's role is closely related to how sin is understood. Paul falsely implies that Augustine obscured the reality of our being created good (p. 64) in seeing Genesis as being primarily about original sin, but Augustine saw both the original goodness of creation and the fall from this state through sin, as central to the drama of salvation.[5] Augustine opposed the Manicheans precisely on this

---

4 See a critical overview of options, and one constructive Reformed way forward: Oliver Crisp, 'Original Sin and Atonement', in Thomas P. Flint and Michael C. Rae (eds), *The Oxford Handbook of Philosophical Theology* (Oxford: Oxford University Press, 2009), pp. 430–51. For a recent Catholic explication see Matthew Levering, *Sacrifice and Community: Jewish Offering and Christian Eucharist* (Oxford: Blackwell, 2005).

5 See *Contra duas epist. Pelag.* I. II. 4; V. 10; III. IX. 25; IV. III; and also *Contra Jul.* II. X. 33. The Augustinian theme of original goodness has been strongly emphasized, along with sin, in the writing of John Milbank.

point, insisting that creation was fundamentally good and to be valued, but sin made us misuse creation, ourselves and each other. Christ came to save us from sin, not irredeemable bodiliness. Buddhism does not suggest 'original blessings' regarding creation, as Buddhism has no doctrine of creation at all. What one sees in Paul's *appropriation* of aspects of Buddhism is a type of Gnosticism (what he calls mysticism), in contrast to the Christian emphasis on revelation (an action initiated by God); and a type of activism (prophetic social activism) that derives from 'insight' regarding Christ, not Christ's actions as such. Paul is in danger of Gnosticism: redemption through right knowledge.

It is clear that much more careful analysis of Paul's position is required. What I have tried to do here is to indicate three things. First, orthodox Christianity can deliver the goals that Paul's unorthodox Christianity seeks: searching for a just international order and openness to learning from the other, but without having to undergo such crippling revisionism, especially regarding the doctrine of the incarnation. Second, orthodox Christianity can attain the goals of interreligious dialogue precisely through its high Christology, upon which the dignity of the human person is based. Third, Paul's own position cannot be internally sustained as he arrives at conclusions that are inimical to interreligious dialogue and thus fails on his own criterion for accepting doctrine (he must reject the Dalai Lama's teachings and see them as false, not to mention the Pope's teachings). He also fails to convince this orthodox Christian that his Christological revisionism is compatible with the Bible and tradition. It is curious to find myself in closer theological sympathy with my Reform rather than my Catholic dialogue partner.

Response to Daniel Strange

Dan has written a characteristically robust paper. I find myself in agreement on a whole range of issues: his suspicion of methodologies that prioritize modernity over Christianity; his clear and unwavering focus on giving glory to God known in Christ, first and foremost, and without reduction; his defence of a high constitutive Chalcedonian Christology; his clarion call for mission; and his arguments for common social action (co-belligerence). In these significant dogmatic areas we are in agreement. However, I am not sure how deep these agreements go because of the deeper Calvinist–Catholic disagreements regarding total depravity and predestination. Dan's Calvinist tradition generates a very different landscape regarding grace, so that only the invisible elect within Christianity (and for Calvin, specifically 'Calvinists') are justified. The rest are damned and deserve damnation through their total depravity. Is this Calvinist–Catholic divide bridgeable?

One issue between us is that which is termed 'invincible ignorance' by Catholics: a person who does not know the gospel through no fault of their own, and who will thus be offered the means of salvation in some manner or other as God is just and merciful and would not leave anyone without the possibility of salvation. Dan denies this category exists. He holds the position that all those who die as non-Christians will be lost. He tentatively rejects any post-mortem solution. He holds that the majority of humankind is asymmetrically 'predestined' for perdition in terms of their being born into depravity. They are guilty by virtue of being born human. Any possible moral strain on Dan's position is alleviated intra-systematically because he holds that all people, in terms of justice, deserve damnation; and God, in his mercy, has predestined some for salvation.[6] This position is problematic to me and finally highlights our tradition-specific differing starting points.

First, Catholic teaching rejects the 'Geneva' position in the Council of Trent (session 6) that God predestines the damnation of anyone. It is not possible to rehearse the complex Molinist debate here. According to 1 Timothy 2.3–6: 'God our Saviour . . . desires everyone to be saved and to come to the knowledge of the truth. For there is one God; there is also one mediator between God and humankind, Christ Jesus, himself human, who gave himself a ransom

---

6 See Strange, *The Possibility of Salvation Among the Unevangelised* (Carlisle: Paternoster, 2002), pp. 265–86. Strange does not fully clarify what kind of predestination theory he holds (single, double, supra or infra-lapsarian, preterition, and so on).

for *all*' (my emphasis). According to Luke 5.31–2: 'Those who are well have no need of a physician, but those who are sick; I have come to call not the righteous, but sinners to repentance.' These passages have often been read to imply that Christ's atonement is for all and is not limited. The Reformers protested that since universalism is false and God's will cannot be thwarted, these verses do not refer to 'all' which would include the damned; rather 'all' means 'all' the elect. However, many of the early fathers, councils and the magisterial tradition interpreted these texts otherwise. The Council of Orange in 529 excluded the possibility of God predestining anyone to evil. Pope Innocent X condemned as heresy the proposition that Christ suffered for the elect predestined only. Alexander VIII refused the assertion that Christ had sacrificed himself for the faithful alone. The controversy against Jansenism consolidated this magisterial position. This tradition certainly does not permit universalism, but it refuses to hold that God's love and mercy is restricted. (In Dan's Reform terms, it is probably analogous to a qualified Arminianism.) Rather, human freedom must be allowed its tragic dimension. This does not mean that God's will to save all is thwarted, because God also wills men and women to choose him freely – and some might not. Hence, we seem to have two irreconcilable starting points, mine and Dan's, Catholic and Calvinist, and each is based on scripture. How do we move forward in this dispute? Straightforward appeal to the Bible is difficult, for each of us operates within a differing tradition of interpretation of the same biblical texts. Whither ecumenism?

Second, the category of invincible ignorance has been particularly developed and deployed in regard to the non-Christian in the nineteenth century, although this tradition begins in the sixteenth.[7] This means that there is an analogous position of: (a) those after Christ who do not know the gospel through no fault of their own; with (b) those who, prior to the coming of Christ, did not know the gospel through no fault of their own. Dan seems to reject the possibility of (a), although he accepts (b). Elsewhere Dan also holds that

---

7 See Francis Sullivan, *Salvation Outside the Church?* (New York: Continuum, 1992), pp. 63–82.

the righteous of Israel were saved through their implicit or proleptic faith in Christ.[8] The specific issue between us thus revolves around whether there is any analogy between the righteous of Israel and the 'holy pagan', both before and after the time of Christ, while respecting the *sui generis* nature of Israel? Elsewhere I offer textual evidence that some of the early church fathers accepted that there were pagans in the *limbus patrum*, the limbo of the fathers, deriving from 1 Peter 3.19 and 4.6 and other biblical texts, and that Christ's descent into hell was soteriological.[9] Interestingly, this type of solution is employed by the Lutheran theologian George Lindbeck, so it is not a Catholic peculiarity.[10] My proposal has ecumenical support.

Some questions to Dan are in order. First, will Dan accept this tradition regarding the descent into hell to redeem some of the righteous Jews and pagans before the coming of Christ? If he does not, how does he explain the Apostles' creed, '*Christus descendit ad infernos*', which is a normative creed for both of us? Second, how does Dan understand the manner in which those pre-Christ were saved? Third, is there no analogy between the implicit faith in Christ that Abraham had and the implicit faith that might be had by a man who has come to believe in theism on the basis of common revelation? Does not true theism have a telos towards Christ? Fourth, what does Dan make of Hebrews 11.6: 'And without faith it is impossible to please God, for whoever would approach him must believe that he exists and that he rewards those who seek him.' Can this suffice for the invincibly ignorant who do not know Christ through no fault of their own? Fifth, if Dan accepts the descent as I have outlined it, what would be his objections to this analogical application of it to those after Christ who are in invincible ignorance?

---

8   Strange, *The Possibility*, pp. 167–89.

9   See *Christianity and World Religions: Disputed Questions in the Theology of Religions* (Chichester: Wiley-Blackwell, 2009), pp. 167–87. See also Jared Wicks, 'Christ's Saving Descent to the Dead: Early Witnesses from Ignatius of Antioch to Origen', *Pro Ecclesia* 13:3 (2009), pp. 281–309, a useful extension to the literature.

10   See Lindbeck, *The Nature of Doctrine*, pp. 46–72.

To turn to a different topic: the role of 'religion'. Dan holds that religions are idolatry for they suppress and substitute truth (the trinitarian revelation) with falsity and error and thus, whatever goodness, truth and beauty may be found in any religion, it is always within the context of greater sinfulness, error and disfigurement. This means that non-Christian religions are always incommensurable with Christianity (not necessarily with each other, as their incommensurability derives from the difference between supernatural truth and human sinfulness). Their ethical practices may resemble elements of Christianity, but the justification for these practices always remains incommensurable with Christian practices. One might say that they are continuous on the human level and discontinuous on the divine.

If I understand correctly, there is an internal dissonance in Dan's position, which possibly reflects his openness to a dynamic situation regarding 'religions' but also may destabilize his fixed category of 'religions'. Let me explain. Dan allows for the action of the Holy Spirit in other religions in terms of common grace which is 'non-salvific', which 'restrains sin and the consequences of sin' and 'excites non-Christians to perform acts of "civic righteousness" and culture building' (p. 118). So far, so good! One can trace a clear parallel with what is taught by the magisterium regarding the actions of the Holy Spirit (which have been interpreted by some as asserting nothing more than common grace).[11] But Dan later allows the possibility that 'religions' may be more than just the effects of common grace, when he speaks of Bavinck's notion of the 'inflow of special revelation', where for example, Plato is seen to be influenced by the prophets, or Leithart's 'plausible' case that morality within another religion might originate in a 'mixture of general and special revelation' (p. 121). If special revelation is operative, then surely two important points are conceded, which seem inconceivable at the outset? Is this a chink in what appears an invulnerable position on 'religions'?

First, while other religions are ultimately false in so much as they do not teach the truth of God's triune self-revelation, they are

---

11   See Mikka Ruokanen, *The Catholic Doctrine on Non-Christian Religions according the Second Vatican Council* (Leiden: Brill, 1992).

capable of mediating 'special revelation', which means that there is the possibility of knowing the one true God within that religion. Is Dan willing to accept that non-Christians can know God through 'special' revelation? This is certainly the direction of the teaching of the Catholic Church, although I would not wish to concede 'special revelation' in another religion, apart from Israel pre-Christ, as I take 'special revelation' to be God's Trinity. I would prefer to speak of the activity of the Holy Spirit. Further, this implication means that the division between a person and their tradition should not be pushed too hard as when Dan writes: 'God through his Spirit does not strive with religious traditions and systems but with individuals made in his image' (p. 121). But if the person in question writes texts that are taken as authoritative, cannot the action of the Spirit also be discerned in religious structures (for example in caring for widows)? What is the logic of isolating the Spirit in the personal inner subjectivity of the person, and not the structures which persons shape and form? I wonder whether our different ecclesiologies shape our attitudes on this point.

If Dan has conceded the possibility of 'special revelation', why is he so reticent to understand the *praeparatio evangelica* more dialectically? He writes, 'I have already indicated the sinful human propensity to pervert and distort the truth of God's revelation which becomes a basis for further judgement rather than a *praeparatio evangelica*' (p. 128). But does it only and always become a basis for further negative judgement and never for positive appraisal such as we saw in *Nostra Aetate* in my chapter above? For example, there are non-Christians who have resisted violence with peaceful forbearance. The Dalai Lama has championed the cause of Tibet against China's invasion with careful Buddhist principled argument, and Aung San Suu Kyi has resisted the military dictatorship in Burma through non-violent action. Both these Buddhists draw from Buddhism, and the first is an authority in interpreting his tradition's texts. Gandhi is a good Hindu example, although he explicitly drew upon the New Testament as well as Hindu scriptures. But his synthesis of the two was definitely a form of neo-Hinduism, not a form of Christianity. In that sense his example surely has some, rather than no elements of a *praeparatio evangelica*? His not becoming a Christian perhaps equally demonstrates Dan's point! My question boils down to this: if Dan allows that God's grace might work as it pleases, why does he make an *a priori* decision against the possibility of a *praeparatio evangelica*, for Eusebius, from whom the term originates, realized the untruth of pagan systems while he also searched for positive bridges that might be crossed in engaging with that non-Christian tradition. Eusebius did not affirm other religions as salvific, but acknowledged elements of positivity within a fundamentally false religion. Are we simply emphasizing different points, or is there a more fundamental disagreement between us? I finally want to say that objectively other religions are in error, but they may be used providentially by God to lead women and men to him.

I think there is an important agreement between Dan and myself regarding the religions, but I want to claim that my emphasis is more properly dialectical and not unduly pessimistic. I think this balance is exemplified in *Dominus Iesus* (21):

> Certainly, the various religious traditions contain and offer religious elements which come from God, and which are part of what 'the Spirit brings about in human hearts and in the history of peoples, in cultures, and religions'. Indeed, some prayers and rituals of the other religions may assume a role of preparation for the Gospel, in that they are occasions or pedagogical helps in which the human heart is prompted to be open to the action of God. One cannot attribute to these, however, a divine origin or an *ex opere operato* salvific efficacy, which is proper to the Christian sacraments. Furthermore, it cannot be overlooked that other rituals, insofar as they depend on superstitions or other errors (cf. 1 Cor 10:20–1), constitute an obstacle to salvation.

Surely this more truly expresses the struggle of a fallen humankind sometimes seeing glimpses of God's grace which always and everywhere point to Christ for its fulfilment? Whether this fulfilment is arrived at is another matter altogether.

Finally, I need to chew on something Dan offers. Could it be that the Spirit's operation in other religions is best understood as common grace and not in any way salvific? I think this catches Catholic theology wrestling with an unresolved question. In On the Holy Spirit in the Life of the Church and the World, *Dominum et Vivificantem*, 53, John Paul II expresses the issue well:

> The Second Vatican Council, centred primarily on the theme of the Church, reminds us of the Holy Spirit's activity also 'outside the visible body of the Church.' The Council speaks precisely of 'all people of good will in whose hearts grace works in an unseen way. For, since Christ died for all, and since the ultimate vocation of man is in fact one, and divine, we ought to believe that the Holy Spirit in a manner known only to God offers to every man the possibility of being associated with this Paschal Mystery.' (*Gaudium et Spes*, 22; *Lumen Gentium*, n. 16.)

If there is really the offer of such a possibility, then must there not in some sense be a supernatural and special revelation in non-Christian religions? But we have seen this is not possible in the light of the Second Vatican Council's teachings or later magisterial teachings, culminating in *Dominus Iesus*. Hence, I have tried to resolve this tension through the solution of a post-mortem encounter with Christ, which keeps three sides of this tension intact: some non-Christians can be saved even if they die as non-Christians; while acknowledging the necessity of confessing faith in the triune God to enjoy the fullness of salvation; while acknowledging that God may be inchoately related to within a non-Christian religion. This would mean that the Catholic position can with Dan hold that the Spirit is operating in terms of common grace, but also proleptically, in terms of saving grace. This seems to do justice to the complexity of the evidence, and while not addressed explicitly by revelation, is not in contradiction to it.

5

Paul Knitter Responds to
Gavin D'Costa and Daniel Strange

Response to Gavin D'Costa

What follows is a conversation between family members who are
also good friends. Gavin and I are both Catholics and friends who
have enjoyed many a brotherly theological conversation over the
years (often, as is the wont of Catholic theologians, accompanied
by a bottle of fine scotch). But friends have the freedom to disagree.
And disagree we do. There are profound, often distressing (for both
of us) differences in the way we understand what it means to be
Catholic – indeed, what it means to be religious.

So, to playfully tease a friend but to seriously engage a fellow
theologian, I would formulate my basic criticism of Gavin thus: He
is not Catholic enough! – I'll try to make that case by following the
main topics we were asked to take up in our opening statements.

Theological method: tradition is traditio not traditum

As Catholic theologians, both Gavin and I are committed to the Christian *tradition* as embodied in the Roman Catholic community. But I
believe we have very different understandings of that word, 'tradition'.
The differences are captured in the two Latin words that might be
used for 'tradition': *traditio* signifies the *process* of keeping truth alive
through the centuries by means of the mutual collaboration of bishops,
priests, theologians, lay people; *traditum* implies truth as a *product*
that has to be passed on in the community under the hierarchical over-
sight of the Pope and the bishops. Tradition can be either process or

product. Now, I know that this distinction is too simple. Yet I believe it points to a fundamental difference between Gavin and myself.

In his opening paragraph Gavin states that the role of the theologian is to 'convey the teachings of the Catholic Church'. Although he attests that this does not mean simply to repeat the early doctrines, and although he sees himself as 'applying and thinking through' those teachings (p. 45), in the end he 'conveys' what has been said rather than 'creating' something new out of what has been said. For Gavin, it seems, tradition is like a wise man living through the centuries, learning to adjust and speak different languages as times and cultures change. For me, the Catholic understanding of *traditio* is better captured in the image a couple procreating new embodiments of truth and so producing a family that will spread into different times and cultures. The truths passed on in tradition are as different as children are from parents – and yet they issue forth and continue to be related to their first parents.

As Gavin himself admits, Vatican II brought forth 'innovations and developments' in Catholic teaching. What develops is really different – although never totally different – from what went before. For tradition as *traditum*, what is conveyed is never really different. For tradition as *traditio*, it is – though never totally different.

This process of *traditio* unfolds within the churches through the interplay and dialogue between the various offices within the community that Paul identified: apostles, teachers, prophets, administrators, preachers (1 Cor. 12.27–9). More simply, this is the dialogue between church leaders and laity. Catholics give a greater role to bishops, especially the bishop of Rome. But that role is never one of absolute or monarchical power. If the Pope and bishops lose touch with people and theologians (and vice versa), there is an abuse of power.[1]

God: where is the God of Aquinas and the Catholic mystics?

Many, if not all, of the differences between Gavin and me – and even more so, between Dan and me – stem from what we mean

---

1 This is the vision of the Church in Vatican II as 'the people of God', of which the hierarchy is one part.

when we pronounce or write the word 'God'. If 'God' is a finger pointing to the moon, I fear we are looking at different moons!

What I'm getting at is caught, I think, in a remark that Gavin makes when he states why he is concerned about the dialogue with Buddhism: Buddhists might lead us to 'overcome the distance separating creature from creator' (p. 41). As I tried to make clear in my opening statement, I want to hold to a non-dualistic understanding of how God and the world relate to each other. In such an understanding, there's certainly a distinction between God and creation. But there is not a distance. God is not a Being among beings who acts now here, now there. Rather, God is the very Ground of all being and beings. Such a God acts but, as Aquinas tells us, always in and through secondary agents.[2] 'This follows from the doctrine of creation by God out of nothing, which leaves *no space between God and the creature*. God is *immediately present* to all creation and thus to all human beings individually.'[3] For Aquinas, God as 'subsistent Being itself' (*ipsum esse subsistens*) 'is the simple fullness of the Act of To Be, undividable into intender/intended or actor/world'.[4]

With such a more mystical, non-dualistic understanding of God as that in whom we live and move and have our being (Acts 17.28), one takes scriptural and dogmatic language about God intervening, acting here but not there, saving the Israelites but calling for the murder of the Amalekites (1 Sam. 15.2–3) as figurative, symbolic, time-and-culture-conditioned language – which means it is to be taken seriously but not literally.

Religions: the majority of Catholic theologians view the religions as possible 'ways of salvation'

Gavin's insistence that the religions cannot be 'ways of salvation' makes him what in the good old days of church Latin we used to

---

2   *Summa Theologica* I, q. 22, a. 3.

3   Roger Haight, 'Trinity and Religious Pluralism', *Journal of Ecumenical Studies* 44 (2009), pp. 525–40, at 539. Emphasis mine.

4   Robert E. Neville, *On the Scope and Truth of Theology* (New York: T&T Clark, 2006), p. 112.

call a '*gallus cantans extra chorum*' – a rooster out of tune with the rest of the choir. The Catholic theological choir is pretty unanimous in recognizing the religions as conduits of God's saving action. Richard McBrien, in his magisterial – and careful – summary of present day Catholic belief, concludes his section on religious pluralism: 'Present official teaching acknowledges the salvific value of non-Christian religions.'[5] McBrien appeals to 'official teaching', because, if there was any ambiguity in what Vatican II said about the religions' capacity to be conduits of grace, Pope John Paul II, the Vatican Council for Interreligious Dialogue and the Vatican's International Theological Commission have removed the ambiguity.

I've tried to assemble the evidence elsewhere,[6] but let me offer a sampling in John Paul II's encyclical *Redemptoris Hominis*, where he states explicitly that the sanctifying action of the Holy Spirit can be found 'not only in individuals but also in society, and history, peoples, cultures, *and religions*'.[7] The Council on Interreligious Dialogue is even clearer: It is 'in the sincere practice of what is good in their own religious traditions . . . that the members of other religions correspond positively to God's invitation and receive salvation'.[8] – So although I'm often a little out of tune myself, may I offer a brotherly tease: 'Gavin, join the Catholic choir!'

Furthermore, it seems to me that Gavin's own arguments to deny the religions any saving function are leaky. He invokes Vatican II and argues that the religions 'can only be seen as part of God's plan in so much as they provide a *praeparatio* to the gospel, but not in themselves as a means of salvation' (p. 35). Well, why can't they do both? They can prepare for the gospel by being a preparatory embodiment of God's love and saving grace. Gavin nobly insists that by denying the religions any role in salvation, he doesn't mean that non-Christians as individuals cannot be saved. But how do they then experience God's gift of grace? If not through the social

---

5 Richard O'Brien, *Catholicism: Study Edition* (Oak Grove, MN: Winston Press, 1981), pp. 280–1.
6 Paul Knitter, *Introducing Theologies of Religions* (Maryknoll: Orbis, 2005), pp. 80–4.
7 Section 28, emphasis mine.
8 *Dialogue and Proclamation*, Section 29.

mediation of religion, it would probably have to be by way of a private, direct injection? But as Rahner reminds us, that contradicts Catholic teaching that grace always needs some kind of sacramental embodiment. That's why we say the Church-as-sacrament-of-grace is necessary.[9] Further, Gavin suggests that the abundance of sin and corruption in the religions shows convincingly that they cannot be vehicles of God's saving grace (p. 35). Careful! With that argument, we could say the same of the Catholic Church.

Finally, I know very well that Gavin is sincere in his call to Christians to engage in interreligious dialogue. But I fear that his theology impedes his sincerity. I simply cannot understand how he can really enter into dialogue with other believers – that is, a conversation in which he is truly open to learning something he didn't know before, something that could require him to change his mind – when his theology insists that God has given him the *fullness* of divine truth and the last word on all other truth? If one has the fullness of truth already, what is there, really, to learn? At the most, one can clarify what one already knows. In the end, as Gavin seems to admit, dialogue turns out to be 'conversations between rival communities' (p. 32). One community will have to win out over the others. I prefer to understand dialogue as conversations between *collaborative* communities. That doesn't rule out disagreements and challenges. But it's a conversation where no religion has 'the fullness of truth' and is a final winner.

The Church: no longer necessary for salvation

Regarding the ancient and official church teaching that 'outside the Church there is no salvation', it seems to me that Gavin, like Vatican II and other Catholic theologians, wants to have his cake and eat it too. He argues that the adage, 'Outside the Church no salvation', is not an exclusive declaration that limits membership in heaven to membership in the Catholic Church; rather, he claims, it is more of an admonition that those who are already members of the Church

---

9 Karl Rahner, *Theological Investigations*, vol. 5 (Baltimore: Helicon Press, 1966), pp. 115–34.

leave it at their eternal peril. Honestly, such a creative theological interpretation seems to me to fly in the face of the very explicit declaration of the Council of Florence (1442): 'It [the holy Roman Church] firmly believes, professes and preaches that all those who are outside the catholic church, not only pagans but also Jews or heretics and schismatics, cannot share in eternal life and will go into the everlasting fire which was prepared for the devil and his angels, unless they are joined to the catholic church before the end of their lives.'[10] That pretty much includes – or excludes – everyone.

Gavin seems to hold on to his cake and eat it at the same time in his interpretation of Vatican II's '*ordinantur*' (that is, well-intentioned non-Christians are 'directed toward' the Church, even though they don't know it); he argues that it means that all these good Buddhists, Hindus, Muslims (Jews too?) are really 'in the Church potentially' (p. 18). So the Catholic Church is 'potentially' necessary for their salvation. May I suggest to Gavin and to other such creative Catholic theologians, that we should just eat and enjoy our cake, and happily recognize that the Catholic Church has changed its mind. It now, finally, acknowledges that God's love is so great as to be able to save people outside the Church. That means that the Church is *not* necessary for God to bring people to the enjoyment of God's life. If you respond that that is not official Catholic teaching, I would respectfully respond that since Vatican II, it really is the actual belief of most Catholic people and the teaching of most Catholic theologians.

This would free theologians like Gavin from what seems to me to be theological contortions about people who do not know Christ and are not members of his Church being stored away in some kind of a limbo until the end of time. In suggesting this, Gavin admits that it bears some 'metaphoric complexity' (p. 21). You bet. Maybe a little fantasy, too.

Christology: Jesus Christ is the sacrament of God

Here we come, I believe, to the underlying – I'd call it the *constitutive* – cause of most of our differences. Both of us, with mind

---

10 Denzinger, *Enchiridion Symbolorum*, pp. 801, 870–2, 1351.

and heart, affirm that Jesus Christ is Son of God and saviour. But we understand those words very differently. For Gavin, I think, these words represent a factual statement of truth; that means a truth that can be grasped well enough to be articulated in one or a series of dogmas (dogmas, he adds, that are normatively expressed in the language of western culture) (p. 37). For me, these words convey a symbolic statement of truth; that means that their truth is not declared but indicated and so will have to be interpreted again and again, in a variety of other cultural symbols.

Our differences can be translated into theological language: for Gavin, Jesus is the constitutive cause of salvation. For me, he is a sacramental cause of salvation. In my opening statement I attempted to describe the difference in this way: as the constitutive cause of salvation, Jesus fixes the rupture between God and humanity; that implies just one fixer, only one saviour. As a sacramental cause of salvation, Jesus reveals the love of God that was never ruptured but that so many of us have lost touch and trust with; that leaves open the possibility of other revealers, other Saviours.

Now, as I understand Gavin's convictions, he, like the Pope and many Catholic theologians, would hold that to question whether Jesus is the constitutive cause of salvation, which means to question his uniqueness as the one and only saviour for all people, is to put oneself beyond the limits of what is allowed for a Catholic or Christian theologian. The Pope insists that, if you're going to call yourself Catholic, such questions cannot be placed on the table.

I would suggest that these questions are already on the table. Many Christians today are struggling with, and suffering from, the obligation to believe that they have the only saviour and the only saving Church. To Gavin's statement that 'Christ is the cause of *all* salvation, and the Church . . . [is] the means by which *all* grace is mediated' (p. 22, emphasis mine), I, and I know many other Christians, would answer: 'I just can't believe that. Can't we sit down and talk about it?' But any Catholic theologian who does talk about it and who questions Jesus' or the Church's uniqueness will find him/herself in trouble with the Vatican and often will find himself forbidden to teach and/or write.[11] Serious theologians are offering serious, careful proposals on how the distinctiveness of Jesus (a better word than uniqueness) can be reinterpreted and reaffirmed without subordinating other religions and religious leaders.[12] Respectfully, but also urgently, I implore Catholic and Protestant church leaders and theologians to open this discussion.

If we can engage open-mindedly and open-endedly in this discussion of how Christians are to understand Christ in their new awareness of the need for interreligious co-operation (which is the discussion embodied in this book), I expect (or should I say, I hope?) that in two or three generations, the mainline Christian churches will have a much more pluralistic theology – one which enables them to affirm and proclaim the uniqueness of Jesus, and at the same time affirm and learn from the uniqueness of Buddha and Muhammad and Krishna and others.

Response to Daniel Strange

With Daniel Strange I do not share the same friendship I have with Gavin. But I do share the same family relationship of faith. In our exchanges, and especially in his opening statement, I see in him a brother who is also a 'disciple of Christ' committed to living and announcing the saving truth made known in Jesus of Nazareth. And while I hope we could therefore sit down and break the bread of the Lord's Supper together, we sure will have some hefty theological conversations afterwards. There are some profound, barnacled differences between us.

---

11 Some examples: Roger Haight, SJ, Jacques Dupuis, SJ, Peter Phan, Jon Sobrino, SJ, Tissa Balasuriya, OMI, Jacob Kavunkel, SVD, Michael Amaladoss, SJ. The Vatican has moved against only priests or religious, over whom it has juridical power (and I might add, who threaten its power).

12 Some examples: Roger Haight, *Jesus, Symbol of God* (Maryknoll: Orbis, 1999), pp. 395–423; Raimon Panikkar, *Christophany: The Fullness of Man* (Maryknoll: Orbis, 2004); Aloysius Pieris, 'Christ Beyond Dogma', *Louvain Studies* 25 (2000), pp. 187–231; Paul F. Knitter, *Jesus and the Other Names* (Maryknoll: Orbis, 1996).

I want to honour and respect those differences. Dan, like many of my evangelical friends, represents a different, a very different, way of being Christian. But as with Gavin, honouring Dan's views does not exclude – indeed, it requires – critiquing them. I will try to offer a respectful response by focusing, not so much on what I believe might be the internal incoherence or the biblical inconsistencies of Dan's arguments, but rather on what I believe are their *dangers*. I fear that many elements in Dan's theology of religions can be harmful – harmful to the individual Christian who endorses them, to the Christian Church that acts on them, and to other religious believers who suffer the effects of them.

As I did with Gavin, I make my case according to the assigned topics.

Theological method: the danger of biblical idolatry and fideism

Simply stated, I fear that Dan gives to the Bible all the attributes that are due only to God. That's what we monotheists would call idolatry. When Dan states that 'there is an ontological relationship between God and his words' and that 'God's actions, including his verbal actions, are a kind of extension of him', he sounds a bit more like a Muslim than a Christian. For all practical purposes, he seems to assert an identification of the transcendent, ultimately ineffable God with a finite book, written through human authors, over a complicated patch of history. Please understand, in raising these concerns, I am not denying that for us Christians, the Bible is God's word. But that makes the Bible a vehicle, a conduit, a human medium for God's truth, which calls for constant, never-ending interpretation.

And when I ask Dan just how he knows that the Bible is the ontological extension of God and therefore endowed with 'ultimate authority', the answer he gives sounds to me very much like *fideism* – when the reason why you believe is given solely in what you believe. Dan states clearly: 'the self-attesting, personal and ultimate authority of divine revelation is what it is solely because it is derived from a God who is self-attesting, personal and absolute' (p. 99). And how does he know that God is self-attesting, personal, and absolute? From the Bible, I guess. He's aware that this sounds very much like a circular argument, so he pre-empts my accusation by reminding us that 'all *ultimate* commitments' are 'self-attesting'. As Gödel tells us, every system, even in mathematics, has a starting point that can't be proven. OK. But if it can't be proven, it has to remain open to criticism and to the possibility of falsification, in the light of which a different starting point may have to be chosen.

This is the danger of Dan's fideistic understanding of the Bible: it's impregnable. I don't mean disrespect but it seems to me that to Luther's hymn 'A Mighty Fortress Is Our God', Dan sings another: 'A Mighty Fortress Is Our Bible'. Like so many evangelicals, when Dan quotes the Bible, that's the end of the argument for him. As he tells us, any of the facts of history or of nature that someone might oppose to the 'facts' of the Bible can be seen for what they are *only if* they are regarded in the light of the Bible. Instead of the old Catholic dictum, '*Roma locuta, causa finita*' (Rome has spoken; that settles it), Dan proposes his Protestant '*Biblia locuta, causa finita*' (the Bible has spoken; that settles it). With this notion of the absolute and exclusively normative authority of the Bible, Dan has a very different understanding of the nature of theology from that I laid out in my opening statement. For me, the authority of God's word and biblical revelation has to be brought into a mutually clarifying and mutually criticizing dialogue with God's revelation in nature and human experience. For Dan, there does not seem to be a dialogue. Just the Bible.

And here I see one of the most serious and, for me, saddest dangers in Dan's position: a denigration of our human nature and an expulsion of any revelatory presence of the Divine in nature or in human life. Because of what he seems to take as a literal, historical event, when Adam and Eve sinned, we were totally cut off from any real knowledge of God (p. 98). We are all the blind men in the parable of the elephant; as Dan makes explicit: 'knowledge of the elephant [God] is only possible because the elephant speaks and tells us who he is' (p. 98). And when God does speak in the Bible, it comes 'in contradiction' to anything we can know from nature or in our human condition; if one wants to talk about the Bible 'fulfilling' what we are and know, 'it will be a contradictive or subversive fulfilment' (pp. 162–3). I have to honestly say that such an exclusive confinement of God's revealing presence to the Bible contradicts my Catholic tradition of finding God in nature and the natural law; it contradicts my biblically affirmed experience that even after the fall we can, like God, 'see' that creation is 'good' (Gen. 1.30–1); and it contradicts my experience of the Spirit speaking in human love and in the courage to be, to hope, to struggle for justice. Like all idolatry, I'm afraid that Dan's understanding of the Bible is a confinement of God.

God: the danger of a patriarchal deity

The worries I expressed above about Gavin's God ending up as a distant dualistic deity, removed and unaffected by what happens outside of him, are stirred even more by Dan's insistence that his God is 'self-sufficient . . . independent . . . self existence . . . [existing in] aseity . . . from within determined, not moved by outside influences . . . a totally independent Creator' (p. 99). And to the question, 'But how could such a self-sufficient, unmoved and unmoveable independent entity ever be capable of love?', he appeals to the Trinity. God doesn't have to love anything outside of God because God is Trinity and can be happy loving God's self! This is 'the self-contained ontological Trinity' (p. 115). Excuse me, but this sounds a bit like divine narcissism.

And although this self-contained, untouchable God does not have to (but does) love anything outside of himself, it seems that he (I'm using the male pronoun deliberately) can indeed be affected by and become very angry with all those creatures outside of himself. Honestly, I could not help but cringe when I read that 'God's holy and righteous wrath is kindled and is being revealed from heaven, a foretaste and warning of God's unrestrained wrath to come' (p. 116). Or that 'divine wrath lies at the heart of the human predicament' (p. 124). Not only is this God wrathful; he is also jealous. 'YHWH is jealous for his own name and will not share his glory with another' (p. 115).

When I take a good look at such a self-sufficient, angry, jealous God, I can't help resonating with the concerns of feminist theologians who warn that we (er, I should say we males) have fashioned a God who bears striking resemblance to a stereotypical patriarchal father, who is always in charge, doesn't need anyone, is jealous of any other male, controls by wrathful fulminations and who is ready to love us, but only if we don't offend him or are ready to pay the price and satisfy him if we do.[13]

Christ: the danger of 'Christomonism'

In Dan's theology, it seems that the necessity of Jesus-as-saviour is predicated on this notion of God as wrathful. In Dan's words: 'God took his own loving initiative to appease his own righteous anger by bearing it his own self in his own Son when he took our place and died for us' (p. 125). Only because Jesus 'endured and exhausted the destructive divine judgment . . . [has he] won us forgiveness' (p. 124). I know Dan and other proponents of this substitutionary satisfaction theory will say that all this is a paradox that joins 'wrath' with 'love'. Love satisfies wrath. To me, it seems more of a contradiction. All I know is that because my parents loved me, if I offended them and asked for forgiveness, they would never insist on my having to satisfy them before they could express their love. That's human love, as I think we know it. If divine love is different, I don't understand it. Here again, I hear the feminist critique: a divine Father who permits or requires his own Son to die in order to satisfy his parental wrath looks very much like an abusive parent.[14] I know that is a hard thing to say, and I don't mean to offend Dan. But that's how it looks to me and to many.

Such a satisfaction theory of course limits salvation only to Jesus. And this leads to what I mean by *Christomonism*. Jesus Christ becomes all of God there is. Not only is God's loving and saving action in the world limited to Jesus; it seems that God's very identity

---

13   Rosemary Radford Ruether, *Sexism and God Talk* (Boston: Beacon Press, 1988); Mary Daly, *Beyond God the Father* (Boston: Beacon Press, 1973).

14   Dolores S. Williams, *Sisters in the Wilderness: The Challenge of Womanist God-Talk* (Maryknoll: Orbis, 1993), pp. 161–7.

is. I know that Dan would balk at this, because it rules out the Trinity. So when he points to 'the New Testament writers' conscious and deliberate equating of the identity and action of the historical Jesus of Nazareth with *the* God of Israel, YHWH' (p. 122–3), I don't know what he's pointing to. The New Testament, from what I hear from biblical scholars, does not equate the identity of Jesus with God. On the contrary, Jesus is distinguished from God, who is called Father. 'The Father is greater than I' (John 14.27–9). The New Testament authors indeed call Jesus 'the Son of God' but not God. Only three times in the New Testament is 'God' used in reference to Jesus, and they are all ambiguous references.[15]

I believe it might be more accurate to say that for the New Testament and the early Church, Jesus *defines* God; but Jesus does not *confine* God.

Religions and mission: the danger of imperialism

From his Christomonism, Dan has to move to what might be called 'religio-monism': only one true saviour means only one true religion. And this leads him to a picture of followers of other faiths that I find impossible to reconcile with the most fundamental law of Christianity: to love our neighbours (who certainly include non-Christians) as ourselves.

Before he even meets or speaks with a Muslim or Buddhist or Hindu neighbour, Dan has defined them as follows: they are 'idolaters' (p. 115), 'counterfeits' who 'only bring disappointment, disillusionment, and destruction' (p. 116); their saviours are 'conjured up by the religions of man'; they have 'lost God'; their 'human fancy and speculation' are to be 'condemned' (p. 116); their religions are full of 'empty deceit' (p. 115). Does not love of our neighbours call us to respect them, be open to them, honour their viewpoints (at least before we hear them), be ready to learn from them? If we can't do this, it seems to me, we can't really love them. If we're not

---

15 Raymond E. Brown, *Jesus, God and Man* (Milwaukee: Bruce, 1967), pp. 23–38.

really loving them, we're not measuring up to the first commandment of Jesus.

All of this is on the personal level. When Dan's general judgement and attitude about the utter worthlessness of other religions and their cultures is translated into the attitude and actions of Christian missionaries and of Christian soldiers and politicians, we open the door to all kinds of cultural and political imperialism. I'm not saying that such convictions about the superiority of one's own religion and the subordination of others necessarily *causes* cultural and political imperialism; but such views surely do provide an excuse for, if not an invitation to, such imperialism.

I ask Dan to imagine how the following sentences sound in the ears of Africans or Latin Americans or Indians: 'Only one imperialism is Christian . . . and that is concern for His Imperial Majesty Jesus Christ, and for the glory of his empire' (p. 132). 'As Christians we are to take every thought captive for Christ' (p. 132). The relation of Christianity to other religions and cultures is not to 'accommodate' or to 'adapt', but 'to take in possession' (p. 134). All of which means that for Dan 'elenctics' takes the place of 'dialogue': 'elenctics is combat' (p. 136). This, as he admits, is 'Christian imperialism'. These very same convictions of having the 'only or the best way' have animated European and American imperialism.

I know that Dan is sincere when he warns against 'an attitude of self-righteous superiority' (p. 44). I just don't see how his theology allows him to take his own warning seriously.

My criticisms have been hard and perhaps harsh. I make them to a fellow disciple of Jesus. The dangers I point out are certainly not dangers that Dan intends. If they are real dangers, however, I hope my words can help him avoid them. If they are not real dangers, he will tell me. And we will continue our dialogue.

6

Daniel Strange Responds to
Paul Knitter and Gavin D'Costa

Response to Paul Knitter

In his essay, Paul has outlined, in typically engaging and eloquent fashion, a thought-provoking theological manifesto (indeed metanarrative), which highlights once again how one's particular 'theology of religions' is inextricably linked to, and indeed parasitic upon, foundational theological loci and perennial metaphysical, epistemological and ethical questions. Such questions are not the exclusive privilege of Christianity but of all religions and worldviews.

I was especially struck by a particular juxtaposition within Paul's essay. On the one hand is Paul's right and proper commitment to and call for praxis: that the myriad horrendous injustices of 'this world' matter and need to be urgently addressed by us all, now. There is a gritty realism here which demonstrates that Paul's faith is not 'cloistered' but seeks to listen to, engage with and learn from, not only the world *in* which we live, but also the myriad of worldviews *through* which we live. On the other hand is Paul's 'incorrigible' optimism about the future, a tenor which, for me at least, is present throughout all of his essay, imbuing it with a certain romantic imagination and idealism, a creativity which of course complements Paul's picture of the Divine. I am sure many will find the presence of both these themes a winsome combination. The question to be asked of Paul, though, is whether there is adequate theological justification for this particular vision he sets before us, justification which separates belief, or maybe 'make-believe', from true knowledge, worthy of faith and hope in bringing the world we all want.

It is at this point in my response that I take a deep breath before proceeding, because I have a number of hard things to say. I am eager to model a pastoral sensitivity to Paul which is respectful to him as one of God's image-bearers and which does not make me guilty of either malice or vainglory. However, I also recognize the need for a certain analytic transparency, which will be pedagogically helpful in delineating Paul's position from my own.

At one level and within an intra-Christian frame of reference, there are many individual aspects of Paul's argument that from the perspective of historic orthodox Christianity are deeply problematic, exegetically, hermeneutically and systematically. Just focusing on the area of Christology, Paul, in the interests of 'liberation' (p. 76) and 'dialogue' (p. 52), and assuming a common liberal evolutionary model of Christological development, wishes us textually to reinterpret what have been historically understood as objective, metaphysical and literal theological statements, as subjective, devotional and symbolic, arguing that this was actually the intention of the biblical writers: 'symbols participate in that which they symbolize but cannot be identified with what they symbolize' (p. 67), and 'So when the first Jesus followers called Jesus the Son of God, they were using a symbol that expressed for them the experience that to meet Jesus was to meet God . . . For them, "Jesus" and "God" were almost the same thing. But they weren't the same thing!' (p. 68). Theologically such reinterpretations enable a fundamental paradigmatic shift from an incarnational and constitutive Christology to a degree Christology and an exemplary model of atonement. On the specific issue of the atonement, and so-called 'satisfaction' models, I believe that Paul is reacting against a gross caricature when he rightly speaks out against a 'petulant and abusive' Father sacrificing his own Son is order to satisfy justice (p. 69). While this may be the picture Paul gets from radio and television, I wonder whether these media are the most reliable sources to understand, in sufficient depth and clarity, Christ's penal and substitutionary crosswork, and which for millions of Christians, past and present, has been the heart of the 'good news' of Jesus Christ.[1]

---

1   I recommend here John Stott, *The Cross of Christ* (Leicester: InterVarsity Press, 1986).

There are numerous other similar revisions of foundational theological loci which Paul calls for in his essay. Others have given detailed criticisms of these proposals, especially Christologically, some of which are worth repeating here.[2] First, and more generally, an evolutionary model of Christology cannot be simply assumed and is indeed disputed by many New Testament scholars.[3] Second, Paul's theory of language is extremely counter-intuitive and speculatively eisegetical, contrasted with a normal straightforward understanding of biblical texts, coupled with the difficulty that textual evidence could never falsify Paul's argument. In other words, how could one ever demonstrate to Paul's satisfaction that the biblical writers were indeed making exclusive ontological statements? Indeed, is all religious language non-ontological for Paul? Third is the false dichotomy drawn between the language of devotion, and metaphysical claims that entail exclusivity, to which I ask: Why cannot they be both? Fourth, that far from colluding with their surrounding cultures, the biblical writers were fully aware of their religiously plural context and the counter-cultural nature of their exclusive claims together with the consequences of making such claims. It would have been entirely conceivable for the New Testament writers to identify Jesus with any number of other deities and yet we see no syncretistic accommodation, and only a wealth of exclusivistic statements.

My problem is that even if one demonstrates all the above, one is still left with the problem of mounting a persuasive critique of Paul in that departure from the usual authoritative sources for determining

---

2 For example see Harold Netland, *Dissonant Voices: Religious Pluralism and the Question of Truth* (Leicester: Apollos, 1991), pp. 162–4, 249–60; John Sanders, 'Idolater Indeed!', in Leonard Swidler and Paul Mojzes (eds), *The Uniqueness of Jesus: A Dialogue with Paul F. Knitter* (Eugene, OR: Wipf & Stock, 1997), pp. 121–5; Gavin D'Costa, *The Meeting of Religions and the Trinity* (Maryknoll: Orbis, 2000), pp. 30–40.

3 See, for example, Richard Bauckham, *Jesus and the God of Israel: God Crucified and Other Studies on the New Testament's Christology of Divine Identity* (Grand Rapids: Eerdmans, 2008); Simon J. Gathercole, *The Pre-existent Son: Recovering the Christologies of Matthew, Mark and Luke* (Grand Rapids: Eerdmans, 2006).

Christian truth is not problematic to him. A deeper and more telling critique focuses on the more systemic question as to what motivates Paul in such a radical revisionism. Viewing Paul's paper as a whole, he appears to have a number of fundamental *a priori* commitments with which he comes to and interprets the Christian faith and other faiths, ultimate commitments and presuppositions which stand behind historic Christianity and which reconstruct and relativize its traditional claims. To put it more religiously (and provocatively), orthodoxy is being offered up and sacrificed to something more basic and cherished. I must name the proverbial 'elephant in the room' here, for if I am to be consistent with the position outlined in my own chapter, the conclusion I reach is that my frame of reference for interacting with Paul is not in terms of *intra-Christian* dialogue but rather *inter-religious* dialogue. Paul's deconstruction and ensuing reconstruction, while superficially borrowing the language of Christianity, and even desiring aspects of Christian 'capital', is substantially not a 'Christian' theology of religions at all but rather has become another 'religion' and worldview with its own exclusive claims, its own god, authority, metaphysics, epistemology, ethics, pseudo-gospel (in terms of creation–fall–redemption) and mission. On many axiomatic points this worldview is antithetical to the one described in my own essay. Gavin has named this religion previously as 'Kantian exclusive modernity' and 'neo-pagan unitarianism', to which I add 'Buddhist-Christian panentheism'. Paul's position, like other religions, and noting the complexities of both discontinuity and continuity, is ultimately an autonomous product of human imagination, not rooted and built up in Christ. It is, as I have attempted to define and then expound, an 'idolatrous refashioning of divine revelation' of which the true gospel of Jesus Christ is both its subversion and its fulfilment.

These are, of course, bold and serious claims, but their blows are softened somewhat in the recognition that Paul should make the same accusation of myself (together with the biblical writers, and those of other religions who make exclusive claims), for to use his own illustration, I have idolatrously mistaken my pointing Christian finger for the moon (p. 50). My contention is that there is no reality more ultimate than the personal, self-contained, self-revealing

Yahweh of scripture and Jesus Christ, who is the fullness of deity dwelt in bodily form. The issue becomes therefore a battle as to whose god is ultimate, whose story out-narrates the other. As with all apologetic debates dealing with ultimate presuppositions, our method must be 'indirect' showing the impossibility of the contrary.[4] Or again to put it in the biblical language of idolatry, we must show how rival worldviews are 'cracked cisterns that can hold no water' (Jer. 2.13). In what remains I would like to point to some cracks in Paul's pot.

First, given the metaphysical ultimacy of the non-duality and impersonality of Inter-Being, epistemologically Paul's final authority is neither the personal God who speaks through scripture, nor some form of magisterium. But how can impersonal Inter-Being be a basis for rationality and knowledge (or display the personal characteristics of 'love' and 'patience' for that matter)? With no help from this mute god, I agree with John Sanders's own critique of Paul, that Paul is left in the ancient tradition known as *theoprepes* (that which is appropriate for a God to be), and *soteriaprepes* (that which is appropriate for salvation to be). As Sanders explains:

> Knitter, very Greek in this regard, uses the same method that Hellenized the gospel in order to achieve the pluralization of the gospel. Accordingly, a particular understanding of ultimate reality and how we should live are used to filter the biblical message in order to determine what may be said. For Hellenism, God was a metaphysical necessity needed to explain reality. For pluralism, God is a soteriological necessity needed to provide a purpose for living. Knitter relies on process and liberationist thought, both which begin with the analysis of human life, to show the necessity of religion. It is humanity in search of meaning. In this method, it is *we* who establish the ground rules into which God must fit.[5]

Paul makes a number of definite claims regarding the nature and character of Inter-Being, including of course the claim of incomprehensibility

---

4 For there is no 'neutral' evidence that falls outside of a worldview, since all evidence is interpreted by our worldviews.

5 Sanders, 'Idolater Indeed!', p. 122.

and mystery. But on what authority does he make these claims? How does he know about this god? How does he know that God cannot reveal himself in an unsurpassable way? Paul's method here places him firmly in the Enlightenment tradition as it is a method *von unten* (from below) and which he claims is based on human experience. But experience is not a secure starting point for theological knowledge, for what is the independent norm by which we judge different and often competing experiences? As Harold Netland notes, 'Hitler spoke in a deeply moving manner to the experiences and needs of the German people, but surely this does not qualify him for revelatory status.'[6] Without the secure mooring of an authoritative revelation from above, epistemologically Paul is cut loose and autonomously drifts between a dogmatic rationalism (for example, by ourselves we know what ultimate reality is like) and a mystical irrationalism (we can never know what ultimate reality is like). The Kantian family resemblances are very much in evidence here as are the characteristics of both modernity and late modernity which I believe account for Paul's playful Romanticism.

Second, given Paul's panentheistic worldview, one can only be pessimistic about his eschatological optimism. Panentheism entails that the future is always open as Inter-Being does not determine, or even know, future contingencies, but only necessities. For Paul, responding to the 'randomness' of events and 'chance happenings' is part of the adventure, but it reveals a god who is finite and dependent, not *a se* and sovereign. However, the spatio-temporal orderliness of the physical universe is another contingency that Inter-Being does not determine or know, which would seem to undercut both Paul's faith in the progress of scientific investigation, and his hope that good will finally triumph over evil.[7] An open future means a radical scepticism both for his god and for us. Ironically Paul's endorsement of Nolan's statement that 'Anyone who thinks that evil will have the last word

---

6 Netland, *Dissonant Voices*, p. 257.
7 I am indebted to James Anderson of Reformed Theological Seminary for this point.

or that good and evil have a fifty–fifty chance is an atheist' (p. 65) now becomes a charge levelled at Paul!

Finally, there are a host of ethical problems in Paul's position. First, Paul rightly speaks out against a 'world of selfishness, violence, and the domination of the weak by the strong'. But does not Paul legitimize, indeed sacralize such a selfish, violent mechanism in his strong endorsement of Darwinian evolution (p. 61)? Surely he cannot have it both ways?

Second, regarding Paul's panentheism, evil has to be necessary to Inter-Being as it is an aspect of the universe, but this means that Inter-Being is not absolutely good and can give no absolute standard of goodness. How then do we make sense of concepts of good and evil? Without an ethical norm, there does seem to be something of a dilution here in the evilness of evil, for while Paul can talk about 'justice' and various inconceivable evils, the essence of sin is 'ignorance' and 'silliness' (p. 64) which through a Pelagian salvation can be remedied by enlightenment. Paul's reference point seems to be more influenced by Buddhism than Christianity in that ethics becomes a matter of self-realization, where we overcome our epistemological deception regarding the metaphysical reality of ourselves and the world. Once again though, such an account is wholly impersonal, raising the question as to how Paul could ever speak of an 'obligation' from impersonal Inter-Being. Is this not a version of Hume and Moore's naturalistic fallacy, which denies one can argue 'ought' from 'is'? I contend that although Paul wants to speak strongly in terms of obligation such as the 'preferential option for the poor', his presuppositions provide no foundations for such universal ethical norms. What we are left with are seemingly arbitrary ethical commands with no justification to obey them other than because Paul and other like-minded Kantian pluralists believe in them. In contrast, true Christian ethics is about interpersonal relationships and interpersonal concepts such as obedience, disobedience and love. The personal absolute God of the Bible gives us an absolute moral standard. Thus Christians do not commit the naturalistic fallacy,

for what God says is never mere fact; it is also a norm. God's word bears his lordship of control, authority and presence, and his authority makes whatever he says normative for us. So whatever he says, we are obligated to believe, and whatever he commands, we are obligated to do. Whatever God says is normative. That is, to whatever he says, there is an ought attached.[8]

I return to the juxtaposition I noted at the beginning of this response. While superficially attractive and exciting, on closer inspection Paul's theological vision is a mirage, for his god is no god at all, and his salvation is no salvation at all. The tragic irony is that in attempting to move beyond the transcendentally unique God of the Bible and the plot-line of redemptive history, Paul has moved away from the only source where humanity will find justice, forgiveness, hope and a lasting peace: the fount of living water, the resurrected Lord Jesus Christ.

Response to Gavin d'Costa

Gavin's essay displays all the usual stylistic hallmarks of his writing and teaching, an attractive combination of great erudition and clarity, deep passion and humility. More substantively, is Gavin's continuing desire to remain both faithful to the historical dogmatic framework of his Roman Catholic tradition and also theologically develop, innovate and contextualize within this tradition for our contemporary situation. From my perspective, critically responding to Gavin is personally and sociologically a difficult task. First, it is hard to critique someone in seniority, who has professionally so inspired and challenged you. Second, and as a Reformed evangelical, my community must acknowledge and be thankful, that as a fellow co-belligerent, it is Gavin who has most persuasively unmasked cherished pluralism as exclusive and intolerant liberal modernity.[9] Third, and again as an evangelical, I am aware of various evangelical scholars and movements who, in the name of unity and ecumenism,

---

8　John Frame, *Doctrine of the Christian Life* (Phillipsburg: P&R, 2008), p. 61.

9　See especially, Gavin D'Costa, *The Meeting of Religions and the Trinity* (Maryknoll: Orbis, 2000), pp. 1–95.

would seek to promote such a creedally orthodox Catholic as Gavin, from co-belligerent to ally. Finally, are a number of self-confessed evangelical scholars who, implicitly and explicitly, have far more affinity and sympathy with Gavin's Roman Catholic 'theology of religions' than my own, certainly in spirit (Spirit?), and possibly (given some minor 'protestantizations') in substance as well.[10]

Given the above, and already giving away my ending, I am well aware of appearing ungrateful and unnecessarily negative. And yet while at an *atomistic* level,[11] there is much to affirm in Gavin's essay,[12] *systemically*,[13] it is Gavin's 'faithfulness' to the theological presuppositions of his Catholic tradition, out of which his own 'theology of religions' is fashioned, which means that as a Reformed evangelical Protestant, I must ultimately reject both his method and argument, for his position is built upon basic foundations very different from my own tradition. I would contend these foundations are fatally weak because they compromise the 'solisms' of the Reformation (*sola Scriptura, solus Christus, sola gratia, soli Deo Gloria* and *sola fide*). For Reformed believers, these are not theologically simplistic slogans[14] but communicate the heart of the gospel of Jesus Christ. Allow me to justify such a conclusion.

Viewing Catholicism as a 'life-system',[15] organic whole and unity is naturally in danger of massive reductionism. However, despite the great diversity within Catholic theology, there are certain distinctive methodological and doctrinal contours within which variegation occurs and of which Gavin's essay is an instantiation. In

---

10 See for example, Clark H. Pinnock, *Flame of Love: A Theology of the Holy Spirit* (Downers Grove: InterVarsity Press, 1996).

11 That is, viewed at the level of individual 'parts'.

12 For example, his recourse to scripture, his trinitarianism, and his high constitutive Christology.

13 That is, considered as a hermetically sealed and interconnected worldview.

14 I am reminded of Newman's statement that 'the Catholic doctrine is after all too great to be comfortably accommodated in a Protestant nutshell', *VIII Lecture on the Present Position of Catholics in England*, 1851 (1904 edition), p. 14.

15 To use Kuyper's description in his *Lecture on Calvinism* (Grand Rapids: Eerdmans, 1931).

outlining these contours, I am largely dependent on the important work of De Chirico, who is in a line of Reformed theologians who have argued that analysis of Catholicism must be at the systemic level.[16] First, and as an over-arching scheme for contrasting evangelical and Catholic systems, Di Chirico focuses on the related but distinguishable distinctions of 'time' denoted by the biblical adverbs *hapax* (once for all) and *mallon* (for evermore). His contention is that what evangelicalism affirms to be Christologically *hapax* in the incarnation, Catholicism mistakenly confuses as ecclesiologically *mallon*, in its understanding of the Church as a prolongation of the incarnation. Such a move has profound implications for other doctrinal loci such as the Eucharist and revelation.[17] Second, at the theological core and 'horizon' of the Catholic system are two *loci*, a particular understanding of the relationship between nature and grace and the self-understanding of the Church as mediator of the system.[18] Third, and as a result of this theological core, De Chirico notes the 'regulative principle' of the system which epistemologically allows for progressive inclusion and integration of truth wherever it is found, towards the goal of the system, 'in this sense the outcome of the et–et or in–in approach can be referred to as a *complexio oppositorum*, i.e the combination into a synthesis of different, even opposite, ideas, principles and assertions'.[19] All these characteristics are present in Gavin's essay.

---

16 Leonardo De Chirico, *Evangelical Theological Perspectives on Post-Vatican II Roman Catholicism* (Oxford: Peter Lang, 2003), pp. 165–202. De Chirico notes a number of Roman Catholic theologians (such as John Henry Newman and Hans Urs von Balthasar) who have seen the tradition as a complex unity.

17 See Leonardo De Chirico, 'The Blurring of Time Distinctions in Roman Catholicism', *Themelios* 29:2 (2004), pp. 41–6.

18 De Chirico, *Evangelical Theological Perspectives*, pp. 218f.

19 De Chirico, *Evangelical Theological Perspectives*, p. 199. He adds, though, 'This epistemological openness, however, is not to be confused with an unprincipled cacophony of voices nor with a tendentially anarchic driving force of the Catholic framework of thought in that it is qualified and controlled by the fundamental unity of the system and serves the Catholic unitary project through the structures of the system' (p. 200).

Methodologically, my criticism of Paul was that he had cut himself loose from authoritative revelation, leading to epistemological incoherence. My criticism of Gavin, given his submission to the extra-biblical *mallon* revelation of the magisterium, is that he is too tied down. The magisterium is an authority I do not recognize as 'revelation' or infallible in my Reformed confession of the *hapax* revelation of *sola* (not *nuda*!) *Scriptura*.[20] Reading Gavin's essay as one 'outside' the tradition, the *complexio oppositorum* is very evident as Gavin, albeit very skilfully, attempts to orchestrate the various dogmatic and what might sound like dissonant themes of Catholic teaching on other religions, and attempts to produce a harmonious symphonic whole. Most strikingly, Gavin attempts to formulate a position which affirms and provides justification for *extra ecclesia nulla salus*, and the salvation of non-Christians. However, while the result is dogmatically impressive, possibly ingenious, I believe Gavin and his tradition become more and more theologically speculative, *not* because they engage in dogmatic theology *per se*, but because they move further and further away from scriptural revelation. For Gavin, of course, scripture is a 'source' (p. 5) of authoritative revelation and he states that his argument is biblically 'grounded' (p. 13). But can we, as he asks us to, take this for granted (p. 13)? Is there a biblical defence that would produce a 'more robust and extended explication' (p. 13) of his position? The soteriological example already cited serves as an example.

Gavin recognizes the 'unresolved lacuna' (p. 21) in the Catholic teaching regarding the reconciliation of *extra ecclesia* with the salvation of non-Christians. Demonstrating his own continuity with the tradition, Gavin fascinatingly describes to the 'bewildered'(p. 5) outsider the highly nuanced terms in which the Catholic Church has described the various ways in which non-Christians can be 'related' to the Church, together with a summary of Thomistic and Aristotelian understandings of 'potentiality' and 'actuality'(p. 20). While

---

20 See my chapter, p. 101. I should note that Gavin and I have an ongoing conversation here. I believe that Gavin thinks my position is that of *nuda Scriptura*, rather than *sola Scriptura*. I refer the reader once again to Keith A. Mathison, *The Shape of Sola Scriptura* (Moscow: Canon Press, 2001).

I have a number of more philosophical questions concerning these categories and their relation to the Catholic understanding of 'freedom', these are trumped by a greater methodological question as to the biblical evidence and justification for such variegated categories.

First, as I indicated in my essay, despite the plethora of worldviews and religions in existence, scripture speaks of only two human spiritual categories that are antithetically related: those rooted and built up in Christ, and those founded on philosophy, empty deceit, human tradition and the elemental spirits (Col. 2.6–10). Not only is this a biblical *theological* reality but a biblical *phenomenological* reality, in that biblical examples of salvation and conversion in the New Testament do not appear commensurable to the Catholic categories of *ordinantur* (p. 17) or potentiality. The appeal to the salvation of those before Christ is also illegitimate and disanalogous because not only were Old Testament believers located in a *sui generis* stage of redemptive history,[21] but the object of their saving faith was still Christocentric (as revealed in the shadows and types of the divinely revealed sacrificial system), rather than 'following the good' (p. 17) through the prompting of grace.

Second, Gavin's eschatological 'release' of this tension is in his affirmation of post-mortem conversion together with the 'revitalization' of a number of historic Catholic doctrines, Christ's descent into hell, purgatory and the *limbus partum*. Although systematically, these doctrines have never been part of the historic Reformed Protestant tradition, significantly it is the exegetical flimsiness for such doctrines that has largely contributed to their rejection. Perhaps 1 Peter 3.18–20 and 4.6 are the most prominent examples here, of two infamously opaque texts, about which the majority of contemporary commentators have a number of far more plausible

---

21 The fact that Gavin has recently not only supervised, but also provided a sympathetic foreword for, a published doctoral thesis which argues precisely this point, means I am somewhat confused as to Gavin's view on the nature and means of salvation before Christ. See Adam Sparks, *One of a Kind: The Relationship Between Old and New Covenants as the Hermeneutical Key for Christian Theology of Religions* (Eugene: Pickwick, 2010).

inter-textual interpretations than the ones offered by Gavin.[22] I do not think these texts can bear the dogmatic weight loaded upon them. Without scriptural justification, though, I am neither persuaded by his 'solution' nor obliged to accept it.[23]

Concerning Gavin's argument proper, we must ask whether the Catholic dogmatic foundations on which Gavin constructs his argument are theologically secure and pass inspection. Do the 'tensions' he seeks to explore and resolve (unsatisfactorily in my opinion), betray more fundamental fissures at the base of the system? I would contest that Gavin's 'theology of religions' is working within the distinctively Catholic construal of the relationship between nature and grace, a construal very different from the Reformed foundations of creation–fall–redemption. While recognizing a wide spectrum of interpretations, anthropologically there is an optimistic continuity between the order of nature and that of grace in Catholic thinking:

> The Roman Catholic system subsumes sin into nature which becomes wounded nature, but, in spite of the wound brought about by sin, it still recognizes the unaltered status of nature in terms of its inherent *capacitas* for grace, and maintains the continuity established protologically between nature and grace which sin has not entangled and cannot disentangle. All Roman Catholic typologies of the nature–grace relationship basically agree on man's *capacitas* for grace which is tainted by sin, but is not restrained from being continually open to grace and grasped by it.[24]

In Gavin's 'theology of religions', this relationship is evidenced anthropologically in his affirmation of 'natural law' through use of 'reason' (p. 11); a liberty of indifference in terms of his understanding

---

22 For a good recent survey of interpretation of these passages, together with a very plausible exegesis, see Karen H. Jobes, *1 Peter* (Grand Rapids: Baker, 2005), pp. 235–73.

23 See Wayne Grudem, 'He Did Not Descend into Hell: A Plea for Following Scripture Instead of the Apostle's Creed', *Journal of the Evangelical Theological Society* 31:1 (March 1991), pp. 103–13.

24 De Chirico, *Evangelical Theological Perspectives*, p. 237.

of human freedom;[25] post-fall humanity as seeking and yearning for the living God (p. 16); religions as exemplifying a 'genuine search for God' (p. 29) and functioning as a *praeparatio evangelica*; and the basis of 'common good' (p. 44) and issues of social justice' (p. 44). Complementing these is a 'prevenient' and potentially salvific work of the Spirit, for 'those who through no fault of their own do not know the gospel of Christ or his Church, yet sincerely seek God and moved by grace strive by their deeds to do his will as it is known to them by the dictates of conscience' (*Lumen Gentium*, 16).

However, the Reformed evangelical tradition has posited that scripture teaches a more radical discontinuity between creation before the fall and creation after the fall:

> The hamartiological breach which occurred at the fall has a significance which is much more far-reaching than a mere wound or stain: in this tradition, sin has a far more serious theological status which impinges on the whole orientation of its worldview, to the extent that nature has definitively lost that inner capacity to correspond with divine grace and has radically changed its protological status into a sin-driven, and utterly corrupted reality . . . Creation is therefore a fallen creation which has irreversibly lost its primordial prerogatives and exists in a state of separation from God, incapable of restoring the relationship in its own strength, nor is it even willing to do so.[26]

As I attempted to outline and scripturally justify in my chapter, first, while the Reformed doctrine of 'common grace' nuances the relationship, the principial status of humanity after the fall is that of 'total depravity',[27] 'antithesis' and 'idolatry'. As a result, 'natural law', 'libertarian freedom' and the 'common good' have found it hard to take root in Reformed soil.[28] Second, the depth of sin in the

---

25   Otherwise known as contra-causal freedom. This is opposed to freedom defined as a 'liberty of spontaneity' or deterministic freedom.

26   De Chirico, *Evangelical Theological Perspectives*, p. 237.

27   Meaning that sin has corrupted every area of human life rather than meaning that men and women are as bad as they could be.

28   See Peter J. Leithart, *Natural Law: A Reformed Critique*, Biblical Horizons Occasional Paper No. 25 (Florida: Biblical Horizons, 1996).

Reformed view means that talk of 'truth' and 'holiness' in other religions must be heavily qualified remembering the indivisible unity of other religions and the dynamic and idolatrous nature of religions to suppress and exchange revelation against the Living God.

Exegetically, and as evidence for some form of internal Christ-given universal enabling, Gavin and his tradition seem dogmatically to make much of John 1.9, 'the true light, which enlightens everyone, was coming into the world', a verse also used by Wesleyan evangelicals in their own defence of a 'prevenient grace'. However, Miller, in one of the most detailed historical and lexical studies of this verse, concludes with a restrictive and 'external' interpretation, that is fully consistent with the Johannine literature: 'the "light" of 1:9 is to be conceived as a *special* revelation, radiating specifically from the incarnate Logos and holding consequences and benefits only for those whose lives are touched by it'.[29] Without a verse like this, such gracious 'positive enabling' appears scripturally thin. Interestingly, Gavin, in the interests of balance, does note more 'ominous and realistic' (p. 35) aspects of other religions in his quotation of *Lumen Gentium*, 16, with its reference to Romans 1, idolatry and deception of the evil one. However, given that, in my opinion, these more negative interpretations of other religions and worldviews are overwhelmingly prevalent throughout the warp and woof of the biblical revelation, what is the basis for Gavin's explicit stress on more positive themes and continuity in terms of other religions functioning as *praeparatio evangelica*?

Gavin's construal of nature and grace also has crucial soteriological ramifications in both the accomplishment and application of Christ's redemption by the Spirit. First, Gavin states that those non-Christians who are destined for an eschatological post-mortem conversion are men and women responding freely to grace and that this is not Pelagianism through the back door (p. 17). In this he is correct, and yet it appears to be semi-semi-Pelagianism through the front door where salvation is understood 'synergistically' (where

---

29 L. Miller, 'The True Light Which Illumines Every Person', in L. Miller (ed.), *Good News in History* (Atlanta: Scholars Press, 1993), pp. 63–82, at p. 81.

men and women have the 'ability' to respond positively or negatively to God's grace) rather than monergistically (where men and women have no ability to respond and rely solely on God's irresistible grace). From the perspective of Reformed theology, the implications of this are profound. First, if works are in any way construed as 'meritorious' then the *hapax* work of Christ (*solus* Christus) is undermined and seen to be incomplete in its efficacy in dealing with *the* problem of the wrath of God. Second, if our acceptance by God is founded on our own 'infused' or 'imparted' righteousness, then this is the undermining of what Luther called the '*articulus stantis vel cadentis ecclesiae*'[30]: the Spirit's mystical uniting of the believer to Christ and the *hapax* forensic and declarative work of justification (*sola gratia*) based on the nonimputation of sin (that Christ's punishment is ours) and the imputation of Christ's righteousness (whereby we 'put on' Christ and stand *simul iustus et peccator*[31]). Third is the role of faith and its object, for the reason that Christ must be object of faith, rather than 'theism and morality', is that faith is merely the instrumental cause whereby we are united to Christ.

In summary, I wonder whether Gavin has not sufficiently heeded his own warning as to the 'danger of playing down the power of sin and exalting the power of human goodness' (p. 8). As a result, there are a number of theological moves that Gavin has to make but which I do not think can be grounded biblically. In contrast these are moves that the Reformed position does not have to make. Given the objective sufficiency of revelation to render men and women without excuse, given the depth of universal suppression and exchange in rebellion against God as seen in the phenomena of other religions, there is no-one 'without blame on their part' (p. 16). Salvation need not be universally accessible for God to be just, but wonderfully through the proclamation of the gospel of Jesus Christ in this life, men and women who deserve nothing are, through the gifts of faith and repentance, made alive by the Spirit of God and united to Christ where they receive him and all his benefits.

---

30 The '*article by which the Church stands or falls*'.
31 Simultaneously righteous and a sinner.

PART THREE

The Dialogue Continues

7

Gavin D'Costa Re-responds to Daniel Strange and Paul Knitter

To both my colleagues I am immensely grateful: for their candid criticisms, for their faithful adherence to the truth of the gospel as they perceive it and for their pushing this debate forward. In what follows I try to listen carefully and then give reasons for my position in the light of criticisms, illuminate the issues involved when there are differences between us, and advance my criticisms of my colleagues.

Response to Daniel Strange

Dan, typically, goes to the heart of the matter with his powerful analytical and biblically shaped mind. I think he is entirely right to focus on systemic differences between us, usefully employing De Chirico, rather than isolate atomistic elements whereby we might concur on a number of points and not on others. His Calvinism and my Catholicism are in some respects worlds apart reflected in serious methodological and substantitive differences.

First, I briefly want to attend to what I take are two basic misunderstandings that occur when Dan's Calvinism looks over into Gavin's Catholicism: the role of the Bible and that of the magisterium. Both can be taken together. Sadly, Dan will not have a right to reply on this matter, but I need to put my case to the reader – and they can judge. Our differences will not be resolved, but the clarity about what they are might be – which will, in the long run, help us to see what is at stake. Nowhere do I or any classical Catholic sources suggest that the magisterium, as Dan implies, is 'revelation'

(p. 177). Admittedly Dan put this term in quotation marks, so he may realize this. The magisterium as an authoritative teaching body (deriving from the Latin *magistra*, which was used of an authoritative office that instructs) is seen as authoritative *only* when it faithfully teaches the deposit of faith to be found both in the Bible and the tradition, in so much as tradition testifies to the truth of 'revelation' in the Bible, which is Jesus Christ. In this sense, the magisterium is bound to the Bible first and foremost, and the tradition's interpretation of the Bible secondarily (which will also include teachings of the magisterium at different levels of authority). The magisterium is required to develop and explicate the understanding of revelation as the Church makes its pilgrimage through history in ever changing circumstances. The magisterium cannot teach anything novel – it is entrusted to teach the truth delivered to us. As Paul puts it in Galatians 1.9: 'if anyone proclaims to you a gospel contrary to what you received, let that one be accursed'. So Paul was quite clear that one could not simply add or change according to whim or preference. At the same time Paul addressed all sorts of new questions emerging in the developing Church applying the good news to these new contexts: eating food that had been offered to idols, what women wear in church, and the headship of Christ in his body the Church. The magisterium (teaching authority), shared by Paul at his time through his baptism and role as a preacher, does the same today – and also must decide which previous decisions relate to core faith and morals and which are peripheral and only applicable to a particular context.

The magisterium, like Paul, also has a decisive role when there is dispute about either the contents of revelation or the implications of revelation as they apply to faith and morals.[1] The Catholic notion of the development of dogma, not a notion of new and enduring revelation, does not compromise the rule that revelation 'ended with the death of the last apostle', as the development of dogma is seen as the unfolding of the truth that has been given to us

---

1 See Avery Dulles, *Magisterium: Teacher and Guardian of the Faith* (Naples, FL: Sapientia Press, 2007).

in Christ.[2] This unfolding requires guidance under some authority when deciding between different practices and theories that claim to correspond to the truth of the incarnation, the once-and-for-all *hapax*. But if the *hapax* is a reality, then it is a reality 'evermore' in the sacrament of the Eucharist (not in the Church as a human institution, but as the sacramental body of Christ). In this sense, Dan and I agree: the Bible is the 'source' and Christ's once-and-for-all revelation is sufficient for salvation, but this does not preclude (but actually requires) his sacramental presence through the power of the Spirit in his Church as part of his faithful promise to be with his disciples 'evermore' (*mallon*). The fruits of Christ's salvation are applicable 'evermore' and are made present in history through the Church's proclamation, witness and sacraments.

To say, as De Chirico and Dan do, that the Church is a 'prolongation of the incarnation' is falsely to conflate Christ with the Church, whereas Catholic ecclesiology as it stands makes clear distinctions between the two which do not obscure the human character of those sinners within the Church, including the Pope, while nevertheless emphasizing Christ's sacramental covenant fidelity to his people and his choice of Peter for a special ministry within the community, despite human sinfulness.[3] Historically, Catholic theologians have proposed triumphalist ecclesiologies that diminish the distinction between the risen Christ and the Church, but none have been accepted by the magisterium, even when formulating the doctrine of papal infallibility.[4]

Dan's own Reformed tradition has its 'magisterium': a series of key thinkers that have defined the tradition and its rules for reading

---

2   See Aidan Nichols's useful survey, *From Newman to Congar: The Idea of Doctrinal Development from the Victorians to the Second Vatican Council* (Edinburgh: T&T Clark, 1990).

3   See Avery Dulles, *Models of the Church: A Critical Assessment of the Church in All its Aspects* (Dublin: Gill & Macmillan, 1976). One can see the logical connection here, for its sacramental authority depends on the understanding that it exists, thus the unity of the sacramental and teaching, related to the unity of praxis and theory (as it is rendered in modern terms) or the unity of prayer and faith: *lex orandi lex credendi* (the law of prayer is the law of belief).

4   See Dulles, *Magisterium,* esp. pp. 59–83; and Peter Chirico, *Infallibility: The Crossroads of Doctrine* (London: Sheed and Ward, 1977).

the Bible. I think the difference between us it that infallibility is seen as one attribute of the Catholic magisterium although rarely exercised. I have argued elsewhere, there is never a pure *sola scriptura* in the Reformation despite the claims made by such Reformers, precisely because *sola scriptura* always requires an authoritative body of Christians to: (a) infallibly decide what will form the canon of scripture – as nothing can be added or subtracted from that canon; and (b) infallibly claim that the canon has 'authority' and 'inspiration'. If it has not, then *sola scriptura* is irrelevant. But there is a third point in the Catholic argument: (c) the infallibility of the magisterium is to be found in scripture itself. The Church thus bears a derived and limited infallible authority from scripture undermining the *sola* in *sola scriptura*.[5] Admittedly, there is an important difference between *sola* and *nuda scriptura*: the latter refusing any authority to the Church; the former acknowledging a derived and contingent, but never infallible, authority to the Church. But I have pointed out a triple logic that shows why there is a restricted and carefully qualified secondary infallible authority attributed to the Church in the Catholic tradition from which I offer my critique. The Catholic position is more coherent and intelligible for it triangulates scripture, tradition and teaching authority rather than subsuming the second two under the first (*sola scriptura*) or refusing the second two any status at all (*nuda scriptura*). Of course, my argument would require much more elaboration, namely (a), (b) and especially (c), and the chance for Dan to speak back. Nevertheless, I have pointed to the ways in which I would respond to Dan's and De Chirico's topography.

Let me return to the important differences of method and substance as they actually bear upon the subject matter of Christian attitudes to other religions. First, Dan raises the question that many of my theological assumptions have shaky biblical foundations in two senses. One point relates to how philosophical distinctions that are crucial to my theological arguments map on to or relate to the

---

5 See my 'Revelation, Scripture and Tradition: Some Comments on John Webster's Conception of "Holy Scripture"', *International Journal of Systematic Theology* 6:4 (2004), pp. 337–50.

Bible (for example: the difference between potentiality and actuality regarding the act of faith). Another point relates to whether the Bible sustains Catholic doctrines (Christ's descent into hell, purgatory, and the *limbus partum*), doctrines that are employed in my arguments to address the question of other religions. Both these issues raise larger interrelated questions: what is the relation of philosophy to theology; and what is the relation of theology to scripture? On the first, the Catholic tradition has held that philosophy can be a handmaiden to theology through philosophy's conceptual rigour and formulation and the drive of the intellect towards the truth. Some philosophies, of course, are inimical to Christian faith (atheism, naturalism, mechanism, and so on). Others, such as Aristotle and Plato, in their openness to realities beyond the sensory world, can be employed, once they have been 'baptized', to try and elaborate the Christian mystery – which is precisely what many of the great masters of Christian theology did, such as Augustine, drawing upon Platonism, and Aquinas, drawing upon Aristotle. Both were critical of aspects of these ancient philosophies while taking up their best achievements and insights and modifying and developing them to form the 'Christian mind'. A Christianized Platonism is no longer Platonism, or if it is, then it is actually a Platonized Christianity.

On the second issue, if theological concepts are not grounded in the Bible (as understood through the tradition), then they are worthless. Dan and I agree about the principle. We differ, I think, on the practice and thus the conclusions that might be drawn. Take two examples.

If we look at the Bible, to flesh these issues out slightly, it is clear from Paul's Areopagus speech (Acts 17.16–34) that Paul sees a 'potentiality' in the believers of the 'unknown God' which could become an 'actuality' if they accept the true faith, precisely because in calling their God 'unknown' they have avoided the idolatry of those others in Athens who had given a 'name' to God. Paul was provoked when 'he saw that the city was full of idols' (v. 16), and amidst all these altars dedicated to named gods, Paul found one, which is the basis of his actual speech, marked: 'To an unknown god'. Paul is not of course saying that their faith and worship to the unknown god is true *per se*, but that they have a potentiality for actual true faith in their refusal to create an idol for worship. In this *via negativa* sense, their 'unknown god' is a preparation for the gospel as it contains elements that should help them hear Paul's message, which is of the true God, who is 'unknown' other than in his Son. And now, with the coming of Christ, the 'times of ignorance' are no longer justifiable. This in no way denies that the gospel is a scandal – as it was to both Jews and Greeks. Even though the gospel was a scandal to Jews it was also in part continuous with, and prepared for through, the Jewish religion – as Dan acknowledges. There is a partial analogical application of this to the Greeks.

Some of the early Fathers recognized fragments of truth in various Greek philosophers, especially Plato. This led to the idea of the *praeparatio*. This did not mean that these philosophies were true *per se*, but rather elements of truth contained therein might prepare the hearer for the fullness of truth, Jesus Christ. Equally, precisely these truths within a wider systemic religion/philosophy which was false *might* inhibit the person from seeing the truth of Jesus.[6] Rather than Dan's picture of only two classes of people, I think this suggests a 'third' which bears an analogy to the world religions. For instance, Islam as a whole is false if Catholic Christianity is true, which I take it to be. This does not mean that some claims in Islam are false: there is one God, that God moved through Abraham, that God commands that we look after the poor, orphans and widows, and that fasting and prayer are required for the spiritual life. These elements might act as a *praeparatio*, which is why Vatican II isolates them in *Nostra Aetate*. None of this requires the affirmation of Islam as a true religion, but it means that Catholic Christians can learn from and affirm atomistic elements within Islam.

Dan also gives the example of the *limbus partum* and its alleged unsustainable dependence on verses of 1 Peter 3 and 4. He cites Wayne Grudem, who also criticizes the other four key New Testament passages from which this doctrine evolved – and urges that we do not keep this doctrine despite it being found in the Apostles'

---

6 For the history of this tradition see Jean Daniélou, *Holy Pagans in the Old Testament* (London: Longmans, Green & Co, 1957); and his *Gospel Message and Hellenistic Culture* (Philadelphia: Westminster, 1973).

Creed. Interestingly, the Reformed theologian David Lauber criticizes Grudem's conclusion. Lauber argues that the descent 'is the logical consequence of a synthetic reading of Scripture, and rigorous reflection on the implications of the *pro nobis* character of Jesus Christ's life and passion'.[7] I cite Lauber to show that there is no easy denominational divide on some of these questions. The really worrying aspect of Grudem's argument, not formally alluded to by Dan, is the ease with which Grudem (and Dan presumably) are willing to drop articles of an authoritative and ancient creed. Why should ancient reflection which was given normative creedal status for more than a thousand years be overthrown by moderns? The ancient biblical interpretations on 1 Peter are not universally rejected by all modern biblical scholars.[8] Oddly, Grudem and Dan's move on this point makes them bedfellows with Paul Knitter: earlier Christians got it wrong in matters of creedal faith.

But Dan is right: arguments must be given for beliefs, and they must derive explicitly, and I would add, or implicitly, from the Bible. I would also add, the continuous tradition of the Church's reading of the scripture must also be considered. I have at least tried to address the methodological issues raised by Dan regarding my position. I have admittedly not been able to provide the actual biblical exegesis. However, I hope these clarifications will help readers decide on the strength and weaknesses of our two positions.

Finally, I want to address one more point that Dan raises against my position and the 'Catholic' position: the near conflation of nature and grace by Catholics compared to the Reformers' stark contrast between fallen nature and redeeming grace. This goes to the heart of the differences between the three of us taking part in this debate, and Dan has done a real service by isolating this issue. While I do not think that the difference in emphasis between Catholics and Reformers can be minimized, I would like to clarify two points: (a) my difference from Paul Knitter; and (b) my

---

7 David Lauber, *Barth on the Descent into Hell: God, Atonement and the Christian Life* (Aldershot: Ashgate, 2004), p. 111.

8 See Lyra Pitstick, *Light in Darkness: Hans Urs von Balthasar and the Catholic Doctrine of Christ's Descent into Hell* (Grand Rapids: Eerdmans, 2007), pp. 30–60.

commonality with Dan, while acknowledging a far deeper difference. I am critical of my fellow Catholic Paul for conflating nature and grace, such that the incarnation is ultimately superfluous for the salvation of the world – see below in my response to him for further elaboration. In this sense, the reality of sin is minimized as well as the necessity of the cross and thus Paul is driven, unwittingly, into a post-Christian position that cannot preach Christ crucified as the cause of our salvation. The Reformers' concerns about a possible trajectory within Catholic theology clearly has foundation. In this sense, Dan and I have more in common in contrast to Paul – we both criticize him on this point.

So where do Dan and I agree and disagree? We agree that without Christ, human nature cannot be transformed by grace into redeemed human nature. That is precisely why I draw upon a doctrine of post-mortem choice so that salvation cannot be prised apart from *explicit* faith in Christ. Here I am critical of various Catholic theologians, not just pluralists like Haight and Knitter, but also of inclusive pluralists like Dupuis, who fail to emphasize this necessity. Within my Catholic tradition the necessity of explicit faith in Christ for salvation has not had any clear magisterial resolution and is a disputed question. My position may well be deemed to be wrong by an authoritative magisterial teaching on this matter. But Dan is right to press our differences here, for at stake also are the questions of total depravity and God's election of only some to salvation (both of which I reject on biblical and tradition grounds). Further, my position does not rely on a dependence on works or fallen human righteousness, but on God's justice and mercy in *providing an opportunity to hear the gospel* for those who strive against their human nature to seek justice, love and forgiveness and who have never heard the gospel through no fault of their own.

I have to admit, before finishing, that Dan is right: there are a number of theological moves that I make that are not to be found in the Bible explicitly. But for the simple reason that the Bible does not address every question: what attitude should we have to nuclear weapons, genetic cloning, Islam and the New Age movement? We have to apply reason and analogical thinking to address these issues as they were not materially part of the biblical writers' explicit concerns, but the Bible provides enough material for this process of rational analogical thinking to take place. The reader has to decide which of the three of us fare best here.

Response to Paul Knitter

Paul raises some important challenges to me as a Catholic: both to be more Catholic, and to recognize that the Catholic Church's answers are not credible on some issues. On the first, yes of course; on the second, if the answers do not convince, they need to be revisited. But before turning to those matters of substance, there is an important methodological issue that requires clarification: what is the meaning of tradition? And this is to return to an issue discussed with Dan above.

I actually hold to both Paul's definitions: *traditio* as a process; and *traditum* as a product. One without the other is meaningless. If it was process alone, *traditio*, what is the 'deposit' of 'truth' that is being kept alive through the centuries through the mutual collaboration of bishops, priests, theologians and the laity? If it is a product alone, *traditum*, what of the process whereby this 'deposit' is reflected upon and thought through in terms of the differing contexts and questions that face the Church through its pilgrimage? We are back to Saint Paul's dynamic in Galatians 1.9: 'if anyone proclaims to you a gospel contrary to what you received, let that one be accursed'. Saint Paul receives the good news (*traditum*), and yet we see Saint Paul in his dealings with the communities in Corinth, Rome, Galatia and so on constantly applying *traditum*, thinking it through, sometimes collaboratively, sometimes not, often developing fresh expressions and challenging new forms that do not simply repeat what he was given (*traditio*). Hence, the rule of continuity is essential regarding *central* matters of faith and morals, but this does not mean that creativity is ruled out, nor novelty in terms of fresh doctrinal expressions – as is exemplified in the Marian doctrines of the Immaculate Conception and the Assumption. Can there be discontinuity? Yes: on Saint Paul's injunction to cover their heads. Yes: discrimination against Jews, the deicide charge against the Jews, and liturgical anti-Semitic elements have all been challenged. Yes: non-usury and slavery have been overturned, although one might argue the first should be revisited. Yes: the Catholic Church has now backgrounded the teaching that 'error has no rights' (which was strongly defended during the political emergence of secularism) to balance it with the teaching of the freedom of religions.[9] But can these discontinuities affect central matters of doctrine and faith? Would that not mean that the good news is itself corrupt?

These are difficult questions. This is precisely where the magisterium comes into play, for it is the role of the teaching authority of the Church to give judgements on these issues, especially when they are contested. Paul is absolutely right – the full and proper understanding of the magisterium includes theologians and laity. As Newman noted, the hierarchy frequently consults the laity before defining doctrine, and this was acutely so regarding Marian doctrine.[10] The theologian also has a particular role. If they are religious or lay and teach seminarians and have been mandated to teach on behalf of the Church, they cannot teach their own private opinions and should not contradict the formal teachings of the Church or they will have forfeited their mandate. Some of the theologians who have been asked not to teach particular subjects in Catholic institutions, or not to publish on certain questions (cited by Paul in his essay above), held such a mandate and have in their teachings and writings broken such a mandate (Haight and Phan for example), or were investigated and found not guilty of breaking such a mandate (Dupuis).[11] The Catholic Church has a

---

9 See my discussion on this matter: 'Hermeneutics and Second Vatican Council's Teachings: Establishing Roman Catholic Theological Grounds for Religious Freedoms in Relation to Islam. Continuity or Discontinuity in the Catholic Tradition?', *Islam and Christian Muslim Relations* 20:3 (2009), pp. 277–90.

10 John Henry Newman, *On Consulting the Faithful in Matters of Doctrine* (Kansas City: Sheed & Ward, 1985).

11 Richard McBrien's 'magisterial' work cited by Knitter has in fact been severely criticized by the United States bishops and both the *nihil obstat* and *imprimatur* were withheld from McBrien's *Catholicism*. See: http://www.catholicculture. org/culture/library/view.cfm?id=541&CFID=121743&CFTOKEN=22026492 (accessed May 2010).

responsibility for overseeing institutions such as Catholic universities that are mandated to teach Catholic faith and morals. This does not mean that the Catholic Church resists healthy discussion and critical debate. If the reader looks at any Catholic academic journal this is evident. It simply means that those who teach in such institutions are hired for a particular purpose with certain limits to their public role.[12] I do not want to sanction any authoritarian politics of silencing or any culture that isn't intellectually vibrant, but that is not what is at stake. One analogical example might help.

If we have a government spokesperson putting forward their own private opinions on fiscal recovery rather than explicating and developing the teachings of the government by which they are mandated, we might expect them to be questioned by their employers. If they persisted such that the government position was in some respects being seriously misrepresented we might even imagine they would be suspended from this public role of spokesperson for the government. They will have failed in their public role. We would of course expect them, if they were intelligent folk, to debate these fiscal recovery strategies among their peers and even to challenge certain tenets held by the government and even to try and get the government to rethink certain matters. But when carrying out their role of spokesperson they are being asked to carry out a different function. However, there is a point when if they failed to share the basic tenets (the equivalence of core matters of faith – the Creed – and morals) we might expect them to move into opposition, change parties, and even resign their post as serving the government. This analogy is problematic and limited, but I hope it illuminates the point I am trying to make.

Are there any questions that should not be placed on the table? Here I agree with Paul totally. As a Catholic theologian, I have to take my fellow Catholics as they come, with whatever questions they have. Everything is on the table that the faithful bring to the table, although the opinions of the faithful cannot be simplistically

---

12 I have defended this view of Catholic universities and argued that they engender new forms of freedom for theological research, in *Theology in the Public Square: The Church, the Academy, the Nation* (Oxford: Blackwell, 2000), pp. 77–112.

equated with the *sensus fidei*, for it is also possible that the faithful (and theologians) can be shaped by the mass media, our wider secular culture and the philosophical presuppositions of the Enlightenment. This latter is especially true of Paul. Questions that theologians put on the table cannot be swept under the carpet or silenced. I teach my students about Paul Knitter and try and show them why he fails to communicate the fullness of the Catholic faith – without any prejudice to his personal holiness and integrity. I also teach them why the Catholic Church answers the questions differently and try and elaborate the arguments employed by Catholic theologians to defend this view. That is enough on methodology. Let me turn to three substantitive issues.

First and second: Christology and the Church. Paul's support of a sacramental Christology as opposed to a constitutive Christology takes us to the heart of the matter. I fully support a sacramental Christology within the context of a constitutive Christology, rather than in opposition to each other. Jesus both reveals the love of God (Paul's definition of sacramental), but without him the breach between nature and grace would not have been healed (Paul's definition of constitutive). Paul would hold his position as a pluralist *if* Jesus did not exist, for strictly speaking God is known soteriologically, adequately, savingly, without Jesus Christ. Scripture, the ancient creeds, and the continuous teaching of nearly two thousand years of nearly all Christian denominations run contrary to Paul's proposal that Jesus is unique, but 'unique' just as are Muhammad, Gautama and other great teachers, and that we should all hold to our own unique truth recognizing there to be alternative, unique and equally valid plural ways to 'the' truth. The claim made in the Bible, and consolidated in Nicaea and Chalcedon, that in Jesus, God has become man, is relativized by Paul, for God works *equally* in the different religions for Paul. What I think is more attractive in the Catholic position is the affirmation that God does work in different religions – thus allowing a joyful and generous openness to God and the 'other' – and which is found in Paul's work, while keeping intact the constitutive Christology that established the new religion of Christianity that was a scandal to Jews and Gentiles and gives us the critical ability to make positive affirmations.

The role of the Church is predicated upon the sacramental presence of Christ in the Church. Christ and Church are distinct but inseparable. Interestingly, Paul and Dan here have more in common because they both criticize what they see as an exaltation of the role of the Church in my approach. I tried to critique Dan's position above on this point. Here, I would ask Paul to heed his own important principle: the necessary mediation of grace through the social tangible historical ('the social mediation of religion' as he rightly puts it – p. 156-7). Thus, if Jesus has the role I argue for, then it follows that that role as the bringer of salvific grace into the world must have a 'social mediation' after the resurrection and that mediation must correspond to Christ in the gospel and must be mandated by Christ. This is precisely the teaching of the Catholic Church about Christ's and the Spirit's own historical sanctioning of the sacramental role of the Church. This point would require a lot more argument, but if the logic is accepted, it is then a requirement of the Catholic theologian to explain how the Church is involved in the salvation of non-Christians since Jesus Christ is the cause of all salvation everywhere.[13]

Third: other religions as a means to salvation. I think we have a misunderstanding. Paul says I reject this possibility. I think I am more dialectical and may well be guilty of not expressing myself well. Let me clarify my position in three steps. First, I agree entirely with Paul – if non-Christians encounter grace, they do so as embodied social beings and thus through their religious cultures. This means that elements of their religious cultures can mediate grace and this is why *Nostra Aetate* affirms various elements within the religions and speaks of them as a 'ray of that truth which enlightens all men' (2). Successive popes have continued this line of teaching. Second, the religions as a whole, rather than in their parts, or systemically, rather than atomistically, cannot be 'salvific' *per se* in so much as they do not preach Christ crucified and God's trinitarian action of redemptive love. Many of them actually teach doctrines that would contradict these Christian truths. This point relates purely to the

---

13   This is precisely the concern of my book, *Christianity and World Religions* (Chichester: Wiley-Blackwell, 2009), pp. 161–211.

objective teachings of a religion, not to the lives lived by adherents of that religion. In this sense, to say that other religions are objectively means to salvation would be to say that doctrinally they teach the fullness of truth revealed in Jesus Christ. This is both manifestly false and insulting to impute to other religions. They must be heard for what they teach rather than what we might wish them to teach. Third, this dialectical position, mediating between Dan's 'all non-Christian religions are error' and Paul's 'all non-Christian religions are means to salvation', holds both these fragments of truth in tension. It means that the Catholic must be radically open to truth in these traditions as well as deeply critical of error in fidelity to Christ and his Church, when critical challenge is warranted. This dialectic is found in *Dominus Iesus*, 21. It states that the Catholic cannot attribute to other religions in their positive role (expressed above in the first point) 'an *ex opere operato* salvific efficacy, which is proper to the Christian sacraments'. It continues, highlighting Dan's point: 'Furthermore, it cannot be overlooked that other rituals, insofar as they depend on superstitions or other errors (cf. 1 Cor. 10.20–1), constitute an obstacle to salvation.' So this is not an either/or question, nor would I agree with Paul's assessment that his view is held by the 'majority' of Catholic theologians on this question.[14]

I hope that nothing I have said in any way detracts from the fourfold Catholic vision of: (a) giving glory and praise to God; (b) working together for the poor and marginalized with other religions striving towards a more just world; (c) listening to and learning from the other religions, for the Spirit will blow where She will; (d) being a sign of hope amidst the nations, critiquing other religions and itself, calling all nations and peoples to repentance and to follow Jesus Christ, who lays down his life for us.

---

14 See *Christianity and World Religions*, pp. 3–54, where I inspect a wide variety of Catholic and other Christian views.

8

Paul Knitter Re-responds to
Gavin D'Costa and Daniel Strange

Unless my heart is hardening or my ears are clogging, I don't believe the responses from Gavin and Dan have brought up any brand new issues in the conversation we broached in our three opening statements. But they certainly are nudging, if not pressing, me to look more deeply and speak more clearly about some of the pivotal points that divide us – and that mark differences between our Christian churches.

In carrying on – or trying to deepen and clarify – my conversation with Gavin and Dan, I'm going to address and engage them together, rather than one after the other. So many of their objections to my understanding of how Christians can better understand themselves so as to better understand others seem to be in sympathetic vibration. In fact, perhaps with a touch of paranoia, I've often felt that in our conversations I'm the odd guy out – that I present much more of a problem for both of them than each of them presents to the other. Or more simply, if we line the three of us up on the spectrum that represents the Christian churches nowadays – with the liberal me on the left, the conservative Dan on the right, and the mainline Gavin in the middle – then it seems to me that the 'middle' is much closer to the right than to the left. So, for the rest of this section, when I refer to views common to Gavin and Dan, I refer to them, playfully but meaningfully, as 'Davin'.

I think this is an accurate picture of how our theological differences sort out. But that also raises not just an interesting but an urgent question: are liberal theologians like myself way out in left field (sorry for the baseball imagery), distant from the crowd who are happy to stay where they are seated? Or are the mainline and evangelical theologians standing in the way of a large number of Christians who want to remain in the same Christian stadium but are looking for different seats?

Clearly, I'm with those Christians who are looking for different seats (whether they are in the majority or not). Davin helps me mainly by constantly asking me whether the seats I'm proposing really do still fit within a Christian stadium. The objections they raise for me in their responses seem to sift out into three major categories: (1) *Theology*: If theology is, as I earlier suggested, a balance between Christian tradition and ongoing human experience, they think I've destroyed the balance; I prefer my experience over tradition and end up a 'liberal liberationist' rather than a Christian believer. (2) *God*: Their concern is that I've levelled the playing field between God and humanity and lost touch with the real difference between the Infinite and the finite. (3) *Christ*: In their view, I end up removing Jesus Christ from the place he has always occupied, and must continue to occupy, for anyone who calls herself a Christian: the centre not just of one's own life but of the universe.

In what follows, my primary intent, and my hope, is not to argue that my interpretation of Christian belief is right and theirs wrong (although there may be some instances of that), but that even though my understanding of the truth made known in Jesus may differ from – or actually contradict – their understanding, it still allows for a following of Jesus, or a praxis of discipleship, that they can affirm. And for that reason, we can all have our very different seats in the same Christian stadium.

Theology: is the theologian a *translator* or an *interpreter*?

If theology is 'faith seeking understanding', which counts more?

In Davin's view, I have 'prioritized' a worldview which he identifies under varying, rather nasty, names such as: 'liberal modernity', 'liberal liberationism', 'universal modern liberalism', 'Kantian exclusive modernity', and finally, 'neo-pagan unitarianism'. Because I have so prioritized, I have fallen into a 'relativizing of all orthodox religions, including Christianity', which is nothing else than 'an idolatrous refashioning of divine revelation' by which 'orthodoxy is being offered up and sacrificed to something more basic and cherished'. In the end (or at the beginning), Davin believes that I have placed humanity above God. 'In this method, it is *we* who establish the ground rules into which God must fit.'

These are very serious concerns and accusations. They are made sincerely and forthrightly; I want to respond in the same way. The two responses that follow retrieve and, I hope, clarify claims that I made in my opening statement and in my first response.

1. *Christianity has never been culturally 'naked'.*

In accusing me of prioritizing 'modernity' over 'Christianity', Davin presupposes that on the one side there is *modernity (or something-ity)* and on the other side there is *Christianity*. This implies, further, that *Christianity* is fundamentally different from all the other '-*ities*' in that, while they are all humanly fashioned and therefore culturally conditioned worldviews, Christianity stands above all these human constructions and can, from such commanding heights, judge their veracity or falsity. Such an understanding fails to recognize that there never was, and there can't be, a culturally or historically *naked* Christianity. There is no such culture-free commanding height from which the truth made known in Jesus can look down on all the others and assess them. There will indeed be assessment, there will be critical engagement, but it will always take place within the fray of culturally and historically conditioned interactions.

Even the revelation embodied in the experience and the teaching of Jesus of Nazareth was transmitted through the at-that-time 'modernity' of his Jewish culture and conditioning. (That's what incarnation means!) And when his followers carried his message from their Jewish birth-place into the radical differences of the Graeco-Roman world, they were faced with the challenge of interpreting Jesus' message in and through a mutually clarifying and mutually criticizing engagement with the 'modernity' of the Roman empire.

What Davin calls 'Christianity' or 'orthodoxy' or even 'revelation' is always clothed in some cultural '-ity'.

Therefore, as Raimon Panikkar reminds us: the truth of Christianity – or what Gavin calls 'the guiding authority' of Christian revelation – is not to be found *super-culturally*, or *supra-culturally*, but *cross-culturally*.[1] The power and authority of what was made known to humanity in Jesus cannot be identified with any one cultural, historical expression of it – even the cultural expression of the New Testament or of the early councils of the Church. That would make of these expressions – that is, the Bible or the magisterium – a *super*-culture, which then can become more important than the very truth and being of God. That, it seems to me, is just as much an example of idolatry as my holding up 'modernity' as the one absolute truth (which I hope I'm not doing).

But neither is the truth and authority of Christian revelation to be found *supra*-culturally. That's the point I've already made: Christian truth does not hover, nakedly and detachedly, above all cultures. It is always an embodied truth, and that means that if we want to call it an *absolute* truth, we can get at it only through its relative, historically and linguistically limited clothing.

Therefore, the 'authority' or the 'orthodoxy' of Christian revelation can be known and engaged only *cross*-culturally. That means in the encounter between the expression of Christian truth contained in the culturally conditioned language and concepts of the New Testament and Christian tradition through the centuries (which has been basically a European tradition) on the one hand, and the ever new cultural and historical contexts in which we live or to which we try to communicate the message of Jesus. There is no other way, it seems to me, than this 'mutually clarifying and mutually criticizing' dialogue between the historically conditioned 'Christian fact' and our always historically conditioned, ongoing 'human experience'.

---

1 Raimon Panikkar, 'Can Theology Be Transcultural?' in Paul Knitter (ed.), *Pluralism and Oppression: Theology in World Perspective* (Lanham, MD: University Press of America, 1990), pp. 3–22.

2. *Neither 'faith' nor 'understanding' has the priority.*

But this brings us to the nub of Davin's concern with me and all so-called liberals: in this conversation between 'the Christian fact' and 'ongoing human experience', I end up *prioritizing* human experience over God's revelation, or in Dan's words, I subordinate the Divine to the human. My honest response: they're right! But only sometimes. What I'm getting at is what I've been trying to express in the previous section: Because 'faith' or 'Christian truth' is never culturally naked, that is, never divorced from human expression based on human experience, there can be no neat separation (although there is a necessary distinction) between faith and understanding, or between the Christian revelation and human experience. What God has revealed in Jesus can be known only in human experience. Only when the power of the biblical message is, as it were, picked up and received by the antennae of our human condition and then expressed in human words can it be called revelation!

Therefore, to ask which has the priority – the truth of the Bible and the magisterium or the truth contained in human experience – is like asking a newly married couple who will have the final word in the decisions they will face, the husband or the wife. There's no neat, either–or answer to that question. Who will have 'priority' will be worked out in the ongoing relationship or conversation between partners that we call marriage – or in our case, the ongoing conversation between tradition and ongoing experience that we call the Christian life. In some instances, it will be 'modernity' (or whatever '-ity' we're living in) that is challenged and revised in the light of our understanding of Christian revelation. And in other instances, it will be our understanding of the New Testament and the creeds that is challenged and revised in the light of what we now know of human psychology or biology or economics.

But, Dan will insist, isn't this placing humanity above God? Isn't it 'we who establish the ground rules into which God must fit'? This question arises from what I feel is the *dualism* between divinity and humanity out of which Dan operates (and which I'll address again below). For me, as I tried to explain in my opening statement, belief in the incarnation means belief in the *non-duality* of the divine and the human. Therefore, I would say that the 'human ground rules' into which God 'must fit' were established by God! This is how we were created and how God continues to act in and through us – through our reason, our imagination, our mystical capacities. So for God to contradict – that is, not fit – what we are as human beings would be for God to contradict God's self.

Let me be concrete: unless we expect God to 'fit' humanity, we run the risk of ending up with a de-humanizing God. (The 'fit', of course, may be either a comforting affirmation or a jolting challenge.) For example, I would like to ask Dan whether he would affirm and accept infanticide if the Bible told him that it was God's will (the Bible does not say that, of course). Certainly not! So how is the Bible authoritative for Dan? Because 'it fits' his humanity – that is, it makes sense to him because it both affirms and challenges and so reveals to him how he can best realize his humanity. If the Bible didn't 'make sense' to Dan's experience – if, in our example, it called him to affirm infanticide – he would reject it. But it doesn't. On the contrary, it reveals how we can more truly be and act as humans. And that's why both Dan and I are, and remain, Christian.

How do we know what is 'objective' or 'ontological'?

Davin fears that not only am I losing touch with the truth of Christian revelation, but that I am cutting myself loose from the truth of reality, or what they call 'the objective', 'the metaphysical', 'the ontological'. Dan: Paul ' . . . wishes us textually to reinterpret what have been historically understood as objective, metaphysical and literal theological statements, as subjective, devotional and symbolic . . .'. Gavin: For Paul ' . . . symbolic understanding renders religious language as fundamentally expressive of an attitude or an outlook without definitive metaphysical or ontological claims'. Again, I say 'ouch'. But again, I suggest that Davin is operating out of a false (non-objective!) duality between the subjective and the objective, or between the 'symbolical and the ontological'. The two orders are certainly different; but we humans cannot have one without the other.

Here I appeal to my revered teacher at the Gregorian University, Bernard Lonergan, SJ, who back in the early 1960s jolted us and then freed us with his pithy declaration: 'Objectivity is authentic subjectivity.' His monumental work, *Insight*, is an over-600-page unpacking of this powerful, challenging and liberative insight. The 'real' or the 'objective' is not an 'already-out-there' something that we know by 'looking at it'. Rather, we know the real and the objective only when we are true to our own human subjectivity – that is, only when we follow what Lonergan called the transcendental precepts: be *attentive* (be open to all the data, wherever it is, no matter how distasteful); be *intelligent* (try to understand what the data means); be *reasonable* (don't judge what you think you understand to be true until you've asked all the necessary questions); be *responsible* (when you judge something to be true, you will really know it is true only by living it).[2] All this sounds a bit complicated, and tomes have been written on Lonergan's transcendental method, but it really boils down to this: truth, or the 'objective', is not a matter of taking a look but a matter of interpreting.

And this is all the more the case when the truth we are exploring is the infinitely mysterious and ineffable truth of God. So to understand the real, objective, ontological truth that God is revealing to us through Jesus in the New Testament, we cannot simply 'take a look'. The truth is deeper than the literal meaning. We have to interpret. We have to be attentive to the literal meaning of words or to the description of events, but in order to understand and make judgements about the meaning of these words and events, we have to look more deeply, more imaginatively, more contextually, more relevantly. For me, this means that even though an event may be indubitably factual, even though we may have grasped the literal meaning that the author intended for a particular word, unless we

---

2 Bernard Lonergan, *Insight: A Study of Human Understanding* (New York: Philosophical Library, 1957), pp. 375–84. See his *Method in Theology* (New York: Herder & Herder, 1972), pp. 3–25.

are recognizing these facts and words as inherently symbolic, we will not be able to understand them for what they are.

This brings us back to a difference between Davin and me that has dogged us all throughout this book: I view all language about God and the mysteries that God has revealed in Jesus as symbolic. But as I have tried to make clear in different ways, to say that a doctrine or word is symbolic does not at all deny that it can be telling us something very true, very real, very ontological. Just as we know 'objectivity' through 'authentic subjectivity', we can know the 'real' truth about God through the real power of symbols and myths. But the truth that we grasp through the symbol or the myth will always be 'more than', it will always 'transcend', what we know through the symbol or myth. No symbol, no historical person, no book, no religion can contain the fullness of the Mystery we call God. If it claims that it does, it is probably a dangerous idol.

And therefore, I can conclude this section with an answer to the question that stood at its beginning: Is the theologian a translator or an interpreter? By translator I understand a person who translates a very particular meaning of a word or statement from one language to another, word for word, literally. By interpreter I understand a person who understands the meaning of a word or statement in its original language or context and then adjusts it, shapes it, grasps it differently so it still-the-same-but-also-different meaning can come through in a new language or context. For me, I can faithfully do my job as a theologian only when I am an interpreter. That makes my job more difficult, even dangerous; but also, a lot more rewarding and enjoyable.

God and the world: do they exist co-equally?

As I believe is evident from what I've said so far in this final response, the disagreements between Davin and me regarding the job of a theologian are rooted in our disagreements about the nature of God. But Dan, much more than Gavin, rubs these differences, cogently but gracefully, in my face. So in this section, I will primarily be addressing Dan.

Accusation: Knitter denies the aseity and sovereignty of God. Plea: guilty!

Dan worries that I endorse a 'god [notice his lower case] who is finite and dependent, not *a se* and sovereign'. On almost all counts, his worries are justified. I do hold to a God [notice my upper case] who is not *independent*, not *a se*, and not *sovereign*. But I do bow to a God who is *infinite* – whose infinity, however, is incarnate in finitude. And that means whose infinity is, as Saint Paul tells us in Philippians (2.5–11), *emptied* into the finitude of creation and humanity. As I tried to explain in my opening statement, if we Christians truly believe in a God who is trinitarian and a God whose essence is love – and if we think about what we believe – then necessarily we believe in a God who is profoundly relational, who has God's being in relationship (both the inner relations of the Trinity and the outer relation of creation). Such a God cannot simply impose God's will; that would be contrary to the very nature of God as love. Such a God must work with, yes in dependence on, creation. On the non-human level that means in dependence on the randomness of the natural order; on the human level, in dependence on the vagaries, the improprieties, the potentialities of free will. Such a God, as the process theologians help us understand, acts in creation not through the coercion of sovereignty but through the persuasion – the persistent, relentless, inexhaustible persuasion – of love.

What I'm trying to express, inadequately I admit, is the mystery – the vital and engaging mystery – of what I've called the *non-duality* between God and the finite order. God remains God, the creator and source of all; but the world and especially humanity are the co-creators and the incarnational expressions of that God. Distinct in their identities, God and the world, however, coexist in each other. As I've already confessed, one of the most powerful symbols of this non-dual mystery – a mystery that has to be felt before it can be understood – is Panikkar's image of all reality as a vital, ongoing, ultimately mysterious *cosmotheandric* relationship: God, the world, humanity are carrying on creation in and with and in dependence on each other. To answer the question that heads this section: they are not co-equal as if all played equally important roles, but they are co-dependent in that they can play their roles only in relationship with the others.

Dan asks me: 'on what authority' do I make 'the claim of incomprehensibility and mystery' of this divine–human relationship? I must admit, his question, coming from someone who knows scripture much better than I (typical of Protestants' advantage over Catholics), baffled me. It seems to me that throughout the Bible, the inadequacy of the human mind to comprehend the mystery of God, even though that mystery is made known in Christ Jesus, is stoutly affirmed.[3] And to what the Bible tells me I add my own limited experience, an experience I find clearly affirmed in the lives of the saints: to experience the living God is to experience a reality that is as real as it is beyond all comprehension. The analogy of human love may help: what brought me to love my wife is something very real that I can see and feel, but what it really is, who she really is, I will never fully know.

But Dan pushes his question about God-as-Mystery uncomfortably but appropriately: 'How does Paul know that God cannot reveal himself in an unsurpassable way?' That took me back a bit, probably because it is something like the teasing question: 'How do we know that God could not create a rock too heavy for God to lift.' There is, I think, an inherent contradiction in both questions. For God to reveal God's self unsurpassably in a finite vehicle – an act, a book, a person – would be a contradiction in terms, for it would mean that something finite can contain the fullness of infinity. To say that a particular, historical and finite medium through which God reveals Godself cannot be surpassed would imply that it contains all of God. That, it seems to me, is not only impossible; it is idolatrous. Jesus, in John's Gospel, clearly states that such is not the case for himself: 'The Father is greater than I' (John 14.28). Incarnation means that the Divine reveals itself in the finitude of the human; that means *truly* but it cannot mean *totally*. Otherwise, the human would no longer be the human.

---

3 I think of Job 11.7: 'Can you find out the deep things of God? Can you find out the limit of the Almighty?' Even more dauntingly, Paul in Romans: 'O the depth of the riches and wisdom and knowledge of God! How unsearchable are his judgements and how inscrutable his ways!' (11.33).

Finally, Dan faces me with some complex questions about evil – questions which, I must admit, I could not fully get a hold on. He tells me that in my 'panentheistic' understanding of God and the world (I prefer 'non-dual'), 'evil has to be necessary to Inter-Being as it is an aspect of the universe . . . '. He further fears that I 'provide no foundations for . . . universal ethical claims', nor can I offer 'hope that good will finally triumph over evil'.

I suspect that Dan's problems have to do with my problems – that is, my inability to state clearly what is contained in the mystical experience of a non-dual God who lives and moves and has God's being in humans and in the cosmos. What we call evil – that is, what certainly disrupts our life in the very real forms of hatred and violence and self-centredness – is also ultimately and profoundly contained in the reality of God. What is called 'moral evil' arises from the selfishness that is rooted in ignorance of who we really are, and it is real in its pain and distortion. 'Natural evil' arises from the randomness of nature as it affects humanity in earthquakes and floods and cancer.

These evils are real. But God is more real. Because of the presence of the Spirit of Inter-being, evil does not have to have the last word. There is always the possibility of a response, a way of transforming the horror of evil (the cross) into the occasion for new life and love (the resurrection.) I do hope for a 'better future'. But whether it will take shape depends on both God and us. – But even if my vision of this better future, because of human beings' refusal to hope and to act, is not realized in my lifetime (or the lifetime of this planet), there is always, always, another chance. Why? Because I trust in a God who is infinitely creative, patient, persistent – within the world and within me.

Jesus: how does he uniquely save?

Which brings us to Christology. Here I deal again with Davin, for there is a ricocheting echo between the objections that both Gavin and Dan raise about my understanding of who Jesus was/is and how he saved/saves. I think most of their concerns can be brought into focus in their claims that I have abandoned an 'incarnational Christology' for a 'degree Christology' and that I have moved from a 'constitutive soteriology' to an 'exemplary soteriology'. Or more simply: I see the difference between Jesus and other extraordinarily holy people to be one of degree rather than one of essence; and I understand Jesus' saving power to be that of revealing the saving grace and love of God rather than causing or constituting it. Again, if this is their claim, I stand happily (but somewhat uneasily) accused.

Their fundamental problem with such Christological assertions seems to boil down to: 'You can't say that and still call yourself a Christian.' But that's precisely the issue I want to explore. Why? Because it is becoming more and more an issue for Christians who are more and more aware of other religions and who are more and more uneasy about having to tell their other-religious friends or relatives that we Christians have the only saviour in town or the final word on all truth. The uniqueness of Jesus is a pastoral problem. That means it's a theological problem. My solution for the problem may not be acceptable. But we have to discuss the problem and the various theological solutions that are being proposed.

So let me take up the particular criticisms of my proposed solution that Davin raises in these responses.

1. I have a false problem with exclusive claims.

Gavin puts it this way: 'Paul does not like exclusive truth claims because they are allegedly inimical to dialogue.' What for Gavin is 'alleged' is for me pretty clear: if someone firmly believes that God gave him the exclusively full, final and definitive truth, how is it possible for that person to learn anything really new, or to change his mind? As I've said before, to what is full or to what is definitive, nothing more can be added. All we can do is clarify or deepen something we already know. If I'm missing something here, I earnestly and humbly ask Gavin to point it out to me.

But Gavin adds a zinger and notes that in denying exclusive and absolute truth claims, I'm disagreeing with the Dalai Lama (so, not only with the Pope!). Now, I've read Gavin's case 'that the Dalai Lama makes rigorously exclusivist truth claims which require one to be a *Gelugpa* Buddhist monk as a precondition of final release'.[4] Well, either Gavin didn't get it quite right or His Holiness has changed his mind, for in his recent book, *Toward a True Kinship of Faiths: How the World's Religions Can Come Together*, in the chapter titled 'The *Problem* of Exclusivism' (emphasis shamefacedly mine!), he states clearly that '. . . for me Buddhism is the best, but this does not mean that Buddhism is the best for all'. He goes on to explain that talk of 'one truth, one religion' is to be made only 'in the context of an individual religious practice'. His Holiness explains that because of differences of karma or personality, different people will have different preferences for their 'one and only way'.[5]

2. *I refuse to accept the clear and conscious claims of the New Testament.*

Dan asks me a point-blank question: What would it take to demonstrate to me that the New Testament really does proclaim an absolute exclusivity for Jesus? – Well, such a demonstration would have to show me that the New Testament authors were asserting that in order to be a disciple of Jesus one *had to* insist that there was no other way to experience the God he was talking about. I've already offered reasons why I don't think that is the case. I trust that I can be (rather, try to be) just as faithful a follower of Jesus as is Davin even though I don't believe that Jesus must be the 'one and only' for all people.

But Dan insists that 'the biblical writers were fully aware of their religiously plural context and the counter-cultural nature of their exclusive claims together with the consequences of making such claims'. I agree. But I would suggest that the early Christians were opposed to these other gods, not because they were *other* gods, but because they were *Roman* gods – that is, the gods of a religious system that was part of an imperial, oppressive system. Such gods had to be rejected not because they were 'other' but because they were

---

4 *The Meetings of Religions and the Trinity* (Maryknoll: Orbis, 2000), pp. 72–95.

5 (New York: Doubleday Religion, 2010), p. 158. See also pp. 145–61.

contrary to Jesus' notion of the Reign of God. Which means (and here I respond to Gavin's concern that I 'relativize' Christian truth claims): to be a pluralist does not mean to be a relativist.

3. *I fall into Gnosticism by reducing salvation to knowledge.*

I don't want to 'reduce' salvation to knowledge, but as a Christian theologian I do want to, because I think I have to, hold that 'right knowledge' does have something to do with salvation. It's called *revelation.* Something is made known to us. But the making known is not simply a dumping of new data into the container of our intellect. It is knowledge that is Spirit-filled. That's the difference between 'knowledge' and 'revelation'. I tried to make this clear in my notion of Jesus as the Sacrament of salvation, both in my opening essay and in my first response. Sacraments, by embodying and symbolizing, transmit knowledge or awareness; and such knowledge transforms. Such transformation I would see as having to do with *salvation.*

So for me, this conversation ends where it began: three followers of Jesus, confronting the newly experienced reality of religious pluralism, sharing their differences, trying to learn from each other and continuing to break bread together. I am grateful to have been part of this conversation. I hope it will extend throughout our communities.

9

Daniel Strange Re-responds to Gavin D'Costa and Paul Knitter

Gavin D'Costa

I thank Gavin for his gracious yet probing response to my initial statement. One of the opportunities afforded us in this exchange is the ability not simply to step into each other's confessional worlds, but rather to dig down into them uncovering the theological tectonic plates on which our interpretations of religion and the religions are built. While pedagogically, such excavation will, I hope, be of great use to those reading this exchange, it should be recognized that there is some personal cost here in such an exercise: both toil and tears.

First, given our different theological authorities, the danger of talking *past* each other, rather than *to* each other is great, let alone the possibility of offering a critique which will penetrate rather than tamely bounce off our respective confessional systems. This partly explains my insistence on us returning time and again to the theological presuppositions and authorities we all sit under as human beings, for I remain convinced that ultimately here lies the 'heart of the matter' and the commitments which separate us. However, for all parties concerned, critiquing someone else's basic and cherished presuppositions is always a hard task both intellectually and psychologically.

Second, and recognizing these differing presuppositions, I sense in Gavin's response that a by-product of such perspicacious theological illumination is the somewhat painful realization that, given our 'very difference landscapes', there remains significant distance between us. Regrettably, I concur with this analysis. Whither ecumenism indeed? I am confident though that despite the recognition of what may well be unbridgeable differences between us, we do not necessarily have to shout louder with an increasing animosity towards each other. Rather, we are both able to model continuing reflection, dialogue and robust critique, within the context of trust and friendship. As part of this process, I will attempt to defend my position and answer some of the questions that Gavin raises.

In my opening statement and subsequent response to Gavin, I highlight the severe anthropological and therefore soteriological implications seen in scripture's understanding of the radical discontinuity between creation before and after the fall. Gavin rightly calls this the doctrine of total depravity and then goes on to highlight, and of course reject, the corollary 'Calvinist' doctrines of 'predestination' and 'limited atonement'. For both Gavin and his tradition, these particular doctrines of particularity appear to be deep-seated 'defeater beliefs' which prevent the acceptance of my 'theology of religions'.[1] However, in defence of these doctrines, I would like to make a number of points of clarification.

First, Gavin is quite right to link these doctrines together, indeed, they make up three of the five so-called Calvinist 'doctrines of grace' famously known under the mnemonic TULIP: Total depravity; Unconditional election; Limited atonement; Irresistible grace; and Preservation of the saints. These doctrines are believed to have strong biblical warrant, and, given biblical unity, strong intra-systematic coherence. In my exposition, I decided to highlight the universality and depth of sin which renders us spiritually 'dead' and guilty before God and the need of a monergistic work of regeneration together with the gifts of faith and repentance. As I said, Gavin is right though that these other doctrines are necessary implications. Where Gavin is wrong is to cast these doctrines negatively with implications of parsimony and restrictiveness. These are, or should be, 'doctrines of grace' to be understood positively for the purpose of Christian edification, encouragement and

---

1 Evidenced by the fact that I did not even mention them in my exposition! As defined previously, a 'defeater belief' is a philosophical term to say that if Belief A is true, Belief B *cannot* be true.

assurance. Let us take Gavin's reference to 'limited atonement', or better 'particular redemption'. Notwithstanding that I think Gavin has misinterpreted the biblical passages he cites,[2] the positive and wonderful affirmation in this doctrine, is that Christ's work does actually procure salvation:

> If we concentrate on the thought of redemption, we shall be able perhaps to sense more readily the impossibility of universalizing the atonement. What does redemption mean? It does not mean redeemability, that we are placed in a redeemable position. It means Christ purchased and procured redemption. This is the triumphant note of the New Testament whenever it plays on the redemptive chord. Christ redeemed us to God by his blood (Rev. 5.9). He obtained eternal redemption (Heb. 9.12) . . . It is to beggar the concept of redemption as an effective securement of release by price and by power to construe it as anything less than the effectual accomplishment which secures the salvation of those who are its objects. Christ did not come to put men in a redeemable position, but to redeem himself a people . . . Security inheres in Christ's redemptive accomplishment. And this means that, in respect of the persons contemplated, design and accomplishment and final realization have all the same extent.[3]

Second, it needs to be remembered that these soteriological doctrines of grace are a microcosm of the larger Reformed macrocosm. As Packer states, 'the five points [of Calvinism] assert no more than that God is sovereign in saving the individual, but Calvinism, as

---

2 Scriptural passages like 1 Timothy 2.3–6 do not mean 'all with exception' (Gavin's reading) but rather 'all without distinction'. This is the positive statement that God wills people from all classes of society to be saved. Similarly, another distinction is often made here, namely that although the atonement is 'efficient' only for the elect (*efficaciter tantum pro electis*), it is 'sufficient' for all (*sufficienter pro omnibus*) meaning 'that had the persons of the Godhead determined to save more people than they did, Christ would not have had to do more than he in fact did'. (Robert Reymond, *A New Systematic Theology of the Christian Faith* (Nashville: Thomas Nelson, 1998), p. 672).

3 John Murray, *Redemption Accomplished and Applied* (Edinburgh: Banner of Truth, 1955), pp. 63–4.

such, is concerned with the much broader assertion that He is sovereign everywhere'.[4] As the Westminster Confession of Faith states:

God from all eternity, did, by the most wise and holy council of His own will, freely, and unchangeably ordain whatsoever comes to pass: yet so, as thereby neither is God the author of sin, nor is violence offered to the will of the creatures; nor is the liberty or contingency of second causes taken away, but rather established. (WCF 3.1)

Shortcutting here the necessary and well-trodden biblical and philosophical defence of this understanding of providence and divine 'concurrence', what Reformed believers uphold is that scripture teaches both God's total sovereignty over all events (a 'determinism' but that of a personal God), together with strong notions of human responsibility, and a 'compatibilist' notion of 'freedom' (a freedom compatible with a divine determinism which still enables us to 'do what we want to do'). This 'freedom' (or better 'heart–act consistency'),[5] is the main concern of the biblical revelation: before the fall, the freedom to do good but the possibility of doing evil (*posse peccare*); after the fall, the bondage of the will and inability not to sin (*non posse non peccare*); in regeneration the possibility for us not to sin (*posse non peccare*), and in glory the inability to sin (*non posse peccare*).

Despite the complexities of this construal of sovereignty and responsibility, the alternative Gavin appears to propose, that of a 'libertarian' understanding of human freedom, is scripturally and philosophically far more problematic and 'tragic'. For God, anything other than him foreordaining all events, leads to some uncomfortable implications as to the nature of God's knowledge and whether there is something/someone more ultimate than God. For human beings, one of the standard critiques of libertarian freedom can be reiterated, namely if our actions are uncaused (by God, or

---

4 J. I. Packer, 'Introductory Essay' to John Owen's *Death of Death in the Death of Christ* (Edinburgh: Banner of Truth, 1959), p. 5.
5 John Frame, *The Doctrine of God* (Phillipsburg: P&R), p. 136.

character, etc.), then they are arbitrary and random rather than morally responsible.[6]

More specifically, let us now turn to Gavin's particular questions concerning the 'invincibly ignorant', pre-Christian salvation, and the *'praeparatio'* nature of religions. I have responded, albeit briefly, to some of Gavin's questions (for example the descent into hell) in my original response to his exposition. I hope I can answer Gavin's remaining questions by attempting to articulate a piece of 'theological religious studies', an endeavour Gavin has persuasively argued for elsewhere.[7] In particular I wish to complement and clarify what I have theologically articulated earlier by resuscitating the seemingly dead topic of the origin and history of religion, as well as the *prisca theologia* tradition which both Gavin and I myself have mentioned in our statements.

Even though we must offer a number of cautions and caveats, I would hope a good conservative Catholic like Gavin would recognize that the best way to understand the Old Testament and even a book like Genesis is 'to combine historical interest with competent appreciation of the literary medium employed'.[8] If we take seriously a monogenetic understanding of human origins which posits, in the words of the apostle Paul, that 'from one man' God made every nation of mankind (Acts 17.26), then we are able plausibly to posit a 'single-source'[9] theory of revelation and knowledge, a period at the beginning of human history from Adam to Abraham, when the whole of humanity was privileged to be in proximity of redemptive revelation, for example the *protoevangelium*[10] of Genesis 3.15.

---

6   Frame, in *The Doctrine of God*, pp. 138–45, outlines in non-technical language an eighteen point critique of libertarian freedom.

7   See his *Christianity and World Religions: Disputed Questions in the Theology of Religions* (Chichester: Wiley Blackwell), pp. 91–102.

8   V. Philips Long, 'Historiography of the Old Testament', in David W. Baker and Bill T. Arnold (eds), *The Face of Old Testament Studies: A Survey of Contemporary Approaches* (Leicester: Apollos, 1999), p. 173.

9   I take this phrase from Peter Harrison, *'Religion' and the Religions in the English Enlightenment* (Cambridge: Cambridge University Press, 1990), p. 131.

10   Traditionally seen to be the first 'embryonic' proclamation of the gospel in Genesis 3.15.

Such revelation defies a simplistic categorization as either natural 'general' revelation or supernatural 'special revelation' for as the Reformed theologian Herman Bavinck comments, 'common grace and special grace still flow in a single channel'.[11] On the *protoevangelium*, Bavinck states that within the tradition, 'the universal idea of the revelation of salvation does not get its due',[12] noting that these primeval events, later recorded, are truly a 'genesis': 'religion and morality, cult and culture have their beginnings there'.[13] As a result, from Genesis 3 onwards we are able to trace both theologically and historically the human reaction to this divine revelation, in other words, the history of human religion, both its preservation and degeneration, both its progress and regress. I am even happy to speak of religion as a *genus*. Given such a religio-genesis we are in a position to make a number of observations.

First, concerning the relationship between Christianity and all other religions, the relationship is one of structural continuity in systemic discontinuity. In their rebellion, both individually (as 'religious beings') and corporately (as part of religious 'traditions'), all revelation from God, whether 'general' or 'special', is taken and assimilated into an idolatrous structure. I distinguished this previously as the difference between the 'thatness' and 'whatness' of religion. As well as the influence Christianity might have had historically on other religious traditions, this also includes what might be called 'remnantal' revelation, a Reformed 'version' of the *prisca theologia*. As Bavinck explains:

> But, according to Scripture, this general revelation is not purely natural; it also contains supernatural elements. The revelation that occurred immediately after the falls bears a supernatural character (Gen. 3.8ff) and via traditions becomes the possession of humankind. For a long time the original knowledge and service of God remains intact in a more or less pure state . . . Pagan

11   Herman Bavinck, *Reformed Dogmatics*, vol. 3 (Grand Rapids: Baker, 2006), p. 216.
12   Bavinck, *Reformed Dogmatics*, vol. 3, p. 216.
13   Bavinck, *Reformed Dogmatics*, vol. 3, p. 216.

religions, accordingly, do not rest only on the acknowledgement of God's revelation in nature but most certainly also on elements that from the most ancient times were preserved from supernatural revelation by tradition even though that tradition was frequently no longer pure . . . Hence the distinction between natural and supernatural revelation is not identical with the distinction between general and special revelation. To describe the twofold revelation that underlies pagan religions and the religion of Scripture, the latter distinction is preferable to the former.[14]

Hence the distinction between general and special revelation does not consist primarily in the fact that the latter consistently and in all parts bears a strictly supernatural character; the difference is evidenced fundamentally and primarily by the fact that special revelation is a revelation of special grace and this brings into existence the salvific religion known as Christianity.[15]

I concede I may have confusingly still called this 'remnantal' revelation 'special revelation' in my opening chapter, implying more positive '*praeparatio*' elements than is indeed the case. However, I remain convinced that given the universality of revelation and the unity of humanity, both theologically *and* historically, there is no-one who is 'invincibly ignorant' or 'without fault':

No concrete case exists in which man has no more than the revelation of God in nature. It is no doubt true that many have *practically* nothing else, inasmuch as in their case the tradition of man's original state has not reached them and no echo of the redemptive principle has penetrated to their vicinity. Yet it remains true that the race as a whole has once been in contact with the living God, and that it was created perfect. Man remains responsible for these facts. Back of this arrangement is the Creator, the sovereign God.[16]

---

14   Bavinck, *Reformed Dogmatics*, vol. 1 (Grand Rapids: Baker, 2003), p. 311.

15   Bavinck, *Reformed Dogmatics*, vol. 1, p. 342.

16   Cornelius Van Til, *Systematic Theology*, 2nd edn (Phillipsburg: P&R, 2007), p. 147.

Second, concerning the relationship between believers before Christ and those after Christ, the relationship is one of historical discontinuity in redemptive continuity. From the *protoevangelium* in Genesis onwards, despite widespread suppression and devolution of true knowledge of God, God by his illuminating and regenerating Spirit preserves authentic and genuine knowledge of himself and his salvation in his chosen people (who of course are meant to be a blessing to others), and that while we may speak of the gradual progression in the specificity of revelation as redemptive history progresses, type and antitype, promise and fulfilment remain in continuity. As Kuyper notes, the revelation Old Testament believers received 'produced in their minds such a fixed and tangible form of the Messiah that fellowship with Him, which alone is essential to salvation, was made possible to them by anticipation as to us by memory'.[17] All this is to say, therefore, that contrary to Gavin, I do not believe there to be a valid analogy between those who, by the regenerating Spirit, responded to God faithfully according to the redemptive revelation given to them at their time in redemptive history (Israel and those engrafted into Israel), and those who respond to God idolatrously with the revelation they have been given in nature or history.

In conclusion, I return to my interpretation of Christianity as being the 'subversive fulfilment' of other religions. This notion, coupled with my construal of God's sovereignty, means we are able to suggest some of the 'purposes' of other religions in the providential economy of God. First, while still affirming the idolatrous and therefore sinful nature of other religions, we are able to say that God may use such religions to 'teach', 'edify' and even 'rebuke' God's Church. The great early twentieth-century Reformed missiologist Samuel Zwemer notes that 'contact with non-Christian thought and life often sheds light on various elements of Christianity, deepens our conception of its truths and brings out forgotten or underestimated doctrines. Against the darkness and twilight shadows of heathenism and Islam, Christian beliefs and ideas are

---

17 Abraham Kuyper, *The Work of the Holy Spirit* (New York: Funk & Wagnalls, 1900), p. 166.

thrown into bold relief, like a sunlit face in one of Rembrandt's paintings.'[18] More recently Peter Leithart has articulated a Christian theology of Islam which argues that as a Judaizing parody and counterfeit of Christianity, Islam 'is designed to expose our failing and to call us to faithfulness'.[19]

Second, we must acknowledge that in spite of the idolatrous presuppositions at the heart of religious individuals and traditions, there is a non-salvific work of the Spirit in other religions, restraining sin and exciting to a civic 'goodness'. As I said before, these elements can be described as being the 'borrowed capital' and 'unacknowledged debt' taken from the Christian worldview. They are not to be seen as 'points of contact' but rather 'points of attack' for the elenctic enterprise. Without them though, such an enterprise would be impossible, and so thanks must be given. With these elements of continuity, therefore, from the perspective of faith of one rescued out of a non-Christian religion by Christ and regenerated by the Spirit *in this life*, it is legitimate to look back and recognize the Spirit's *praeparatio* here. However, without such a saving work of subversive fulfilment, and for those who die as non-Christians, this '*praeparatio*' becomes the basis for God's just judgement, for we remain accountable for the good gifts from God that are spurned, for in spurning the gifts we are spurning the Giver. For those without Christ, this is a preparation not for eternal life but rather for eternal death.

In response to Gavin's concerns, whether such a clarification here is 'more properly dialectical' and absolves me from being 'unduly pessimistic' is doubtful, but let our dialogue continue.

Re-response to Paul Knitter

It has been a privilege to be able to take part in this dialogue with Paul. As I predicted in my initial statement, sparks were always

---

18   Samuel Zwemer, *The Origin of Religion* (London: Marshall, Morgan & Scott, 1935), p. 45.

19   Peter J. Leithart, 'Mirror of Christendom', www.marshillaudio.org/resources/pdf/Leithart.pdf at p. 4.

going to fly when very different theological worldviews collided, but I hope that as well as the inevitable heat generated, there has been some helpful light which illumines our respective theological visions. As Paul recognizes, both he and I share less of a personal and confessional history than each of us does with Gavin, and so it is perhaps inevitable that, like any fledging relationship, the possibility of misunderstanding, miscommunication and even caricature is very real. If our exchange here does nothing more than help move along a process whereby Christian traditions like mine and Paul's are able to represent each other's position in a way that the other can recognize, then I think we have a platform for ongoing constructive dialogue. It is to this end that I wish to focus my closing response to Paul. I recognize that much of the subject matter over which Paul and I engage may appear somewhat removed and tangential to the topic at hand. However, it is necessary that we start further back with these more elementary theological ABCs showing once again the interconnectivity and dependency of the theology of religions to more basic theological loci.

At the end of his response to my chapter, Paul asks whether his criticisms of me have been hard and perhaps harsh. My answer here is that I don't think he has been hard or harsh enough! Given the importance of the biblical revelation, both methodologically and substantively, in the construction of my 'theology of religions', Paul passes up the opportunity to offer what might have been some penetrating and potentially wrecking 'biblical inconsistencies' he perceives in my position. Rather he merely focuses on possible 'dangers' within my position. While I appreciate that Paul takes this approach because he wants to be respectful towards me, I think the overall result is a much weakened and 'impressionistic' critique which does not have the force to really challenge the presuppositions on which my argument is constructed. How much am I being helped here to really question my own 'theology of religions', a 'theology of religions' so markedly different, indeed in conflict with the one offered by Paul? Perhaps given the epistemological implications of Paul's religious pluralism, pointing to the possible dangers of another position is as much as Paul is able to say without falling foul of the fallacy of self-referential incoherence.

In responding to these 'danger signs' that Paul has put up as a warning against a position like mine, I want to agree with him that idolatry, fideism, 'abusive' descriptions of God, divine narcissism, christomonism, and oppressive imperialism are all *possible* avenues down which one may dangerously stray. However, I firmly believe that I have not succumbed to these darker byways but kept to the 'well-lit' highway that is historic Christian orthodoxy. I thought I had made an attempt to pre-empt a number of these misconceptions in my opening statement.

In terms of theological method, I wish to reiterate the following. First, concerning the nature of scripture, I am neither committing bibliolatry nor adopting a Muslim view of scripture in recognizing the intimately close identification between persons and their words. In the Bible identifying itself as *theopneustos* (God-breathed) (2 Tim. 3.16), I used Ward's linguistic analysis concerning the 'speech acts of Scripture' with implication that God is both 'semantically present' and personally present through his Spirit. It may help for Ward to explain further this 'semantic presence':

> There is, then, a kind of personal presence in the words that someone utters. It is mysterious in some ways, and hard to spell out conceptually, but is nonetheless real. We may call it the 'semantic presence' of persons in their words (in those words as they are used as the means for the performance of actions). We extend the reach of our selves by uttering or writing words that can then travel across a room or around the world, and that, in written or recorded form, can remain beyond our death. *This is of course not to say something absurd, such as that to have in your hand a letter from me is the same thing as having me in the room with you.*[20]

Paul's 'caution' against me committing idolatry here, once again raises for me the question as to Paul's own authority for judging what is idolatrous and what is not. How do we know what counts as a 'confinement' of God and what does not? Is it not the

---

20   Tim Ward, *Words of Life: Scripture as the Living and Active Word of God* (Nottingham: InterVarsity Press, 2009), p. 65 (italics mine).

self-revealing God who in the Bible both defines and describes this particular concept, prescribing the ways he wishes to be known to his creation? As Motyer notes on God's self-revelation in Exodus 3.14, 'It is worth remarking that the Bible knows nothing of different "names" of God. God has only one name – Yahweh. Apart form this, all the others are titles or description. This fact is often imperfectly grasped.'[21]

Second, concerning the charge of fideism, I again plead not guilty. Depending on how Paul is defining this term, fideism is often associated with a form of subjective irrationalism, but my epistemology is strongly committed to thinking through rationally the implications of a biblical worldview and non-Christian worldviews. Such actions never bypass the mind and reasoning but involve persuasive argumentation and refutation. I find Paul's charge here somewhat ironic in that a tradition like mine is so often labelled not 'irrational' but rather 'rationalistic'. Indeed, a double irony is that I see good grounds to lay the 'fideist' charge at Paul's door given his own stress on the existential and experimental side of faith. Kierkegaard's dictum that 'A dogmatic system ought not to be erected on the basis: *to comprehend faith*, but on the basis: *to comprehend that faith cannot be comprehended*'[22] would appear to be a fair summary of the position Paul has outlined.

What Paul mistakenly labels as 'fideism' in my position are two fundamental aspects of my 'presuppositional' epistemology and methodology. First are the role and importance of presuppositions and the 'all-encompassing grids' that are the worldviews through which we interpret the world and decide what counts for evidence and what does not. Paul admits that we all have 'starting points' and so he must be included with Gavin and myself on his own list: '*Experior locuta, causa finita*' (Experience has spoken; that settles it). Paul is rightly worried that any ultimate commitment like mine (the Bible) cannot be criticized or falsified. In other words, if there

---

21   J. A. Motyer, *The Revelation of the Divine Name* (London: Tyndale, 1959), p. 31, fn.18.

22   Søren Kierkegaard, *Journals and Papers L–R*, vol. 3 (Bloomington, IN: Indiana University Press, 1979), p. 635.

is no epistemological 'no-man's land' or 'neutral zone', how can we ever critique each other? Of course, given his ultimate commitment to experience, we are all in the same boat. Given the 'unprovability' of our ultimate starting points, I concede that one cannot argue 'directly' for or against them, but we can argue 'indirectly': that is we show the 'impossibility of the contrary'. That is to say, we may not be able to prove a certain position, but we can show that the inevitable consequences of rejecting that position are disastrous on all levels intellectually, practically, culturally, and so forth.

I maintain that Paul's ultimate appeal to experience over revelation is an unstable foundation on which to build his theology of religions and that this can be demonstrated in a number of ways. My claim about the Bible, which of course is not immune to challenge, is that if it is indeed what it claims to be, then the Christian cannot appeal to any higher authority than God's word, for to do that would be to deny its final authoritative status.[23] Second, in affirming the 'absolute and exclusively normative authority of the Bible', I am by no means denying the existence of revelation or knowledge of God outside of the Bible, indeed I maintain that *all* creation reveals God, the clearest 'revelation' being the *imago Dei*, which is metaphysically ineradicable and which renders us 'without excuse' in knowing God. The objectivity, perspicuity and goodness of revelation in nature, history and the Bible are not in doubt. Where Paul and I do part company is that scripture is clear that all men and women suppress this truth and exchange it for idolatry leading to a subjective and moral inability, a spiritual blindness. As I noted before, given this state what we need is both new sight and new light which God graciously gives by his Spirit in the message of the gospel found in scripture.

Concerning the dangers Paul sees in my doctrine of God and Christ, the following can be restated. First, the descriptions of God's nature and character that I sketched out previously are biblical descriptions, and so I believe divinely revealed descriptions. For any Christian who has the Bible as either *a* or *the* source of authority, this biblical evidence has to be recognized and explained. Second,

---

23   Hebrews 6.13–20 gives us a biblical form of this argument.

Yahweh reveals himself to be both absolute and personal, the self-contained ontological Trinity. Divine narcissism is avoided here precisely because we are not speaking of an impersonal monad, but Father, Son and Spirit who from eternity love and adore each other, glorify each other and serve each other. Because God in the beauty of his perfections is God, both self-exaltation and creaturely exaltation is not a vice but rather a virtue.

Third, and concerning religious language, I noted that given the Creator/creature distinction, our language about God is neither univocal nor equivocal but rather analogical. All speech about God is anthropomorphic but perhaps even more importantly 'theomorphic' in that God designed creation with divine communication in mind. Without even asking Paul whether he believes 'jealousy' or 'anger' to be at times perfectly legitimate human responses to unfaithfulness or injustice, he appears to take these imperfectly human manifestations of jealousy and anger and project these onto God. In doing so he forgets their analogous nature, and the fact that for God, all his perfections include the others, so his anger is always a holy and righteous anger. Methodologically it is wrong to argue simply from *our experience* of these characteristics, but rather we must start from God's own self-revelation of these characteristics in scripture. Fourth, Paul in siding with a number of feminist theologians, associates various negative images of God with a certain view of human masculinity.[24] While it is important to recognize what might be called more subtle 'feminine' descriptions of God in scripture,[25] the preponderance of this imagery is masculine not arbitrarily or simply 'culturally'[26] but for important theological reasons concerning God's authority and covenantal headship.

---

24   There is a certain ambivalence within feminist theology as to whether the argument here is against stereotyping gender (that these 'characteristics' are actually common to both men and women), or that they are typically male characteristics (and so should be avoided in describing God). See Frame, *The Doctrine of God*, pp. 379f.

25   For example, Isa. 42.14–15, which uses the metaphor of a woman in childbirth.

26   For as Frame points out, female deities were well known to the biblical writers, *Doctrine of God*, p. 384.

Fifth, and concerning the doctrine of penal substitution, there are a number of misunderstandings that need to be addressed. First, there is no trinitarian division in the cross which would lead to Paul's worry over this constituting a case of divine parental abuse. Jesus was no passive victim but went willingly to his death (John 10.17–18), and the purpose of the cross was not the personal gratification of the abuser but for Jesus to bring glory to himself (Phil. 2.8–9) and to his Father, and to save his people (Rom. 5.8). Second, and amazingly, divine love is the motivation behind the sending of the Son to die, not its consequence. As Murray notes, 'it is one thing to say that the wrathful God is made loving. That would be entirely false. It is another thing to say the wrathful God is loving. That is profoundly true. But it is also true that the wrath by which he is wrathful is propitiated through the cross. This propitiation is the fruit of the divine love that provided it.'[27] Third, while it is not contradictory that God can be both wrathful and loving at the same time, as with God's wrath, the biblical doctrine of the love of God is not a simplistic concept but complex, having different objects and both universal and particular aspects.[28] Paul's illustration of parental love is the privileged particular love of the believer who has been adopted at great cost: 'Penal substitution affirms that, on conversion, our status changes from rebellious outsiders to adopted children, and as a result we enter into an experience of God's *fatherly* love we did not know before (1 John 3.1). But the change occurs in us not in God.'[29]

Finally, we turn to Paul's claim that believing in the exclusivity of Christ for salvation together with a belief in the idolatrous nature of non-Christian religions provides an excuse for, and even invites, a harmful imperialism both personally and politically, which cannot be reconciled to the command to love our neighbours. While

---

27 John Murray, *Redemption Accomplished and Applied* (Edinburgh: Banner of Truth, 1961), pp. 31f.

28 See D. A. Carson, *The Difficult Doctrine of the Love of God* (Nottingham: InterVarsity Press, 2010).

29 Steve Jeffrey, Mike Ovey and Andrew Sach, *Pierced for our Transgressions: Rediscovering the Glory of Penal Substitution* (Nottingham: InterVarsity Press, 2007), p. 292.

unfortunately we might be able to point to historical instances where this invitation to harmful imperialism has been accepted, these abuses should never stop us proclaiming, as his ambassadors, the lordship and mediatorial kingship of Jesus Christ. We are not to be embarrassed by Christ's imperial claims knowing that these claims are never to be equated with just one cultural manifestation. Rather God's triunity of unity in diversity is displayed and celebrated as all cultures and ethné's come under his rule, be they African, Latin American or Indian. As Gavin has so cogently argued elsewhere, an explicit and 'thick' theological interpretation of another religion is as legitimate as, indeed is more legitimate (and therefore more loving) than, more 'secularized' or 'neutral' readings that for ideological reasons seek to dissolve difference.[30] Although we must ultimately interpret all other religions through the prism of God's revelation in scripture, this does not mean that in our engagement we do not work hard to understand how a religious culture intra-textually understands itself (an 'insider reading'), or respectfully listen as to how they perceive reality. Indeed missionary communication depends upon this accurate reading if 'subversive fulfilment' and *possessio* is to occur.

In all our engagement, our approach should be *fortitier in re suaviter in modo* (bold in our defence, gentle in the manner of our defence), and we must never be motivated by malice or vainglory because we ourselves have been saved by a grace we do not deserve. We proclaim the exclusivity of Christ for salvation and hope, motivated by love, for we know that although we always retain the dignity of being created in the *imago Dei*, without Christ we are lost and hope-less. As D. T. Niles famously said, 'Christianity is one beggar telling another beggar where he found bread.'

---

30   See Gavin D'Costa, *Christianity and World Religions: Disputed Questions in the Theology of Religions* (London: Wiley-Blackwell, 2009), pp. 91–102.

Further Readings

Gavin D'Costa

Veli-Matti Kärkkäinen, *Trinity and Religious Pluralism: The Doctrine of the Trinity in Christian Theology of Religions* (Aldershot: Ashgate, 2004).
A helpful overview of various attempts to think about this question from a trinitarian perspective across different denominations.

Francis Sullivan, *Salvation Outside the Church? Tracing the History of the Catholic Response* (New York: Paulist Press, 1992).
Still probably the best overview in English of the history of Catholic responses to the question.

Jacques Dupuis, *Toward a Christian Theology of Religious Pluralism* (Maryknoll: Orbis, 1997).
The second best overview of the debate also taking into consideration wider issues and developing a neo-Rahnerian viewpoint.

Riccardo Lombardi, *The Salvation of the Unbeliver* (London: Burns & Oates, 1956).
A comprehensive coverage of views prior to Vatican II within Catholic theology, which is excellent in outlining the issues at stake and the key dogmatic principles to be used in attempting answers – also see Eminyan below. Both are much neglected jewels.

Maurice Eminyan, *The Theology of Salvation* (Boston: St Paul, 1960).

Good read with Lombardi above covering similar ground, but vital for appreciating the developments in the Catholic Church since Vatican II.

Karl Josef Becker, Ilaria Morali, with Maurice Borrmans and Gavin D'Costa (eds), *Catholic Engagement with World Religions: A Comprehensive Study* (Maryknoll: Orbis, 2010).
Provide careful studies on numerous dogmatic aspects related to this question as well as individual studies of world religions and their evaluations.

Gavin D'Costa (ed.), *The Catholic Church and the World Religions: A Theological and Phenomenological Account* (London: Continuum, 2011).
Provides a close study of relevant Vatican II documents to indicate a proper Catholic orientation, followed by a study of the major world religions and New Age movements, analysing them in this theological manner.

Gavin D'Costa, *Christianity and World Religions: Disputed Questions in the Theology of Religions* (Chichester: Wiley-Blackwell, 2009).
Examines four disputed areas: the modern theological approaches; the concept of religion; the resources for religion in the public square (Catholicism and Sunni Islam); the descent into hell as a means to resolve theological questions.

Gavin D'Costa, *The Meeting of Religions and the Trinity* (Maryknoll: Orbis, 2000).
Offers a critique of 'pluralism' in Christianity, Judaism, Hinduism and Buddhism and develops a trinitarian Catholic approach to theology of religions.

Gavin D'Costa (ed.), *Christian Uniqueness Reconsidered: The Myth of a Pluralistic Theology of Religions* (Maryknoll: Orbis, 1990).
A response to Paul's number four entry below in which a group of international theologians from different denominations criticize pluralism and present alternative approaches.

Paul Knitter

John B. Cobb, Jr., *Transforming Christianity and the World: A Way beyond Absolutism and Relativism*, ed. Paul F. Knitter (Maryknoll: Orbis, 1999).
A collection of Cobb's efforts to find a dialogical path that will honour both particularity and universality – and that will address the needs of the world.

Catherine Cornille, *The Im-Possibility of Interreligious Dialogue* (New York: Crossroad, 2008).
An identification and an analysis of the virtues that are necessary to engage in authentic and productive interreligious dialogue.

John Hick, *An Interpretation of Religion: Human Responses to the Transcendent* (New Haven: Yale University Press, 1989).
A classic statement of a pluralist understanding of religious history and religious experience.

John Hick and Paul F. Knitter (eds), *The Myth of Christian Uniqueness: Toward a Pluralistic Theology of Religions* (Eugene: Wipf & Stock, 2005). (Originally published by Orbis, 1987.)
A collection of various Christian theologians and philosophers seeking to lay the foundations for a pluralist theology of religions that would move beyond claims of absolute uniqueness.

Jeannine Hill-Fletcher, *Monopoly on Salvation? A Feminist Approach to Religious Pluralism* (New York: Continuum, 2005).
Using feminist understandings of hybridity, an effort to find a middle path between the particularity of the post-liberals and the universality of the pluralists.

Paul F. Knitter, *Introducing Theologies of Religions* (Maryknoll: Orbis, 2002).
A broad overview and a critical analysis of the pros and cons of four models for a Christian theology of religions: Replacement, Fulfilment, Mutuality, and Acceptance.

Paul F. Knitter, *One Earth, Many Religions: Multifaith Dialogue and Global Responsibility* (Maryknoll: Orbis, 1995).
Makes the case that a shared concern for the sufferings of the planet and its inhabitants can serve as an arena and starting point of inter-religious dialogue.

Paul F. Knitter, *Jesus and the Other Names: Christian Mission and Global Responsibility* (Maryknoll: Orbis, 1996).
Reasons why Christians can move beyond exclusive claims for Jesus without losing their commitment to Jesus and his mission.

Paul F. Knitter (ed.), *The Myth of Religious Superiority: A Multifaith Exploration* (Maryknoll: Orbis, 2005).
Spokespersons for diverse religions show the resources in their own tradition for a pluralist approach to other traditions.

Marjorie Hewitt Suchocki, *Divinity and Diversity: A Christian Affirmation of Religious Pluralism* (Nashville: Abingdon Press, 2003).
Shows why traditional Christian beliefs such as creation, Trinity, incarnation, and the reign of God call Christians to a positive engagement with other religions.

Daniel Strange

D. A. Carson, *The Gagging of God: Christianity Confronts Pluralism* (Leicester: Apollos, 1996).
In this wide-ranging study, the evangelical New Testament scholar tackles 'cherished' philosophical pluralism head-on.

Leonardo De Chirico, *Evangelical Theological Perspectives on post-Vatican II Roman Catholicism* (Oxford: Peter Lang, 2003).
A comprehensive analysis of evangelical interpretations of Roman Catholicism post-Vatican II, with the author favouring a 'systemic' interpretation.

Timothy Keller, *The Reason for God: Belief in an Age of Skepticism* (New York: Dutton, 2008).
Keller is an influential pastor in New York City. In this work he defends historic Christian orthodoxy against its cultured despisers. His response to the defeater, 'There can't just be one true religion,' is especially powerful.

Hendrik Kraemer, *Religion and the Christian Faith* (London: Lutterworth Press, 1956).
Another missiologist coming from the Dutch Reformed tradition and a genuine polymath, Kraemer was a towering figure at the World Missionary Conferences in the 1920s and 1930s. This later work represents his mature thought and is a classic defence of Christian uniqueness and particularity.

Harold Netland, *Encountering Religious Pluralism: The Challenge of Christian Faith and Mission* (Leicester: Apollos, 2001).
A contemporary defence of Christian particularity that engages with the pluralism of John Hick.

Alvin Plantinga, 'Pluralism: A Defense of Religious Exclusivism', in Thomas D. Senor (ed.), *The Rationality of Belief and the Plurality of Faith* (London: Cornell University Press, 1995).
Plantinga is one of the most significant and influential analytic philosophers of religion of the last 30 years. In this essay he defends 'exclusivism' by demonstrating the self-referential incoherence of pluralism.

Daniel Strange, *The Possibility of Salvation Among the Unevangelised: An Analysis of Inclusivism in Recent Evangelical Theology* (Carlisle: Paternoster, 2000).
A detailed study of the 'soteriological problem of evil' focusing especially on contemporary evangelical inclusivism.

Daniel Strange, 'General Revelation: Sufficient or Unsufficient', in Christopher W. Morgan and Robert A. Peterson (eds), *Faith Comes*

by Hearing: A Response to Inclusivism (Nottingham: Apollos, 2008), pp. 40–77.
An exegetical and theological essay on the insufficiency of natural revelation for salvation.

Timothy C. Tennent, *Christianity and the Religious Round Table: Evangelicalism in Conversation with Hinduism, Buddhism, and Islam* (Grand Rapids: Baker Books, 2002).
In the style of Martin Luther's Tabletalk, Tennent stages several fictional conversations between historic Christianity and other religious traditions.

Kevin Vanhoozer (ed.), *The Trinity in a Pluralistic Age: Theological Essays on Culture and Religion* (Grand Rapids: Eerdmans, 1996).
A collection of essays showing how a full-orbed Trinitarian doctrine, with a proper emphasis on both the One and the Three, provides the necessary resources for successfully addressing the problems and the possibilities of contemporary pluralism.

Index

INDEX

religions
as conduits of grace 155–6
dialogue between 25–32, 51–2,
139–40, 157, 165–6
origin 217–19
pluralism 34, 95–7, 103, 156,
196
relativity 139–40
theology of 94–6, 174–5, 179–80
religious language 49–50, 141,
169, 226
resurrection, of Christ 70–2
revelation 99–102, 109–16, 125,
172, 177, 217–19
in the Bible 163
and culture 202
and development of dogma
186–7
fullness of 208
and salvation 212
special 121, 126, 150, 181
Vatican Council on 152
rights of Christians 45
Roman Catholic Church
Declaration on . . . Jesus Christ
see Dominus Iesus
Dogmatic Constitution on the
Church see Lumen Gentium
teaching role 3–4
see also Vatican Council

sacraments 70, 157, 212
and Christology 158–60
salvation 13–22, 215
in Christianity 76–8
and church membership 7–8
as corporate and social 19
and liberation theology 73
of non-christians 8
none outside the Church 15,
157–8, 177
in religions 155–6
and revelaiton 212

Sanders, John 171
saving grace 152
science, and poverty 12
second coming of Jesus 86
selfishness 63–4
sin 62–4, 115, 118, 123, 144,
173, 180–1
and freedom 216
sincerity 111
Sobrino, Jon 75
social justice 44–5, 75, 142, 167
in Judaism 75
sola Scriptura 100–1, 177, 188
Son of God 66–8
special revelation 121, 126, 150,
181
Spirit 57–9
Strange, Daniel, writings 233–4
Suchocki, Marjorie Hewitt 232
suffering 64
Sullivan, Francis 229
Sunyata 56–9
symbolic language 49–50, 74,
141, 206
symbols 56, 67

Teilhard de Chardin, Pierre 62
Tennent, Timothy C. 234
theology
defined 47–52
of religions 94–6, 174–5,
179–80
role in Roman Catholic
Church 3
translation or interpretation?
200–6
thief on the cross 20–1
Thomas Aquinas
on God as Being 155
and the unbaptized 18
and the unevangelized 10
Tillich, Paul 55–6, 74
total depravity 146

239